NEW JERSEY

THE AGE OF URBAN REFORM

Kennikat Press
National University Publications
Interdisciplinary Urban Series

General Editor
Raymond A. Mohl
Florida Atlantic University

[by] MICHAEL H. EBNER
and
EUGENE M. TOBIN
editors

THE AGE OF URBAN REFORM

NEW PERSPECTIVES ON THE PROGRESSIVE ERA

National University Publications
KENNIKAT PRESS // 1977
Port Washington, N. Y. // London

Manufactured in the United States of America

Published by
Kennikat Press Corp.
Port Washington, N.Y./London

Library of Congress Cataloging in Publication Data

Main entry under title:

The Age of urban reform.

(Interdisciplinary urban series) (National university publications)
Bibliography: p.
Includes index.
1. Cities and towns—United States History—Addresses, essays, lectures. 2. Progressivism (United States politics)—Addresses, essays, lectures. I. Ebner, Michael H. II. Tobin, Eugene M.
HT123.A615   301.36'0973   77-4959
ISBN 0-8046-9192-4
ISBN 0-8046-9204-1 (paper)

CONTENTS

TABLES

MAPS

ACKNOWLEDGMENTS

A knowing historian warned us as we initiated this project, in April 1974, that a composite volume never yields its fruits without preliminary anguish during the germination process. Fortuitously, we have been blessed with contributors from far-flung locales, most of whom we still have not met, who shared our early enthusiasm. Particular thanks must be extended to Michael P. McCarthy, Center for Policy Research, whose gentle and timely prodding was instrumental in moving the manuscript beyond the stage of a good idea and whose trenchant questions helped to clarify our thinking as to its direction; to Edward J. Kopf, Virginia Commonwealth University, and Martin J. Schiesl, California State University at Los Angeles, who served as sounding boards for our queries about a variety of matters; to Bruce M. Stave, University of Connecticut, who offered wise counsel to two neophyte editors; and to Raymond A. Mohl, Florida Atlantic University, academic advisory editor for Kennikat Press, whose encouragement eased our labor. We appreciate the assistance, at various stages, of Timothy Crimmins, Georgia State University; William W. Cutler III, Temple University; Lewis L. Gould, University of Texas; Otis A. Pease, University of Washington; Stanley K. Schultz, University of Wisconsin; and Tom Ticknor, Lake Forest College. Arthur Zilversmit, Lake Forest College, deserves special thanks for his advice concerning both the introductory essay and the bibliographic compilation.

The institutions of higher learning that have employed us—The City College of New York and Lake Forest College, and Jersey City State College and Kutztown State College, respectively—have generously, if not always knowingly, provided supportive services. Lake Forest College has made secretarial assistance available to satisfy deadlines—most notably the service of Phyllis Shrock, whose assiduous devotion to detail we valued—and never questioned our reliance on photo-duplication machines, endless mailings, numerous and long-distance phone calls. A National Endowment for the Humanities fellowship-in-residence at Vanderbilt University provided intellectual stimulation, in the seminar of Dewey W. Grantham, during the final days of this project. Also, colleagues in the Columbia University Seminar on the City offered a most congenial and often exciting environment in which to think about urbanism and share our ideas. Finally, the New Jersey Historical Commission, a model public agency that other states should emulate, has facilitated our friendship, intellectual as well as personal, by means of its superb grant-in-aid program for scholarly research.

Happily for us, and we trust for them as well, there are our teachers: J. Joseph Huthmacher, then at Rutgers University; Morton Keller, Brandeis University; Norman Blume, University of Toledo; and William H. Harbaugh, University of Virginia. Scholars and teachers who have devoted themselves to the American polity, they have passed much of importance along to generations of students. We trust that each will recognize his respective influence in this book.

Darryl Tucker Ebner, Ian and Brooke have tolerated occasional absences for visits to "work with Gene" and welcomed his own visits—always with note cards, manuscripts, and tennis gear.

M. H. E. & E. M. T.

THE AGE OF URBAN REFORM

MICHAEL H. EBNER and EUGENE M. TOBIN

INTRODUCTION

One of the most notable recent occurrences in American historiography has been the sustained attention accorded urban politics during the early twentieth century. In the twenty-two years since Richard Hofstadter published his provocative study *The Age of Reform,* the Progressive Era has assumed the forefront of historical debate.[1] Though historians disagree over Progressivism's exact beginnings and end, the years from 1880 to 1920 are generally recognized as a watershed marking the emergence of a modern technological society. Such widely read interpretive analyses as *The Response to Industrialism, 1885-1914,* by Samuel P. Hays, and *The Search for Order, 1877-1920,* by Robert H. Wiebe, emphasize this view. Indeed, within the last decade the sense of security and permanence with which historians originally confronted the world of bosses, reformers, and moralism has all but been displaced by concern with the impact of industrialization on society.[2]

Hofstadter's seminal explanation that a "status revolution" motivated urban, professional, middle-class Protestants to enlist as progressives has undergone searching reexamination.[3] The fact that men and women became reformers has been attributed by Wiebe to the impact of modernization resulting from the industrial revolution.[4] Both James Weinstein and Samuel P. Hays emphasize the role played by corporate-minded leaders in the quest for social order.[5] J. Joseph Huthmacher and John D. Buenker developed a different focus—the interest of ethnic-stock politicians in social welfare legislation.[6] Ultimately, each of these interpretations has contributed to David P. Thelen's universal framework emphasizing the progressives' multiple interests as consumers, taxpayers, and citizens.[7] Actually, the very word "progressive" has been so misused that it has become a timeworn cliché that describes too little because it has characterized too much.[8]

Recent Progressive Era scholarship has produced a number of quality studies whose diverse conclusions emphasize the period's ambiguities and inconsistencies.[9] The rapid onslaught of technological innovation, industrial supremacy, and business consolidation, once warmly embraced by civic opinion leaders and decision makers, had unforeseen consequences. The coalescence of industrialization, urbanization, and immigration telescoped urban development far beyond the existing capabilities of most city dwellers and their institutions. Cities grew, but did so haphazardly. Municipal charters designed to meet the needs of less complex communities could not readily adjust to the highly differentiated residential life and sophisticated economic institutions of the early twentieth-century city. Yet physical and human expansion prompted proliferating demands for urban services—police and fire protection, gas, electricity, streetcars, adequate housing and sanitation, education, and recreational facilities. The long-standing belief of civic officials that city government should not provide such services placed the burden upon the private sector. Ambitious businessmen, recognizing the opportunity for potentially unlimited gain and public adulation, legitimately filled the vacuum, though occasionally with the assistance of political bosses who functioned as brokers for the city's resources. The panic and depression of the mid-1890s temporarily slowed urban development and revealed the imprudence of total dependence upon corporate wisdom.[10]

Private citizens and public officials revised long-standing assumptions about limited government and individual rights and set about humanizing the urban environment. In rhetoric that often posed dramatic, though misleading dichotomies, the more radical reformers questioned why the rapid growth of progress had been accompanied, in Henry George's phrase, by the concomitant growth of poverty. Others wondered aloud about a society that allowed its wealth to fall into fewer and fewer hands while ignoring the problems of the poor, elderly, and incapacitated. The Progressive Era did not, of course, present such clear-cut choices; yet, historians have occasionally ignored long-term American values and accepted the eloquent interpretations fashioned by reform spokesmen, including Herbert Croly, Walter Lippmann, William English Walling, and Walter Weyl.[11] This is not to say that the various social and political reforms were imaginary—but they were deceptive enough to require further study.

There have been repeated calls for systematic analyses and descriptions of particular communities and the social processes that molded them over time.[12] This collection of essays presents urban case studies by a new generation of historians. Heretofore, because of a preoccupation with the uniqueness of particular communities, criticism has been directed toward local studies to the extent of ignoring systematic comparative evidence. The fact remains, however, that while urban progressivism produced a universal commonality, each community shaped and in turn was shaped by forces peculiar to that city. A major value of this volume lies in the conceptual, methodological, and geographic diversity of its individual contributions. As Edward J. Kopf suggests in discussing the Chelsea experience, any "attempt to understand early twentieth-century 'reform' must place at least as much emphasis on the uniqueness of its varied local, state and national manifestations as on its unity. . . . The meaning of political behavior can be comprehended only in the full context of each particular community."*

But, for all its apparent diversity, this volume also represents a group effort by ten young historians whose exploration of urbanism and politics provides the basis for a comparison of community experiences during the Progressive Era. Most early twentieth-century cities shared, in varying number and degree, common problems: haphazard growth, municipal corruption, substandard housing, inadequate public health enforcement, rising property taxes, poor utility service, and impure water supplies. The differences in their individual responses, however, can be best appreciated when emphasis is placed upon distinct residential configurations, geographic location, the varying quality of political leadership, and community perceptions of crucial priorities.[13]

Some of our contributors are interested primarily in ideology; others, in bureaucratization and professionalization; and still others have studied voluntarism and modernization. Each chapter represents a distinct case study reflecting an individual community's response to widely shared urban problems. In some instances our contributors examine the implementation of social reform: public health and housing in Philadelphia and New York, progressive education in Atlanta, and civil service reform in Los Angeles. Other essays deal with the complex social environments that shaped reform: city-building in Houston and Chelsea, centrifugal growth in Chicago, urban land use in Jersey City, and partisan politics in Passaic and Seattle. By studying aspects of common problems in different ways, each essay provides insights that vividly convey the constants and variables of urban reform.

The collection is organized around a triad of themes that provide a sense of intellectual continuity: the qualitative implications of urban growth; the disparate, often distinctive, political issues and leadership that emerged in particularized settings; and the theoretical as well as

---

*Internal sources, drawn from the essays in this book, have not been footnoted.

applied responses to specific social and economic problems. Our contributors, sharing Eric E. Lampard's contention that "good political history of American cities" is woefully weak, have endeavored to analyze not only why elections were won or lost but also what the results have to tell us about the nature of urban development.[14]

The ramifications of urban growth, an experience shared by residents of most Progressive Era cities, presented a multiplicity of pressures and opportunities. Edward J. Kopf's study of Chelsea, a suburb of Boston, analyzes how the response to commission government was shaped by diverse economic, ethnic, and geographical groups. A fire of catastrophic proportions that burned its way across the entire community in 1908 left this compact town decimated. Seeking to maintain municipal stability while rebuilding during an emergency situation, its leaders proposed commission government as the best means for achieving civic unity. But fires, as Chicago's experience attests, did not always prompt calls for a change of government. Kopf's essay describes the economic, cultural, and political factors that figure in the change-of-government movement. Chelsea's recently arrived ethnic and occupational groups, whose political influence paralleled the city's growing industrial importance, did not believe that expert government was worth the price of their exclusion from the political process.

Although commission government was ultimately defeated, voters never completely rejected the notion of urban reform and, in fact, later adopted charter revision. The rhetoric of reform utilized in Chelsea was, of course, similar in type to arguments presented in other cities, and the response to industrialism that shaped events reflected but one variation of local-level community concern. Kopf's essay is especially valuable in fulfilling the need for a study of commission government that moves beyond formal political institutions to an examination of the social processes that shaped a community's response to structural reform.

Each city may have defined progressivism in its own way, but the results were almost always related to an underlying similarity of urban development. For instance, the response to industrialism that helped defeat commission government in a relatively established New England city produced the reverse effect during an earlier stage of growth in the Southwest. In the 1890s, Houston, already a regionally important commercial and transportation center, was still in a formative period of city-building. The immediate result, as Harold L. Platt details, was a fifteen-year era of intra-urban conflict among competing socioeconomic, geographic, and political interests. As in so many cities caught in this process and enduring similar ramifications, local officials in Houston were blamed for the failure of private utility services to keep pace with the city's expansion. Ultimately, contends Platt, its growth, which was accelerated by the discovery of nearby oil reserves and by a hurricane that devastated its major rival, Galveston, forced Houston's civic leadership to reevaluate the scope and authority of local government. In a subsequent series of physical and structural changes between 1901 and 1905, the city government initiated its first period of annexation, expanded the municipal bureaucracy, and revised its charter to reflect the increasing economic importance of business and professional groups. But the modernization of public authority was consummated only after its polity had been restrictively redefined—with the passage of Jim Crow laws, a state poll tax, and suppression of the only viable labor union. Unlike Chelsea, what Houston achieved featured the exclusion of the lower classes, white as well as black, from direct participation in decision making. The adoption of commission government in 1905 provided expert service at the expense of direct democracy.

Many late nineteenth-century cities responded to growth by extending their hegemony into expanding suburbs, whose middle- and working-class residents alike sought essential urban services. This spatial growth had considerable implications for municipal reform. The centrifugal expansion of large metropolises, as Michael P. McCarthy suggests in his essay on Chicago, enfranchised a variety of middle- and working-class voters who shared common problems related to growth. But McCarthy argues that Chicago's suburbs were neither homogeneous nor completely middle class; nor was there a simple cause and effect relationship in political terms through annexation. Some of the suburban wards were middle class, others working class. Only by perceiving the problems of growth as common to both classes does the success of a citizens' group like the Chicago Municipal Voters League become understandable. Its middle-class leadership represented but one part of a cross-class coalition that supported a program of grass-roots activism. Immigrant newcomers, like white-collar workers, had no special love for the ward bosses who picked their candidates.

After 1920, in Chicago and most other older cities of the East and Midwest that coalition disintegrated, as earlier growth problems that had once provided the bond became less significant. More importantly, the racial and ethnic composition of these suburban wards changed so drastically that the sense of commonality disappeared. In essence, when annexation declined and the middle classes moved away, the healthy mix of class and growth that had provided the dynamic for municipal reform was destroyed. While calling for closer scrutiny of physical setting as a determining factor in municipal reform, McCarthy also has provided an urban model and political typology readily adaptable to other localities.

government, we shall be able to see how the diversity of national progressivism was rooted in the diverse social environments in which Americans responded to industrialism. In this essay, we shall examine how a unique and complex interplay of ideology, ethnic identity and economic interest produced a reform in that particular city that was, of necessity, different from many other forms of that complex historical beast.

In 1908 Chelsea was a growing industrial city. Residents had every reason to expect that its population and economy would continue the expansive course of the preceding eighty years for the foreseeable future. But on a quiet Sunday morning in April of that year, all expectations suddenly had to be revised. One resident described the fire that shattered the continuity of Chelsea's growth:

The Chelsea fire started near the Everett line a little before eleven o'clock, Palm Sunday morning, 12 April 1908, and before it was out had swept the center of the city, covering a space a mile and a half long and three-quarters of a mile wide. It destroyed practically all the business section, most of the municipal buildings, twenty-eight hundred and twenty-two other buildings, and made seventeen thousand and four hundred and fifty people homeless. . . .
It is the third largest fire in point of area in the history of this country. The insurance loss was $8,846,879. The taxable value of property destroyed was . . . $20,000,000.[3]

In terms of its impact on the life of the city, no American urban fire has matched this one. Almost all of the municipal buildings and schools, seven hundred business firms and professional offices, and 2,400 residences were wiped out in twenty-four hours. The infrastructure of local society was destroyed.[4] No one was untouched. The most distant parts of the physically compact town, a mile from the holocaust, were seared by flames that were visible as far away as Portland, Maine.

The immediate reaction to the fire was stunned horror. But this was soon replaced by the desire of the political and business leaders of Chelsea to restore what they had lost. The newspaper, owned by the mayor, understandably called for a "firm determination that from these ashes will arise a new Chelsea. Let all citizens work in harmony, this is no time to discuss or quibble over petty affairs. What is needed is unity; success is then assured."[5]

Success did indeed come. By December 1908, the Chelsea *Gazette* (which like most local papers liked to look at the bright side of things) commended the rapidity, solidity and beauty of the rebuilt city. The paper estimated that $3 million had already been committed for reconstruction. Two years later, with the value of local property approaching the pre-fire level, an "Achievement Number" of the paper was able to tout the city's "marvelous recovery." Less biased observers confirmed the weekly's upbeat version of the rebuilding process.[6] The growth of Chelsea, far from being stopped by the fire, continued for twenty years thereafter.[7]

But this success was not achieved through the unity that Mayor John Beck had called for. Chelsea had developed as a part of a nationwide process of industrialization and urbanization that promoted not only growth but also profound differentiation and division in the population of the expanding cities. When this process began for Chelsea in 1830, it had been a small farming town on Boston Harbor about a mile distant from Boston proper by boat. Only thirty persons were to be found in 1830 within the 1.5 square miles that would comprise the twentieth-century city. However, by 1860 the growth of Boston as an industrial metropolis and the advent of improved transportation to Chelsea stimulated the creation of a community of 12,000 people in what had become a booming commuter's suburb.[8]

This expansion marked only the first stage of the impact of urban growth in this former farm village. After the Civil War, industrial as well as residential Boston expanded into the town across the harbor. As early as 1885, a significant amount of industrial activity had penetrated Chelsea. Printing, food preparation, building, leather and iron goods and other industries employed a total of almost 2,000 persons.[9] By the first decade of the twentieth century, 50 percent of the city's locally employed work force was engaged in manufacturing; production was four times that of 1885.[10] Yet the city did not lose its earlier function as a "bedroom" suburb. In 1915, one-third of Chelseans still commuted to Boston and more than one-third of those locally employed were engaged in trade and service occupations directed (for the most part) at the residential population. Chelsea had become highly diversified economically.[11]

Supporting the growth of the industrial economy was a striking increase in population. By 1905 Chelsea's total population had reached 37,300.[12] As in many other industrializing American cities, a large portion of this new population was made up of alien immigrants. In fact, in 1905, 37 percent of the residents of Chelsea had been born abroad. Before 1890 Irish and other northern European immigrants constituted the bulk of the newcomers. After that date streams of Jews, Italians, and Poles from eastern and southern Europe became more prominent. In 1905, English-speaking persons included 48 percent of the total of 13,883 foreign-born in Chelsea. But Jews from Russia, with a much smaller number of Poles, already constituted 32 percent of all immigrant residents. Italians comprised almost 3 percent of this population.

Immigrants and their children outnumbered the old settlers of Chelsea two to one in 1905.[13]

Thus, when Mayor Beck called for unity in the effort to rebuild after the fire of 1908, he was appealing to a city far from unified in either its origins and culture or its economic pursuits and interests. In addition, the diversity, and even divisiveness, of Chelsea were sharply reinforced by the high degree of residential segregation in the city. The topography of Chelsea encouraged this. When industry invaded the residential suburb, the largely native commuter element of the population was able to retreat eastwardly from the early harborside settlement to a series of hills (see Map 1-1). Far more suitable for residences than industry, "Mounts" Bellingham and Washington, as well as Powder Horn Hill, became in the early twentieth century exclusive and most pleasant residential neighborhoods. The flatlands near the harbor were occupied by the factories and the industrial workers.[14]

This functional division of Chelsea resulted in ethnic and occupational segregation. The hills tended to be the home of the more highly skilled and the professionals; the flats, of the less skilled (see Table 1-1 and Map 1-3). Associated with this tendency, but still stronger, was the separation of the recently arrived southern and eastern European immigrants from the "older stock," which had origins in the British Isles. Data available for 1915 (and probably reflecting a situation similar to that of 1908) clearly demonstrates this. Using the Index of Dissimilarity (a statistical measure of segregation), the Jews of Chelsea can be shown to have been almost as well segregated from the older stock as blacks and whites are from one another in contemporary American cities. The Poles were even more segregated than this from all other groups.[15] Map 1-2 clearly indicates that the old stock was concentrated in the eastern, occupationally elevated part of town, and the Jews in the western lowlands. The extremely dense Polish community was found in the immediate vicinity of the docks[16] (see Table 1-2).

These ethnic and occupational divisions were reflected in Chelsea's political life. The city government was organized on a mayoral-aldermanic basis. One alderman was elected in 1908 from each of ten precincts, organized into five wards; five were elected (like the mayor) at large.[17] Naturally, the aldermen tended to reflect the interests of the particular group dominant in their home precincts. Wards II and IV roughly corresponded to the immigrant and workers' sections. Wards I, III and V were heavily weighted toward the more highly skilled natives.[18]

The political, social, and economic context in which Mayor Beck called for unity was one of heterogeneity and diversity of interests. The decentralized aldermanic system functioned to balance differing cultural and economic elements. It was not aimed at rapid and efficient action, but at politic compromise and accommodation. In the eyes of many, this political system, which mirrored social reality so well, was incapable of providing the unity of aims and actions called for in an emergency. It could not produce the unity called for by Beck. In particular, the leading financial and industrial figures in Chelsea, confronted by devastation, concluded at the time of the 1908 fire that inefficient and inexpert partisan governance could no longer be tolerated. Recurrently, voices were raised that decried the continuance of politics as usual.[19] Within a few days after the fire, representatives of "37 of the various institutions" involved in local financial and manufacturing affairs met and concluded that only a commission form of government could undertake the recovery effort. The meeting was followed by the formation of a widely based Citizens' Committee, which immediately submitted a bill to the state legislature calling for the creation of a city commission. Fifty-two days after the fire, Acting Governor Eben Draper appointed five commissioners to replace the aldermen and mayor.[20]

The Chelsea commission, called the Board of Control, was a striking political innovation in the East. It centralized in the hands of the commissioners almost all political authority. They assumed the powers of mayor, aldermen and, temporarily, the school board. The immediate justification of this concentration of power was the need to "assure to the city a government that will command the confidence of the money and insurance interests" during the rebuilding process.[21] A small group of apolitical experts appointed by the governor surely would inspire more confidence than the highly political and inefficient aldermen. In accord with the legislation establishing it, the new board would supplant the aldermen for five years of concerted effort at reconstruction.

The members who were appointed to the new Board of Control did have considerably more claim to technical expertise than did the displaced aldermen. The latter included Alexander Cook, a compositor; Horatio Delano, a bricklayer; and James C. Denning, a carpenter. In all, at least five of the fifteen aldermen in 1908 were skilled workers who appeared to be unqualified for a massive executive responsibility during the recovery. Even professionals on the Board of Aldermen, including lawyers Clarence A. Warren and Melvin D. Breath, hardly seemed to have the stature or experience to undertake the reconstruction of the city.[22] In contrast, the Board of Control appointed to carry out the rebuilding was headed by William McClintock, a prominent civil engineer. Other members included Mark Wilmarth of nearby Malden, also a civil engineer; A. C. Ratshesky, an important Boston banker; George Dunham, a local manufacturing executive; and Alton Briggs, principal of Chelsea High School. The acting governor chose the "best" men even if they were not Chelseans.

members of this group and of the professionals who aided them were of the older, Protestant stock. The favored members of this group identified the city itself, as well as its successes, with themselves. The Chelsea *Evening Record*, a strong supporter of the Board of Control, approvingly quoted the assertion in the *Christian Science Monitor* in 1910 that "the intelligent businessmen, the heads of families, the owners of homes" represent "more than all others the city itself."[46] At the heart of the philosophy that endorsed commission government, and much of the rest of progressivism in Chelsea, was the belief that the expert and responsible persons who had led the city to material success could represent its common interest in encouraging future growth. The *Evening Record* heartily approved the view of one J. J. Hamilton: "The city is physically, socially and economically a unit. There is a common mind in the community . . . voiced by the local newspaper press."[47] The assumption was that the editors of the press and their commercial and manufacturing allies could best express a common mind on behalf of the community. From this perspective, the composition of the Board of Control was both sensible and democratic. Responding to Mayor Beck's plea, it provided the unity of direction needed to meet the challenge to the city.

The view of the immigrant or worker was quite different. Rather than seeing the board as reflecting a unified society, members of these groups saw quite clearly the ethnic, religious and economic divisions in the city that industrialization had augmented. The geography of Chelsea made these divisions literally visible. The First Precinct of Ward V was north and east of the railroads and Broadway (the major shopping street), which decisively marked the precinct's boundaries. At the heart of the eastern end of town and including Powder Horn Hill, this precinct was the only political unit of the city in which a majority of the population was employed in white collar positions (see Maps 1-1 and 1-3). It was overwhelmingly native and heavily Protestant. Politically, the precinct was strongly Republican.[48] Of particular interest is the fact that this precinct contained a street, Crescent Avenue, on which William McClintock and Alton Briggs, two of the three local members of the Board of Control resided. Just around the corner, in the same precinct, was Tudor Street and the home of the only other local Board of Control member, George Dunham. The physical and social contrast between this section and Ward II at the western end of town, inhabited by large numbers of unskilled and immigrant workers, made the ideal of social unity most implausible.

From the first debates on commission government, opponents of the progressive plan recognized that it would be far more beneficial for the residents of wealthy areas than for others. One resident, W. W. Tucker, commented in May 1908 that "if a referendum was taken, Ward V would be for it and Ward I would be against it."[49] Tucker was quite right. When the referendum occurred, Ward I did decide that its interests were quite distinct from those of the residents of Ward V, who had been running the Board of Control. Only three of the fifteen aldermen of 1908 had been from Ward V. In 1911, Chelseans selected only two residents of that ward among the nine men elected aldermen.[50] By returning to the aldermanic system, Chelseans appear to have asserted that the city was a congeries of ethnic, economic, and geographic interests, each of which required its own representation. This was a fact that the proponents of the commission misunderstood at their peril.

To try to reduce such a complex conflict as Chelsea's to simple economic terms or, alternatively, to purely cultural considerations would be a gross distortion.[51] A number of coincident group interests were reinforcing one another in the controversy over the attempt to install a commission in Chelsea. Economics did play an important role. It was indeed the manufacturers of the city who initiated the commission movement with the intent of stabilizing economic conditions after the fire of 1908. And support for the plan had been derived from the most wealthy portions of the city. The commission plan was, in part, one way of insuring the advantaged group that the relationship of wealth and influence was not unduly diluted by the growth of "the ignorant population . . . only of importance to the city as a laboring class."[52]

But we have seen that the desire for efficiency and economy in government became entangled with an attempt by the dominant Protestant business group to deny the growing ethnic and social heterogeneity of the city. John Higham and others have demonstrated how often progressive thought was related to racial and religious exclusiveness. This tendency to identify American progress with traditional American Protestantism and Anglo-Saxonism during the Progressive Era yielded a series of putative reforms, including eugenics and immigration restriction, that now seem anything but progressive.[53] The attempt to reform Chelsea's city government was intended to retain and consolidate the favored political, cultural, and economic position of the wealthier native Protestants. The culturally threatening immigrants were excluded from and hostile to the reform. In a city like Chelsea, it was difficult to separate economic from ethnic or religious politics. The basic divisions of the community were founded in many spheres of overlapping social differentiation. This created a context in which geography, economics, and ethnicity all inevitably became engaged in the major issues of community conflict.

The failure of the commission plan in Chelsea was clearly not due to the total opposition of the population to "progressivism." The city charter that replaced the Board of Control included several of the reforms central to urban progressivism. The 1911 document included the referendum, the initiative, nonpartisan elections, and strict campaign regulations among its provisions. This was the charter that received heavy support in immigrant and working-class sections. Nor was the failure of the commission plan due simply to the attempt of the wealthier and more established elements in the population to exercise their influence; that attempt would continue unabated after the defeat. In 1915, Chelsea's mayor lived in the exclusive First Precinct of Ward V. Two of the four aldermen-at-large elected in that year lived on or within that precinct's lines. The city clerk, city treasurer, city engineer, clerk of committees and the superintendent of public buildings also lived in that precinct—an area containing only 8 percent of the city's population.[54] The possession of wealth was still closely related to the possession of influence.

The defeat of the commission proposal is fully explicable only in light of its interaction with the totality of the city's social life. If the rhetoric of progressivism and the interests of a modernizing economic elite had not been so tenaciously tied in Chelsea to the retreating hegemony of a religious and ethnic group, the course of "reform" might have been quite different and more successful. In Chelsea, as was often true elsewhere, the leaders of the industrial economy were also the conservators of the Protestant, Anglo-Saxon tradition. They pursued their twin goals of economic and cultural hegemony through the same political reform. The support for the commission came most particularly from those areas in which wealth and Protestantism reinforced one another. By overreaching themselves, by alienating other ethnic and economic groups, this small privileged elite defeated itself. It failed to recognize the full complexity of the society.

Increasingly, students of progressivism have been avoiding this same error and as a result have been discovering the full complexity of reform. In Chelsea, a northeastern industrial town, the evolving ethnic distinctions came to the fore in shaping the divisive reactions to one vital element of urban progressivism. History had determined that ethnicity would be at the heart of political life. This may also have been true elsewhere in the Northeast. In other parts of the nation, where ethnic divisions were less significant, such universal concerns as public utilities were often more important in defining a unified community view backing reforms.[55] Still elsewhere, where politics was dominated by immigrant organizations, other varieties of urban progressivism were experienced.[56] The rhetoric of reform was common to many cities. But in each case, the response to industrialism was guided by the total nature of local society. In a nation as diverse as the United States at the start of this century, the wide range of "reform" experiences was surely one of progressivism's most significant and interesting characteristics. With varied ethnic, economic, and cultural environments, every type of community had to define progressivism in its own way, according to its own history and conditions. Progressivism did, no doubt, have some unified identity, if only in its response to new conditions and in the consciousness of those who used its rhetoric. But the attempt to understand early twentieth-century "reform" must place at least as much emphasis on the uniqueness of its varied local, state, and national manifestations as on its unity. If the Chelsea case makes anything clear, it is that the meaning of political behavior can be comprehended only in the full context of each particular political community. Only by examining the social tensions within a particular city can we understand what progressivism meant there. Only after such an understanding is achieved in many instances can the national commonalities of experience emerge—and with them a fuller meaning for "progressivism" in the nation as a whole.

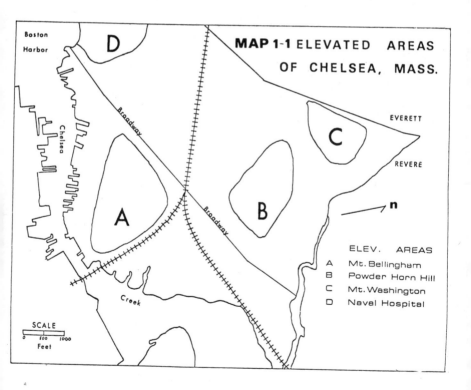

MAP 1-1 ELEVATED AREAS OF CHELSEA, MASS.

ELEV. AREAS
A   Mt. Bellingham
B   Powder Horn Hill
C   Mt. Washington
D   Naval Hospital

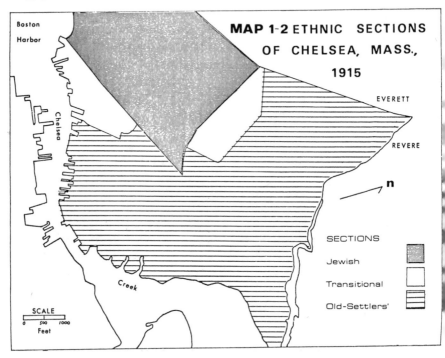

TABLE 1-1. Occupational Composition of Precincts: Chelsea, Mass., 1915
(Males, Twenty Years of Age and Over)

Occupation	I,1	I,2	II,1	II,2	III,1	III,2	IV,1	IV,2	V,1	V,2	All
Unknown:											
No.	9	2	8	5	2	5	5	4	6	6	52
% of row	17.3	3.8	15.4	9.6	3.8	9.6	9.6	7.7	11.5	11.5	100.0
% of column	12.3	5.0	10.7	8.3	3.4	9.3	12.5	7.4	12.2	12.0	9.4
Unskilled:											
No.	31	8	29	7	4	10	6	5	2	5	107
% of row	29.0	7.5	27.1	6.5	3.7	9.3	5.6	4.7	1.9	4.7	100.0
% of column	42.5	20.0	38.7	11.7	6.9	18.5	15.0	9.3	4.1	10.0	19.3
Semiskilled:											
No.	13	7	6	15	14	8	10	15	2	12	102
% of row	12.7	6.9	5.9	14.7	13.7	7.8	9.8	14.7	2.0	11.8	100.0
% of column	17.8	17.5	8.0	25.0	24.1	14.8	25.0	27.8	4.1	24.0	18.4
Skilled:											
No.	8	10	11	19	18	22	7	12	13	12	132
% of row	6.1	7.6	8.3	14.4	13.6	16.7	5.3	9.1	9.8	9.1	100.0
% of column	11.0	25.0	14.7	31.7	31.0	40.7	17.5	22.2	26.5	24.0	23.9
White Collar:											
No.	12	13	21	14	20	9	12	18	26	15	160
% of row	7.5	8.1	13.1	8.8	12.5	5.6	7.5	11.2	16.2	9.4	100.0
% of column	16.4	32.5	28.0	23.3	34.5	16.7	30.0	33.3	53.1	30.0	28.9
All:											
No.	73	40	75	60	58	54	40	54	49	50	553
% of row	13.2	7.2	13.6	10.8	10.5	9.8	7.2	9.8	8.9	9.0	100.0
% of column	100.0	100.0	100.0	100.0	100.0	100.0	100.0	100.0	100.0	100.0	100.0

Source: Sample Data. See Kopf, "The Intimate City," Appendix A.

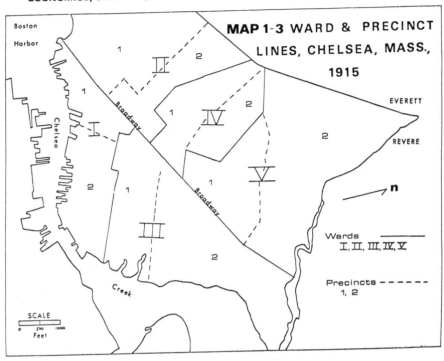

MAP 1-3 WARD & PRECINCT LINES, CHELSEA, MASS., 1915

TABLE 1-2. Proportion of Population of Precincts in Major Ethnic Groups Chelsea, Mass., 1915 (Males Twenty Years of Age and Over; Percentage)

	I,1	I,2	II,1	II,2	III,1	III,2	IV,1	IV,2	V,1	V,2	All
Old Settler	47	80	47	21	87	81	38	63	80	84	61
Jewish	19	18	41	63	10	0	55	33	10	2	26
Other	34	3	12	16	3	19	8	4	10	14	12
Total	100	100	100	100	100	100	100	100	100	100	100
(N)	(73)	(40)	(75)	(62)	(60)	(57)	(40)	(54)	(49)	(50)	(560)

Source: Sample Data. See Kopf, "The Intimate City," Appendix A.

TABLE 1-3. Election Results in Chelsea Referendum on City Charters, November 7, 1911

	I,1	I,2	II,1	II,2	III,1	III,2	IV,1	IV,2	V,1	V,2	Total
Plan 1 (Commission Government)	80	86	98	63	172	137	45	282	421	347	1731
Plan 2 (Aldermanic Government)	161	166	347	165	153	357	68	191	167	186	1961
Total	241	252	445	228	325	494	113	473	588	533	3692

Source: Chelsea *Evening Record*, November 8, 1911.

HAROLD L. PLATT

2. CITY-BUILDING AND PROGRESSIVE REFORM:

THE MODERNIZATION OF AN URBAN POLITY, HOUSTON, 1892–1905

The Progressive Era was the first period in which urban reform permeated the entire country. Its pervasiveness was in large part generated by national economic developments, particularly in communications. Interdependence insured the simultaneous diffusion of novel ideas and innovations everywhere, irrespective of city size and location. Yet, the impacts of the powerful new agents of change, from electric rapid transit to budgetary theory, were far from uniform. A configuration of indigenous conditions—community socioeconomic fabrics, stages of growth, and local-regional perspectives—shaped a unique path of experience in each place. Progressivism's blend of uniformity and diversity makes comparative analysis of individual case studies vital to an understanding of the period.[1]

Houston's experience provides insight into the age of urban reform, for it exposes the interface between national forces of modernity and localistic reactions against the accelerating pace of change.[2] In constructing a modern city, Houstonians contended over the propriety of promoting growth as opposed to improving the quality of their immediate surroundings. This clash of values and interests was transmuted into a political struggle for leadership of the municipal government, which was being transformed into the central agency of control over the community's welfare. Ward-centered politicians expressed neighborhood-narrow perspectives and Southern fears of relinquishing self-determination to Northern intruders. The aldermen conducted a disorderly and inefficient if democratic process of decision making about the fate of the community. The resulting instability became intolerable to elite business groups, whose success was tied to fostering growth by securing Northern capital and expertise. After 1901 these groups acted forcefully to take over local government in order to link Houston into the national economic system.

Political alignments and reform results in the Gulf Coast city were structured by at least two major concurrent developments. Houston entered the nineties largely disconnected from national events and ill-prepared to cope with rapid change. The initial cause of concern was a metamorphosis in physical scale; steady growth had outstripped essential public services and their institutional supports. Houston underwent a basic change from town to city that repeated many dynamic characteristics common to nineteenth-century city-building. A step-by-step series of adjustments was wrought amidst confusion and crisis over priorities, leadership, and the reach of the police power. Conflict within the community became endemic as increases in population and organizational effectiveness promoted the active pursuit of self-interest by more and more groups.[3]

For the first time, in this period local brokers of outside information, capital, and technology were offered unprecedented, almost irresistible, weight in the political balance of power. The second major transformation affecting Houston, its vertical integration into the national urban hierarchy, tipped power at first gradually, then suddenly, toward these broker groups. The 1901 destruction of rival Galveston by a hurricane and the discovery of oil a brief time later raised Houston to national importance as the leading city of the Southwest region. A New South style of accommodation with Northern developers and financiers now became imperative to the city's commercial-business elites, whose opportunities dramatically expanded. After capturing municipal power in 1902, these elites made fundamental alterations in party machinery, municipal institutions, and government relationships with utility corporations. Northern techniques of urban structural reform allowed new modes of city planning and social control. Possessing a holistic image of Houston as a single politicoeconomic unit, the "metropolitan" elite came to consider ward-centered democracy inimical to the mutual growth of their own and the city's fortunes. By 1905 the metropolitans were able to defeat and exclude more parochial groups and to consolidate power under a novel commission form of government.

Rapid urbanization in Texas was based on a steady economic revival and diversification that began during the early 1880s. The state experienced extensive railroad expansion and agricultural growth, with rice, grains, cattle, and timber harvesting added to cotton production.[4] Since its inception in 1836, Houston had been a commercial and transportation center. The initial advantage Houston gained in the 1850s as the region's rail terminal had neutralized Galveston's superior location fifty miles downstream on the Gulf Coast. This advantage had brought accumulating benefits, especially the operation of railroad repair shops and agricultural processing plants. The high cost of importing fuels, however, retarded industrial development.[5]

Productive activity in the hinterlands was reflected in evolving spatial and demographic patterns within the city. The municipality's nine square miles was divided into two specialized areas by a shallow waterway. Buffalo Bayou had been an important shipping route to the coast until the 1879 completion of East-West rail lanes. Industries and depots bordered the bayou's northeastern side; a business district paralleled the opposite bank. As the population grew from 27,000 to 45,000 between 1891 and 1901, the inauguration of electric rapid transit shifted residential construction towards the western portions of the town. The first planned suburban subdivision further enhanced the real estate boom. Harris County's 71 percent growth rate was boosted for the first time above the city's.

Even in the early nineties, Houston's size contrasted sharply with restricted public utility services and environmental improvements. Water, gas, telephone, and electric light and power lines were tightly concentrated in the business district, which also possessed eight miles of wooden-paved streets. Only the street railway, with a fifty-mile series of twelve belt lines radiating from a central downtown loop, served the entire community.[6] Under local ownership that was short of capital, technical expertise, and managerial vision, utility corporations primarily accommodated commercial rather than consumer needs. Municipal government functioned with similarly limited resources and perspectives.

Houston's experience seems "typical" of nineteenth-century American urban development—haphazard, unplanned, underfinanced, privately oriented. Municipal government was unequipped institutionally and financially to manage the city-building process. Local politics before and after Reconstruction was a brief biannual Democratic affair dominated by ward-level meetings that culminated in a primary election. A prominent businessman was usually selected mayor, while retail proprietors, skilled laborers, and white-collar workers filled the ten aldermanic positions. In 1892, for example, a united Democracy chose John T. Browne to end small but constant budget deficits. The new mayor, who had worked his way up from brickcarrier to large mercantile wholesaler, was representative of Houston's first-generation leadership. For Browne and other leading commercial entrepreneurs, involvement in municipal government, promotion of city growth, and personal business success were closely tied together. Browne's previous experience as council finance chairman determined his selection.[7]

Nevertheless, an interrelated process of clarifying issues, ordering priorities, and forging organizational identifications occurred over the next four years. Unresolvable problems and shocking incidents helped focus attention on the necessity to formulate public policies. But growth was most responsible in forcing a redefinition of urban government's role in the community. Older arrangements for supplying most services and facilities were breaking down under the impact of demographic, industrial, and physical expansion.

During the early 1890s Houston reached a turning point. New levels of institutional, fiscal, and technological sophistication were essential. Social and economic patterns had already begun responding to the city's enlarged complexities. The number of formal organizations more than doubled between 1885 and 1895 and increased another 300 percent over the following decade.[8] Neighborhood, business, and other special groups emerged as powerful vehicles of concerted political pressure on city officials.

The Browne administration's initial efforts followed a traditional pattern: restoration of a balanced budget through retrenchment of governmental functions. It faced the difficult task of balancing limited tax revenues against rising current expenses (see Table 2-1). Public officials, moreover, were determined to implement at least some projects on their lengthening list of vital public works. The mayor and the council attempted to freeze spending for such services as police and education, while stalling insurance underwriter demands to professionalize the firemen. At the same time, Browne sought to use municipal bonds to finance construction of more schools, an electrical fire alarm system, and a refuse facility.[9] Expensive street paving and sewer costs were paid through special direct taxes on private property owners. A solid tax base and efficient collection machinery belatedly had been established in 1888, after a fourteen-year bond default contest with creditors and the U. S. Circuit Court.[10] Yet, property valuations stagnated at $22 million for five years following the 1893 depression. Until tax assessments could be raised, Houston's ability to issue new bonds was circumscribed tightly by old debts and recent state legislation.[11]

It was within this context of fiscal dilemmas that the mayor and the aldermen began serious inquiry into the feasibility of municipal ownership. An inflexible tax base and chronically poor quality service from franchised companies pointed policy-makers toward novel uses of the public authority. In 1893, Browne concluded that large savings in the

$180,000 budget could be achieved only in the city's utility bills. He argued that instead of paying $35,000 annually for water supply and electric street lighting, lesser amounts could finance permanent municipal assets. The next year appraisers estimated it would cost $900,000, a 50 percent increase in the debt, to purchase even the existing unsatisfactory systems. Their initial expectations of quick, cheap solutions shattered,

TABLE 2-1. Allocation of Public Revenues, 1892–1905[a]

Year Population	1892 30,000	1897 40,000	1901 46,000	1905 56,000
Interest				
A. Amount	$109,400	$ 88,000	$170,000	$320,100
B. Percentage of Total	38.1	23.8	29.4	33.5
C. Per Capita Expenditure	$3.64	$2.20	$3.70	$5.72
General Expenses				
A. Amount	$ 30,000	$ 33,500	$ 58,600	$ 86,900
B. Percentage of Total	10.4	9.5	10.1	9.5
C. Per Capita Expenditure	$1.00	$ .84	$1.28	$1.55
Public Safety				
A. Amount	$ 37,000	$ 82,000	$108,600	$150,700
B. Percentage of Total	12.8	22.2	18.7	15.7
C. Per Capita Expenditure	$1.23	$2.05	$2.36	$2.70
Health				
A. Amount	$ 10,000	$ 22,700	$ 32,800	$ 12,400
B. Percentage of Total	3.5	6.1	3.9	1.3
C. Per Capita Expenditure	$ .33	$ .57	$ .50	$ .22
Roads and Bridges[b]				
A. Amount	$ 40,000	$ 52,000	$ 60,800	$ 97,700
B. Percentage of Total	14.0	14.0	10.5	10.2
C. Per Capita Expenditure	$1.33	$1.30	$1.32	$1.75
Utility Services				
A. Amount	$ 30,000	$ 43,000	$ 45,800	$ 81,700
B. Percentage of Total	10.4	11.6	7.9	8.5
C. Per Capita Expenditure	$1.00	$1.07	$1.00	$1.46
Education				
A. Amount	$ 30,000	$ 51,000	$ 81,000	$123,200
B. Percentage of Total	10.4	13.8	14.0	12.8
C. Per Capita Expenditure	$1.00	$1.27	$1.76	$2.20
Sanitation[b]				
A. Amount	c	c	$ 15,900	$ 55,300
B. Percentage of Total			2.7	5.8
C. Per Capita Expenditure			$ .35	$ .99
Recreation				
A. Amount	c	c	$ 15,900	$ 9,500
B. Percentage of Total			2.7	1.0
C. Per Capita Expenditure			$ .35	$ .17
Totals				
A. Amount	$286,400	$372,200	$589,400	$937,500
B. Percentage of Total	100.0	101.0	99.9	98.3
C. Per Capita Expenditure	$9.05	$9.25	$12.60	$17.10

[a]Calculated from: Houston, *City Council Minutes*, Books H-P (Houston: City Secretary's office, 1892–1907); Houston, *Annual Message* (Houston: Coyle, 1913), 70-96; and U. S. Bureau of Census statistics as listed in *Texas Almanac* (Dallas: *Dallas Morning Star*, 1972), 63.

[b]Includes only current budgetary appropriations.

[c]None.

the administration renewed more traditional techniques to secure larger concessions from utility companies.[12]

City government had found few effective means to regulate these firms after twenty-five years of experimenting with various franchise strategies. While the introduction of competitive ventures had produced immediate rate reductions and service extensions, businessmen rapidly merged their enterprises to restore monopolies. The consolidation of the two railway companies, as well as the electric firms, by outside investors in 1891 convinced many Houstonians that the maxim "competition is the life of trade" was a misleading myth.

In June 1894, the council rejected franchise proposals from new water and electric light ventures in favor of reaffirming existing contracts with the two established firms. Two months later, local government's incapacity to insure the performance of franchise obligations was tragically demonstrated. A fire consumed a residential block and St. Joseph's Infirmary; two nuns died in the blaze as volunteer firemen stood helpless with limp hoses attached to dry hydrants.

The council launched a full investigation, which took testimony from corporation executives, fire insurance underwriters, and, for the first time, consumers. Water company president Thomas M. Scanlan's accurate explanation that compliance with the pressure levels defined in the original 1878 franchise was impossible did not appease the outraged community. Central pumping methods of fire-fighting had become outmoded along the expanding sixty-mile distributive network, and many older mains simply were too small. Scanlan responded to unanimous consumer complaints of overcharges by liberally redrawing rate schedules, and he recited current projects for upgrading facilities to correspond to the city's greater scale. The company president also offered to sell the utility to the public for a price to be determined by an arbitration board.

Local and state insurance men provided the most complete analysis and scathing criticism of Houston's water supply system. Their reform proposals were enacted within a year because they had imposed a special tariff on fire coverage premiums that placed the city in an inferior and more expensive category than other urban centers. The underwriters' principal recommendations were a fully paid fire department, a rapid expansion of the alarm system, and a stiffer building code. These reforms greatly improved the city's fire protection, but solutions to the basic problem, a new water pressure system, were evaded.[13] The council's course was marked by policy drift rather than initiatives to either enforce the franchise, enact better controls, or assume financial responsibility. Efficient regulatory mechanisms also continued to elude the aldermen in their search for answers to other utility problems, such as testing streetlamp quality and enforcing the transit firm's paving obligations.

In April 1895, the state supreme court completely upset the city government's uncertain groping for a fruitful mix of public and private means to enhance urban services. In *Higgins* v. *Bordages,* the court held that special assessment tax liens were unenforceable against homeowners. Overruling twelve years of harmonious precedents, the court ended the efficacy of financing street and sewer improvements with this tax system. The city could no longer threaten every delinquent with certain loss of property.[14] In Houston the surprising judicial reversal threw more than $850,000 in unpaid and previously collected assessments into legal limbo, leading one reporter to observe that "the whole situation which was yesterday so serene, is [today] all turmoil and commotion."[15]

The "public calamity" created by the Higgins case forced the administration to begin the city's first systematic planning. The clarifying and ordering of public improvement goals marked a watershed in Houstonians' perception of urban problems. The definition of alternatives meant the start of a protracted struggle for political control. The council immediately hired local experts to institute better methods of fiscal accountability. They calculated that a maximum of $1 million in bonds could be issued over a five-year period. Browne and most councilmen wanted the entire amount spent on road-building projects. Since any bond issue over $100,000 needed approval from a two-thirds majority of voting taxpayers, the aldermen scheduled a special election for September. Citizens had considered paved streets the primary engine of internal growth and a powerful magnetic symbol of urban modernity for over a quarter century. The equation of paving and progress reflected property owners' predominant influence in municipal affairs.[16]

By 1895, however, groups with different priorities were organized to intervene in decision making about the allocation of the community's limited resources. The Labor Council, for example, had started an educational program in local government after the shocks of the infirmary fire and a subsequent report by physicians that the water supply was "detrimental to the public health."[17] Representing over a thousand white skilled workers and closely allied to another three thousand railroad repairmen, the labor federation campaigned against the bond proposal. They argued for municipal ownership of the existing water and electric services. The opposition of the Labor Council and others who raised informed doubts about the city council's plan, signaled most citizens to vote against their leaders; the proposition was defeated, 525 to 497.[18]

The repudiated administration allowed policy planning to drift, but the issues propelled Houstonians into their first real political battle since Reconstruction. As the April 1896 general elections approached, some middle-class professionals and small proprietors formed a moralistic Good Government League. This truly nonpartisan party was too radical and quickly foundered against continuing attachments to the Democracy. A more viable intraparty movement was spearheaded by Henry Brashear, a large landowner and county officer. Democratic dissidents denounced the closed and dishonest methods their party's executive committee used to select candidates, notably H. Baldwin Rice for mayor. The Brashear forces bolted to conduct a separate primary election. Rice, also a member of the city's inner elite of wealthy pioneer families, drew on party loyalty to sweep the general election with 3,600 votes, against 2,800 for the dissidents and 300 for the Leaguers.[19]

Reform ferment was largely internal at first, a common response to urban growth from town to city. Although the regular leadership retained office, the issues debated during the campaign exposed deep political fissures. Many different groups, now armed with specific programs and priorities, began to demand vindication of their understanding of urban progress. Strident competition to direct municipal decision making generated a state of tension and suspicion. Increasingly, the community at large became involved in a divisive series of crises over allocation priorities and political leadership.

Control of urban policy was, however, becoming increasingly important to larger economic concerns. By the 1900s Houston would become locked into webs of regional and national interdependence. Consequently, city government's power to influence the outcome of competing private aspirations swelled. The limits of municipal authority to supervise community development more closely were frequently contested in the courts. The judiciary's enlarging role in adjusting relations and making policy paralleled other institutions' greater management of the city-building process.[20]

The rapid metamorphosis of public utilities during the nineties provides a good illustration of the tightening net of interdependence enveloping Houston. While utilities are most pertinent here, similar developments were occurring in other industries, such as timberland-lumber, cotton processing, machinery repair, and brewing. Houston's industrial integration rested upon a foundation of earlier linkages into national transport, communications, and financial networks.

The Citizens' Light and Power Company, like other franchised enterprises, responded to increased consumer demand for services by extending distribution lines and expanding outputs. Central stations grew organically with bigger, more advanced units connected to previously accumulated equipment. These improvements were financed through mortgage bonds sold in New York and Boston. The electric firm's fiscal integrity was linked to policy decisions made at city hall. The municipal corporation held critical sway over the company's prospects as both its major customer and the source of large but vaguely defined regulatory power.

In 1897 a municipal ownership movement, which had been gaining strength and respect during the depression, threatened the electric corporation's survival.[21] The city council began considering a resolution to construct a light plant. Advocates chose this priority because of a low, $100,000 initial expense, and the dismal performance of the private facility. Company officers counterproposed a 20 percent rate cut in exchange for a seven-year contract that effectively precluded a public alternative. Mayor Rice's supporters on the council joined the city ownership minority after winning agreement to establish a Board of Light Commissioners chosen by the mayor. A bond referendum to finance a municipal plant was approved; strongest support was registered in the newer, middle-class sections on the west side.[22]

The uncertainties created by local government stimulated anxious investors to place their venture in bankruptcy for bond defaults since 1896, even though the light commissioners appointed by Mayor Rice opposed municipal ownership. Under a U. S. Circuit Court receivership from 1898 to 1902, the utility was completely rebuilt. Infusions of Eastern money and managerial expertise were required to create modern services, which attracted substantially more consumers.

The street railway underwent two similar reorganizations.[23] By 1905 control of every franchised service except the water supply would pass from local businessmen to holding companies that operated on a national scale. Modernization under private initiative shifted general attention and support for municipal ownership towards the old-fashioned waterworks.

The organizational changes being wrought in public utility structures were typical of broader trends binding Houston's internal affairs to external events. The Browne and Rice administrations hoped to accelerate these developments by pursuing the New South prescription for attracting Northern capital and industries. In 1898 parochially centered groups reacted forcefully to protect their narrower interests. Samuel H. Brashear, a state district judge and nephew of Rice's previous challenger, headed an opposition slate. Political struggle was now contained within the party through reform of primary procedures and the exclusion of blacks, who comprised 40 percent of the population. The ensuing debate between Rice and Brashear revealed essentially different visions of the best means to enhance the general welfare. The incumbent defended policies aimed at encouraging growth of the private sector, but Brashear insisted that government should first correct current problems facing the community and its investors.[24]

A second confrontation, with violent overtones of local self-determination battling Yankee intruders, began on the eve of the March primary. Recently unionized transit workers started a strike against the Houston Electric Street Railway Company. In Houston's first disruptive experience with a business-labor clash, sympathetic policemen refused to intervene. Angry mobs enforced the Labor Council-sanctioned shutdown, while the mayor promised to summon troops to protect company property. Rice's unpopular stand contributed to his three-to-two margin of defeat at the polls. The triumph of the localistic perspective was further highlighted by widespread support of the strike, which was settled unfavorably for the Boston-owned corporation.[25]

Brashear's administration vigorously pursued coherent programs designed to expand controls over the environment and essential service functions. Progressive attacks on public utility company tax-dodging were enhanced by the administration's emphasis upon efficiency and professional expertise. New offices, such as a city auditor and electric and gas inspectors, were added to the burgeoning bureaucracies of established departments. The work force employed by local government also grew from projects that laid miles of asphalt pavement and began construction of a unified sewage treatment/electric power plant.[26] In augmenting the machinery of government, the municipal corporation became a big business. It had a large impact on the local economy and the general well-being of its inhabitants. In 1901, the city spent almost $600,000 (see Table 2-1), one-third more per capita than four years earlier.

Municipal services were upgraded, expanded, and extended to previously neglected areas. Brashear's brand of reform fulfilled neighborhood-narrow concepts of urban progress. The council's ward-centered logrolling insured a fairly equal distribution of the benefits among geographic sections. The mayor also waged an unrelenting fight against rich foreign corporations, especially the utility enterprises. For example, the administration withheld payments from the light and water companies, granted franchises with lowered rates to new telephone and telegraph ventures, and took the street railway company to court to force collection of $100,000 in unpaid paving taxes.[27]

The costs of Brashear's innovative policy thrusts caused steadily rising municipal debts, with mounting resistance from large taxpayers, utility firms, and promoters of the New South creed. These opposition forces united in 1900 behind former mayor Browne, who campaigned against the incumbent's "nagging" posture towards outside corporations and "spoils" system of patronage. The contest became one of the rare instances when localism was openly denounced. But the opposition lacked a forceful positive direction, because Browne was unable to visualize the New South for the voters. Administration supporters among labor, homeowners, and small businessmen rallied in record numbers to tip the close election by 240 out of 8,100 votes.

Brashear's victory was short-lived, however. A coordinated revolt by council conservatives and administration opponents brought decision making to a standstill. The pivotal issue in producing the stalemate was the aldermen's refusal to follow the mayor's plan for selling municipal light and power to consumers. Brashear's bold, if parochial, progressivism had pushed too far ahead of its political support. Utility company counter-suits and delayed expansion programs amplified the political crisis at city hall. Brashear resigned, finally, in January 1901; retrenchment and restoration of council leadership became the watchwords of the conservative backlash.[28]

Yet, the momentum built into the enlarged administrative machinery effectively resisted any significant curtailment of public sector responsibilities. Although spokesmen continued to blame the mayor, the council's frustrations resulted from failures to establish levers of control over the growing bureaucracy. Divided into small committees, the aldermen long had exercised the chief role in supervising departmental operations, in addition to their legislative duties. The twelve part-time officials were little aware of the inadequacy of piecemeal arrangements for maintaining checkreins on the emerging complex of governmental activity.

A sense of crisis and bewilderment was becoming common in Houston. This divisive state of affairs became intolerable to businessmen whose success was dependent upon the city's political and economic stability.[29] The rising importance of Houston in regional and national calculations jumped sharply in 1901, as the result of two fortuitous events. A hurricane devastated Galveston just four months before the largest petroleum reserves in the country were discovered near its inland rival. The local economy in Houston boomed from the rush for black gold and an acute drop in energy costs.[30]

Houston's now undisputed dominance over the area's development and the nation's future oil industry expansion emphasized the urgency to end disorder. Yet, factional struggles seemed to throw solutions to the dilemmas of rapid urbanization out of reach. Two members of the city's business elite, Oran T. Holt and John Kirby, intervened in the 1902 municipal elections to determine the winners. Holt, a retired attorney for the Southern Pacific and the state Democratic chieftain, was promoted by Kirby, the biggest baron of timber and oil lands in Texas. *Houston Post* editor Reme M. Johnson joined them to conduct a well-orchestrated campaign against "ring" politics. Local political leaders such as Brashear and Rice defended the incumbents seeking reelection, but two of every three voters chose Holt and his hand-picked ticket of aldermanic newcomers.[31]

The 1902 election represented a second major watershed in Houston politics and government. Both Brashear and Holt were progressive leaders committed to municipal innovation and expansion of public expenditures to advance the general welfare. But in contrast to Brashear's uncompromising localistic perceptions, the new mayor possessed a holistic or metropolitan image of the city. Holt pursued an accommodationist approach to achieve mutually beneficial settlements that ensured steady urban improvement and growth. He and like-minded men identified themselves with the municipal reform currents running through the nation.[32] The ascendancy of the metropolitan perspective among business and professional groups also inspired related attempts to exclude parochial interests from the political process.

The new mayor's first proposal, to install advanced budgetary techniques, mirrored the novel thrust of reformer orientations. Holt and Kirby persuaded the council to employ the nationally respected accounting firm of Haskins and Sells instead of using cheaper local talent. Kirby, who had worked with the experts in setting up the Houston Oil Company, promised to pay the New Yorkers' fees if even greater savings were not gained from their reforms.[33] Within a year, Haskins and Sells had tied a unified system of fiscal checkreins on to the city's bureaucracy.

In a similar fashion, outside expertise was injected into the 1903 revision of municipal governance. Because the administration drew heavily on the National Municipal League's model charter, it disclaimed innovation. But the *Post*'s comment that the final product represented a "radical departure" from the past was a more accurate assessment.[34] Structural adjustments implemented in the municipal corporation reorganized power and responsibility along lines commensurate with government's augmented scale and scope of operation. Public authority was broadly extended over such areas as utility rate levels, welfare and educational agencies, and city employee pensions. The inability of the council to manage the complicated machinery of government was recognized in provisions that separated legislative and executive functions more completely. Peripheral territory was brought under municipal jurisdiction through the first annexation in Houston's history. City boundaries were enlarged from three to four miles square.[35]

Analogous modernization processes greatly enhanced the quality and range of services supplied by public utility corporations. In 1904, for example, the Houston Light and Power Company's 5,500-horsepower generators fed a variety of circuitry; the firm's gross sales were $200,000, as compared to $50,000 in 1897, when the facility had a 600-horsepower capacity. During the receivership, the General Electric Company had constructed a technologically efficient facility, and now continued to provide managerial advice. The innovative Boston engineering firm, Stone and Webster, operated the vastly improved rapid transit system.

Implementation of major technological changes in both the production and the appliance ends of the gas business also stimulated parallel increases in consumption and reductions in costs.[36]

These utilities' owners found Holt to be a tough but businesslike negotiator in unraveling the convoluted disputes wound during Brashear's term of office. A spirit of cooperative accommodation on both sides encouraged settlements that produced immediate gains for each party as well as consumers. The agreement with the street railway in 1902 provided for the inauguration of crosstown transfers, construction of additional suburban lines, installation of vestibules to protect motormen, and payment of $80,000 in paving charges. In exchange, the city granted franchise privileges for route and tenure extensions and dropped litigation that made financial transactions relatively expensive for the company.[37] The detente between the city government and the utility enterprises reflected acknowledgment of their mutual interdependence and sealed the permanency of these relationships.

The contrast presented by the irreconcilable dispute between the water company and its president Thomas Scanlan on the one hand and public officials on the other exposed the rising price paid by the community for policy deadlocks. Despite sizable increases in wells, machines, and pipes, the waterworks remained only an enlarged version of the original system. Badly contaminated bayou water was still funneled throughout the meterless distribution network to boost fire-hydrant pressure, which always proved insufficient in serious emergencies. Failure to decide who was responsible for solving this problem created alarming health and safety hazards; political support mounted for municipal ownership. Scanlan rebuffed city offers to buy the company for $350,000 less than an appraisal board's figure of $1 million. Attorneys then engaged in a complicated series of legal contests in state and national courthouses. The matter stayed under cautious judicial care until the city bought the firm in 1906 for $900,000.[38]

Except for the waterworks, Houstonians were provided more technologically advanced, professionally managed services. Structural and regulatory adjustments were based on the current and future wealth generated by the steady growth of the city. From 1894 to 1904, population and property tax valuations doubled, to 54,000 persons and $34 million, respectively.[39] Both fueled the municipal corporation's muscular assertions of authority over a widening range of urban activities. Prosperity also broadened consumer demand for utility services. *Post* editor Johnson summarized contemporary observations: "Houston is no longer a town, to be operated along lines that prevailed 10 or 20 years ago. It is a city now, the metropolis of a great state."[40]

Political realignments were also wrought by the dual emergence in governmental and business sectors of a new level and scale of corporate organization above older, small-scale patterns. Before the 1904 Democratic primaries, a fusion was forged between Holt supporters and displaced representatives of middle-class taxpayers who had been defeated in the previous election. The reconciliation of elite reformers with Browne and Brashear made certain victory at the polls.[41] Their confidence was reflected in the choice of their candidate, an unknown political neophyte, Andrew L. Jackson. These arrangements were cemented inside the Business League, which Johnson had started in 1895 and helped promote to major importance. The League became the central metropolitan booster association, with a membership by 1904 that listed 150 corporations and 400 individuals.[42] The combined strength of the community's proprietary interests overpowered the strange coalition of opposing forces that brought organized labor and the water company briefly together.

The election allowed the victors to isolate further their last viable adversaries, skilled workers, from meaningful influence. The exclusion of blacks from the Democracy had allowed local legislators in 1903 to enact the city's first Jim Crow ordinance, which segregated streetcar seating. A state poll tax law passed during the same year, moreover, had eliminated other poor citizens from registration rolls, which were cut drastically from 76 to 32 percent of the potential electorate. Almost immediately after the March 1904 primary, transit company executives began maneuvers to destroy the railway workers' union. A seven-month strike ensued, but in contrast to the earlier conflict, only Labor Council members and blacks, who were already boycotting the company, stayed off the scab-driven cars. Armed and trained motormen drawn from sister companies in the Stone and Webster group made a large difference in the defeat of Houston's union men; but the most important factor was the managers' curtailment of public antagonism toward the utility because of its improved performance. Houston's labor movement suffered long-term setbacks in prestige and finances from this defeat in the costly strike.[43]

The political and economic eclipse of organized workers opened the way for the Business League to consolidate their hold on public policy through commission government. Holt, Jackson, and other top officials were League members. Yet, the total abolition of ward-level politics remained a persistent goal of the metropolitans. The examples of Galveston's commission rule after 1901 and Dallas's more limited earlier experiments became ideal models to contrast against perceived omissions at home. Between July 1904 and March 1905, the League spearheaded a drive for structural change that successfully overrode the stubborn resistance of a council majority. The new municipal charter provided for the at-large election of four commissioners and a mayor and gave the mayor much greater power than did the Galveston model.[44] In April the League's candidate, H. B. Rice, and his slate were installed.

Rice directed city government along a set course for the next eight years. The young native son personified the completed bridge between local and larger concerns. The popular mayor's unprecedented term of office stemmed in part from leadership in arbitrating between these varied interests.[45] Rice's tenure, moreover, reflected the high degree of political stability reached in Houston after a decade of divisive agitation. The absence of strife was a combined product of the disenfranchising of most dissident elements and the mayor's broker role of accommodation. Commission government supplied an efficient instrument for the fulfillment of policy goals and allocation priorities established by the Holt administration.

The transformation of Houston between 1892 and 1905 was double-edged; physical and structural modernization occurred simultaneously with racial and social exclusion. Initial periods of ferment defined alternatives and expanded governmental responsibilities over a wide range of community concerns. After 1903 centralized institutions were created that placed a system of control levers on the agencies of urban development. Structural adjustments substantially increased public and private sector capacities to make environmental and service improvements. The reform impulse to impose planning over the city-building process produced a related drive to end disorderly conflicts among local groups. But the antidemocratic results of governmental "reform" eliminated any need to consider the interests of the lower classes in public policy calculations.

This case study reinforces the conclusion that urban progressivism was a mixture of singular and common components that produced a diverse range of results. Houston's experience suggests that city size, regional position, and national economic importance were basic elements in determining the course of reform. Large-scale corporations, municipal and business, acted as powerful agents in cementing the growing links of interdependence. They promoted the victory of a growth strategy for urban improvement over more parochial orientations narrowly focused on current neighborhood deficiencies. National trends of economic organization, technological diffusion, and communication flows greatly accelerated the pace of reformer ideas. National connections also largely supplied the means to insure the eventual triumph of the metropolitans and their New South creed.

MICHAEL P. MCCARTHY

3. THE NEW METROPOLIS:
CHICAGO, THE ANNEXATION MOVEMENT, AND PROGRESSIVE REFORM

In 1902 and 1903, Lincoln Steffens visited several cities in the East and Midwest for *McClure's Magazine.* He was on a research assignment for his famous muckraking articles, which soon appeared in book form as *The Shame of the Cities.* To his surprise, Steffens found New York and Chicago to be exceptions to the state of corruption and public apathy that the book's title characterized; in fact, Steffens saw them as exemplary models for municipal reform across the country.

What is interesting to note is that these two cities were not only the largest and most heterogeneous in population but also the largest in area. Moreover, they had grown dramatically since the 1880s: New York from 44 square miles to 299, and Chicago from 43 to 190. Other cities that were leaders in reform had also experienced significant area growth in the same period (see Table 3-1).[1] Historians of the municipal reform movement by and large have neglected the physical settings of their communities. But it is clear that much of the progressive movement and its success has to do with a common set of problems related to the growth of late nineteenth-century cities. The Chicago experience provides a case study of the rise and decline of reform in that "urbanizing world."[2]

In the late 1880s, Chicago had firmly established itself as the regional capital of the Midwest. Located at the edge of the rich agricultural prairie, with strategic lake, canal, and rail connections, the city was a diversified marketing and manufacturing center, with a population of some 850,000 and an area of forty-three square miles.[3]

Beyond the city limits were the suburban townships of Lake View, Jefferson, Lake, and Hyde Park, some 125 square miles in area and with a population of approximately 220,000 in the late 1880s (see Map 3-1). These towns had grown rapidly during the decade as downtown commuters took advantage of increased steam railroad service and new cable

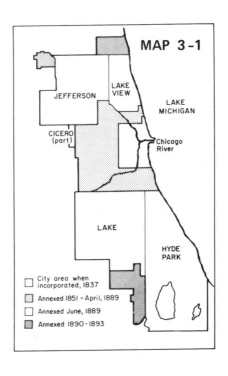

TABLE 3-1. Size of Chicago and Selected Cities in Square Miles, 1860-1910

	1860	1870	1880	1890	1900	1910
Chicago	17	35	35	178	189	190
Cincinnati	7	7	25	25	39	50
Cleveland	9	12	27	28	32	46
Detroit	13	16	22	28	28	40
Los Angeles	29	29	29	29	43	101
Minneapolis	5	8	12	53	53	53
New York	22	22	22	44	299	299
Seattle	11	11	5	13	34	71

Table data from varied sources.

and electric lines to find suburban homes, and as workers followed the movement of many industries to the metropolitan periphery, particularly to the Calumet district of Hyde Park.[4]

On the north side along the lake in Lake View were substantial middle-class neighborhoods that dated from the 1870s. Further north were a number of new housing developments, of which Edgewater was typical. In the early 1880s, H. Lewis Cochran, a real estate speculator from Philadelphia, bought 350 acres of woods and corn fields along the right-of-way of the Chicago, Milwaukee and St. Paul Railroad. He began building attractive houses at moderate prices (between $5,000 and $10,000), replaced the shed station that served surrounding farmers, and obtained more frequent train service from the railroad. By the early 1890s, Edgewater would have over three hundred homes, a thousand residents, Methodist and Episcopal churches, a boat and shooting club, plus a bath house, and seemed assured of a "very fashionable character" indeed.[5]

West of the lakefront neighborhoods on the north side, in Gross Park and Ravenswood, were more modest homes of foremen and skilled workers, many of them German or Scandinavian, who took the Clark Street trolley or the Northwestern Railroad (only a seven-cent train fare from Ravenswood) to their jobs at brick works, the Deering farm implement factory, or other industries along the north branch of the river. Beyond Ravenswood, the built-up area thinned out rapidly. One "pioneer" in Ravenswood remembers finding, to his surprise, open land to the west. With the exception of Norwood Park and a few other small settlements along the Chicago and Northwestern line in Jefferson township, Chicago remained rural all the way to the city limits and beyond in the early 1890s.

On the south side along the lake from 39th Street to Jackson Park in Hyde Park township were a string of middle-class communities such as Kenwood, Hyde Park, and Woodlawn, similar to those on the north side. South of Jackson Park, beyond Woodlawn and across stretches of prairie, was George Pullman's model village on Lake Calumet and a growing industrial district at South Chicago near the Indiana state line. West of the lakefront commuter villages, between 39th and 47th streets in Lake township, was the sprawling Union Stock Yards, one mile in width from Halstead to Western Avenue and surrounded by blocks of working-class homes. Away from the yards, south of Garfield Boulevard at 55th Street to the area of 63rd Street, was the solid but unpretentious middle-class community of Englewood, which, like Morgan Park in the suburbs beyond, enjoyed good commuter service on the Rock Island line.

In September 1887, residents in the suburban towns petitioned to join Chicago by means of a referendum vote that November. Although rapid growth had affected the suburbs most, there were mutual benefits in annexation. The towns could share the city's water supply and fire and police departments; Chicago could centralize administration under its control and tax for services it had long been offering on a voluntary basis, particularly the loan of fire-fighting equipment and personnel.

Annexation had widespread support for other, more subjective, reasons. "Why should we hesitate to join our destiny to that city which must march on until she becomes greater than imperial Rome?" asked the superintendent of schools in South Chicago. "'Rogers Park in Chicago' sounds better than 'Rogers Park near Chicago,'" that village's newspaper commented in another example of suburban affinity characteristic of the late nineteenth century. For other supporters, consolidation provided the means of creating a greater sense of community among residents in the suburbs. Englewood had little in common with the stockyards; the commuter villages of Hyde Park and Lake View, little with Pullman or west Lake View. As one suburban resident noted: "What is common to all these places? Chicago, Chicago, Chicago alone. In Chicago unity under a government looking after the interests of all."[6]

In all the towns the annexation leaders were the traditional community elite of businessmen, ministers, lawyers, doctors, and other professionals. The coalition they led, however, was varied in class as well as motive. The older and wealthier sections of Hyde Park near the city, for example, felt they were paying a disproportionate share of taxes to develop the periphery; south end residents in turn resented these "kid-gloved gentlemen" who, one annexationist claimed, could find money for a costly drainage works in Woodlawn but none for sidewalks in his neighborhood. The only organized opposition came from suburban officeholders who would lose their jobs through consolidation. They issued pamphlets warning of the perils of joining the city. Their supporters also disrupted speakers at annexation meetings. Despite such "mean and petty" annoyances, those in favor of joining Chicago were still confident they would carry the vote.

The results of the referendum were mixed. Voters in Chicago, Hyde Park, Jefferson, and Cicero approved; those in Lake and Lake View rejected the referendum. Although the local bosses were strongest in these latter towns, there were many reasons for the defeat and opposing votes in other towns as well. Many homeowners, especially those in Lake and Lake View, were worried about the higher cost of stone construction if Chicago's "fire limits" building code were extended to the suburbs. Others fretted over the future of prohibition districts enacted under town laws. Many in Lake, including the influential meat-packing companies, were unhappy that the annexation bill had provided them with new tax assessors. Still others had opposed the referendum because whole towns had not been included in the petitions; southwest Hyde Park had been omitted; so had the western part of Lake, the northern half of Lake View, and most of Jefferson. Whatever the reasons for voter disapproval, the results of the referendum were quickly challenged. The Hyde Park trustees filed a suit to test its constitutionality and found themselves upheld in a state supreme court decision the following year.

In the spring of 1889, the state legislature passed another, more carefully worded, annexation law. This time its supporters were more organized. They created a central committee to work on a metropolitan basis; and in May some three hundred official delegates from suburban towns met in a convention at the Grand Pacific Hotel in downtown Chicago. Within days, the central committee had printed and distributed petitions that included the entire surrounding towns. In Lake, annexationists traveled by wagon into the thinly settled sections beyond Western Avenue to get signatures from farmers; in southwest Hyde Park, they profited from growing resentment toward George Pullman and the paternalism of his company town to gain support.

To avoid the partisanship of regular November elections, and to prevent confusion with a proposal for the regional sanitary district that would then be on the ballot, the annexationists sought to hold the referendum in June. To do that, they needed court approval. They scoured their towns for the signatures of registered voters far in excess of the 250 needed to petition for a referendum. Within days they had secured 4,000 names, shortly thereafter a total of 12,000, more than enough to convince a Cook County judge.

In other ways the annexation campaign was going better for its supporters than had the earlier one. The revised law left intact the township as an administrative unit for taxes, with locally elected assessors. The Chicago city council also helped by passing ordinances that permitted the suburban neighborhoods to stay exempt from the city's fire code and retain their prohibition districts. As the referendum neared, the only doubtful town was Lake, where the People's Party, with its strength in the Irish, Democratic neighborhoods of the stockyards, organized the opposition under the leadership of the popular James "Buck" McCarthy, a one-time prizefighter and former county commissioner.

With the fire limits issue resolved and the meat packers now in support, not even McCarthy was able to block annexation this time. On June 29, 1889, the referendum carried in Lake as well as in all the other towns. Overnight Chicago added some 220,000 to its population of over 850,000; and the additional 125 square miles made the city, at 168 square miles, the largest municipal area in the United States.

Shortly after the election, the city council drew lines for ten new wards to represent the suburban towns. With the total number of Democrats and Republicans roughly the same as they were in the central city, the council created a few safe wards for each party, such as the Democratic Twenty-ninth in Lake's stockyard area and the Republican Twenty-fifth in Lake View, east of Ridge Avenue along the lake, where Edgewater and the other commuter villages were located. Most wards, however, were as mixed in their loyalties as in class and ethnic composition, largely because they covered such broad areas in the thinly populated sections. The Twenty-seventh included nearly the whole town of Jefferson; the Thirty-third and Thirty-fourth stretched for miles across the prairie of south Hyde Park.

By the fall of 1893, South Englewood, the villages of Washington Heights, West Roseland, Fernwood, Rogers Park, West Ridge, Norwood Park and a part of Gano had joined the city and were added to the outer wards, increasing Chicago's size to 185 square miles.

This consolidation was not unique. London took steps toward a regional government in 1888; New York would join Brooklyn and their smaller neighbors in 1898. These were only the most dramatic examples of nineteenth-century growth, which in many respects created new cities, with new constituencies and new patterns of power.

The political implications of the annexation movement in Chicago were shortly realized amid the depression years of the mid-1890s when a group of businessmen and professionals created the Municipal Voters' League. The immediate cause behind the League's founding was a council scandal in which a handful of aldermen from downtown wards had engineered the passage of a utility bill that cheated the city. Amid hard times, tax dollars were scarce and civic leaders in no mood for so-called "boodle" ordinances.

As its first objective, the League set out to improve the caliber of the sixty-eight aldermen, half of whom were elected every spring for a two-year term. In the first campaign the League obtained its objective of securing a council with a few more than one-third "safe" aldermen to sustain a mayor's veto if another utility ordinance incident occurred.

After that, it did even better. By the early 1900s, two-thirds of the aldermen were considered honest, and the council enjoyed a reputation as one of the best in the country.[7]

The Municipal Voters' League was one of the biggest success stories of the Progressive Era, its leaders lionized by fellow reformers across the country and by such noted journalists as Lincoln Steffens and Ida Tarbell. Although a later generation of historians by and large has been less admiring, the League's achievement remained undimmed by time. A handful of "old stock" businessmen and professionals—the traditional community leaders—did oversee a major political reform movement in a city in which native-born of native parents constituted less than 30 percent of the population.[8]

How did the League manage to do it? Clearly, the suburban additions of the late 1880s and early 1890s created a new political environment in structural terms. The ten new wards represented nearly 30 percent of the seats in the expanded council and gave the League its most consistent support. With the lakefront commuter wards the most enthusiastic, the League could be considered a coordinating agency for a native American middle class whose power was increasingly fragmented by wards and centrifugal movement. But it would be misleading to view the League in these terms, because even the elite lakefront suburban wards were composed of a majority of "new stock" residents; moreover, the League won many victories in the inner city, where the population was overwhelmingly foreign-born.[9]

The League seems to have been successful for a variety of reasons. One was its exceptional personnel during the formative years. For the first president the League founders chose George B. Cole, a crusty, freewheeling printing company president who had served in the Civil War with the Tenth Michigan Volunteers. Cole was a natural political showman with a style for dramatizing issues that Tom Johnson of Cleveland would later make famous. He was also idealistic and independent. He attracted a talented group of younger men, mostly in their thirties, to work with him on the League's small staff: men such as William Kent, a Yale graduate whose father had made a fortune in Chicago real estate; Charles R. Crane, another young wealthy second-generation Chicagoan; Walter L. Fisher, lawyer and son of the president of Hanover College in Indiana; and Allan B. Pond, an architect whose father had been a warden in a Michigan state prison.

Like Cole, the other officers of the League had little awe for establishment figures; Kent and Fisher would not hestitate to lecture Theodore Roosevelt on what they considered a poor patronage appointment in the city, or scold the arch-conservative Marshall Field, who opposed the League because it was scaring off business investors. For Cole and the others, the utility scandals represented a failure of civic leadership. The old deals between political and economic elites no longer served the interest of the community. By their betrayal of the public trust, the bosses and the business leaders involved with them had forfeited their right to civic stewardship. A new political order was necessary that would redistribute power by returning decision making to the electorate.[10]

The reformers neither blamed the immigrants for the existing corruption nor doubted that they would meet their civic responsibility once given the chance. With the city council as the instrument of reform, the League made explicit its faith in both democracy and "new stock" Americans.[11]

The League built on the ward as a community by emphasizing issues that mattered in the everyday lives of residents. Was the alderman keeping the streets clean? What about garbage collection and the like? The League underscored an alderman's accountability in many visible ways related to a ward's self-image and pride. At the same time, the League reinforced the metropolitan perspective of the earlier annexationists by picking community-wide issues that cut across class, ethnic and occupational lines. Stiffer public utility ordinances, for example, meant cheaper rates and more money in the city treasury for other services.

The League also had very simple criteria for a candidate: he had to be honest, hard-working, and popular enough in his ward to have a chance of getting elected. It was not particularly fussy about occupation, backing plumbers, carpenters, blacksmiths—even saloonkeepers.[12] Not surprisingly, the ideal was a businessman, but this was more for knowledge of finance, bookkeeping, administrative procedures, and the like than for any elitist values.

Only in a handful of river wards, where the old ward bosses retained their power, did the League meet repeated failure. The highly transient character of these wards, with many boardinghouses for seasonal workers and a high residential turnover as a result of immigrants' moving on to better areas, may have been a factor.[13] Immigrants there may also have felt patronized and demeaned by the middle-class Americans who often assisted ward insurgents. But it would be a mistake to conclude that the success of anti-League candidates represented a reaction to reform values. Many residents, being unnaturalized foreign-born, could not vote. Also, the ward bosses often used their own brand of nonpartisanship, by deciding on a candidate who would represent their collective interests and having him run unopposed—as was the case in the First, Seventh, Eighth, and Nineteenth wards in 1900 (see Map 3-2). Under such circumstances the League often conceded defeat and did not even bother to field a candidate of its own.[14]

Whatever the reasons for voter behavior, clearly no single variable that can be measured in a quantifiable way explains completely the League's success. With all its activities and community involvement, the League offered something for nearly everyone. Like reformers in New York, Cleveland, Cincinnati, Minneapolis, Seattle, Los Angeles, and other cities both in the United States and abroad that were experiencing rapid territorial growth, the Chicagoans found themselves dealing with issues that cut across the traditional social barriers and created new, broad-based coalitions. To some extent, they made the "new citizenship" work.[15]

The annexation movement peaked in 1899, when the Illinois legislature gave serious consideration to a bill that would have joined Chicago and the rest of Cook County into a single administrative unit. The measure

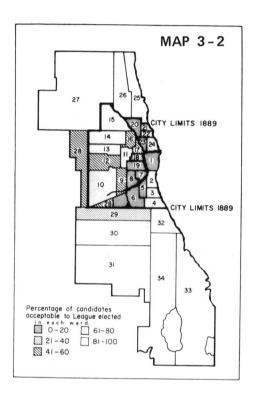

MAP 3-2

CITY LIMITS 1889

CITY LIMITS 1889

Percentage of candidates
acceptable to League elected
in each ward.
0-20
21-40
41-60
61-80
81-100

had wide support; even the mayor of Evanston, a city that long had kept its self-identity zealously, considered such a union inevitable. At the last moment, however, there were second thoughts by both political parties—the Democrats saw too many Republicans in the suburbs, and Republicans feared the loss of their control of Cook County offices—and the bill was defeated. After that, the sentiment swung the other way. Cicero, Oak

Park, Evanston, Elmwood Park, Blue Island, and Norwood Park—all defeated annexation attempts by referendum. Only Morgan Park—and only after four unsuccessful referenda—joined the city after 1900. The same thing occurred in other cities of the East and Midwest that were leaders in the reform movement. Some continued to grow in the 1920s, but by 1930 these cities had reached nearly the same physical size that they would have four decades later (see Table 3-2).

Why did these cities stop growing? There were many factors involved: the declining faith that centralization would bring greater efficiency; a lessening dependence on the central city for utilities and services; new transportation patterns in an automobile age that weakened older ties between suburb and central city; and for those who continued to grow into the 1920s, the fiscal crisis that followed the crash of 1929 discouraged further expansion.

TABLE 3-2. Size of Selected Cities in East and Midwest in Square Miles, 1870-1970

	1870	1890	1910	1930	1950	1970
Boston	13	39	39	44	46	48
Chicago	35	178	190	207	212	228
Cincinnati	20	25	50	72	75	78
Cleveland	12	28	46	71	81	81
Detroit	13	22	41	140	140	140
Minneapolis	8	48	48	54	54	54
New York	22	44	299	299	299	299
Philadelphia	130	130	130	130	127	127
Pittsburgh	23	27	40	51	52	52
St. Louis	61	61	61	61	61	61

Table data for Chicago from official "Map of Chicago Showing Growth of the City by Annexations and Accretions" (revised, 1974). Data for other cities from tables in Jackson, "Metropolitan Government," 443, 445.

But is is also clear that the middle classes were no longer pulling the city limits along with them for psychological and social reasons. Great numbers of black and eastern European immigrants had poured into Chicago and the other major cities of the East and Midwest in the period from 1900 to 1920, in many ways altering neighborhood residential patterns.[16]

In 1900, most blacks had lived on the south side in a two-block "black-belt" between 16th and 32nd streets. By the 1930s, blacks comprised 90 percent of the population between Wentworth and Cottage Grove Road (ten blocks east) and between 31st and Washington Park at 51st Street; west of the park, between Wentworth and South Park, the black neighborhoods extended to 63rd Street. By then, black areas in other sections of the city had also grown. The largest was on the west side, near the rail yards at Western and Lake, where another narrow residential corridor was emerging east and west in aging neighborhoods along the Lake Street elevated line.

After 1910, there were also significant changes in the ethnic composition of the inner city. In the 1890s, a few blocks around the church of St. Stanislaus Kosta contained most of the Polish community; by 1920, Poles lived a mile north in Logan Square, west near Humboldt Park, and south in the old Seventeenth Ward. The scattered Italian communities also grew greatly in size; Russian Jews moved west along 12th Street to North Lawndale and north on the elevated line to Albany Park; the Czechs spread westward from Blue Island Avenue to South Lawndale, where the massive Western Electric plant on the west, rail and elevated lines on the north, and the industry east and south along the canal created a "natural" community area.

Perhaps the most dramatic change occurred far from the rapid transit lines in the northwest and southwest sections that had been largely open land in the late nineteenth and early twentieth century. There land costs were much lower and developers could still make money on low density housing; more important, they found a demand for inexpensive homes from working-class and lower-middle-class buyers.

In a classic example of supply and demand, these outer areas boomed, as did comparable districts of Philadelphia, of Brooklyn and Queens in metropolitan New York, and other spread-cities during this period. Between 1910 and 1930, the population jumped from 26,006 to 329,510 in the community areas of Portage Park, Hermosa, Belmont-Cragin, Montclair, Dunning, Gage Park, Archer Heights, Garfield Ridge, West Elson, Chicago Lawn, and Auburn Gresham.

Portage Park, Belmont Cragin, Gage Park, and Chicago Lawn were typical. Between 1905 and 1929, 34,963 residential structures were built, representing 91.6 percent of the housing when the Chicago Land Use Survey inspected these areas in the late 1930s. Single-family homes represented 66.1 percent of the housing there, compared to a city average of 15.7 percent. Another 19.7 percent was two-family "decker" homes (two flats), which many buyers preferred because they would have rental income from the second-story apartment to help meet the costs of a new home.[17]

Most of those who bought homes worked in nearby factories, rail yards, or shops and stores in neighborhood commercial districts at major street intersections. Nearly all were foreign-born or children of immigrants. Like the rest of the city, their neighborhoods were highly mixed in terms of ethnicity; most immigrant groups, however, moved toward the suburban periphery in a linear pattern along streetcar lines, so that the northwest had more Poles, Germans, Scandinavians and Italians, while the southwest had more Irish, Czechs, and Lithuanians from older residential areas near the canal and stockyards.

The political implications of all these changes were clear by 1919. That spring, William Hale ("Big Bill") Thompson, a playboy millionaire with Republican machine connections, won reelection to a second term as mayor despite the opposition of the city's reform groups and a poor showing in the lakefront suburban wards that had backed him so strongly four years earlier. Support in the burgeoning black and ethnic communities had been largely responsible for his victory. Here Thompson had found a new coalition, and in a symbolic sense the votes of the black south side and west side immigrant neighborhoods in that 1919 election marked an end to the politics of the Progressive Era.[18]

LEE F. PENDERGRASS

4. URBAN REFORM AND VOLUNTARY ASSOCIATION:
THE MUNICIPAL LEAGUE OF SEATTLE, 1910-1916

The Municipal League of Seattle is representative of twentieth-century voluntarism. Founded to combat chaotic urban growth, it offered the emerging middle class training in political decision making and integrated it into the body politic.[1] Although the League and other similar associations were not alike in every respect, they drew heavily from common American and European experiences and programs.[2] The League's story offers a potential resolution of the long-standing historical debate over the nature of progressive reform.[3] Was it a radical movement that attempted to alter the established order?[4] Was it a conservative movement by an older capitalist class to defend its social and economic position?[5] Was it an effort by individuals rising into the middle class to amplify their influence and power?[6] Was it a liberal movement to expand opportunities for already established members of the middle class?[7] How did its supporters differ from other groups? How was it affected by changing social and economic conditions?[8]

In Seattle progressivism began as a vital middle-class movement with radical features but was transformed into a rather elitist movement with conservative overtones. The Municipal League's acceptance of political conflict as a tool for restructuring the decision-making process increased middle-class representation and power but decreased middle-class militancy. Initially its members were at odds with Seattle's older capitalist class because Leaguers were an emerging elite seeking a share of the realm carved out by the older capitalists. But as members increased their influence in city decision-making circles, their antagonism dissipated.

The Municipal League successfully confronted the established political order because it tailored its rhetoric and recruiting drives to the prevailing social and economic order. Founded in 1851, Seattle was a typical upstart western city. Like many such cities, its growth was propelled by an influx of immigrants and native-born Americans from other parts of the country. By 1910 Seattle's population consisted primarily of Anglo-Saxons of western European descent; together, blacks, Japanese, and Chinese constituted no more than five percent of the population. Many owned their homes, unlike Easterners, who were more likely to rent. The majority engaged in commerce rather than industry. A visible minority were unemployed transients. Although basically homogeneous, Seattle contained distinct social interests.[9]

To mold these interests together, the League was forced to travel in different directions. This required a delicate balance between extremes, which, if not handled properly, would result in indecisiveness or even polarization. In its early years the Municipal League achieved a perfect balance between traditionalists concerned about morality and moderates seeking to manage bureaucracy scientifically. By appealing to both groups, the League captured the support of those who identified with the small town and rural America and those who identified with the modern industrial city.[10]

Prior to 1910, Seattle reform lacked overall structure, as individual associations tried to implement specific proposals. Some sought municipal ownership of public utilities; some clamored for efficiency in city government; others attempted to regulate public morality. By 1910, this scattergun approach was no longer appropriate. The Municipal League hoped to coordinate city-wide reform efforts.

The League's founders pointed out that within the previous ten years Seattle's population had quadrupled. There had been substantial economic growth, but community services had been disrupted and the established capitalist class refused to remove inequities for the middle class. Concerned about solidifying middle-class influence in local politics, Leaguers were supremely confident that the city could continue to grow if citizens accepted their recommendations, which would control bureaucracy and create a sense of community. If their advice was not heeded, Seattle would experience the urban blight so common elsewhere.

This rhetoric captured the hopes and fears of the middle class. It offered an opportunity to end organizational chaos.[11] Although the League's initial members belonged to the same social station, they were a highly amorphous lot. These Mugwumps, Populists, Democrats, Progressives, and Republicans were linked together by their common desire to make Seattle great and to assume a meaningful role in shaping public policy.[12] Most agreed that it was essential to establish a political balance of power between them and the old-time elite. Some thought structural reform offered the best chance, while others preferred social reform.[13] Thus, progressivism in Seattle was not born in the economic turmoil of the late nineteenth century as was, for example, Wisconsin reform. Seattle reform appeared almost two decades later, in the midst of economic prosperity, and provided the unorganized middle class with the institutional means to deal with its predicament. Like its Wisconsin counterpart, however, Seattle reform was not confined to narrow, specific issues.[14]

Because the Municipal League united a variety of groups with diverse interests, it needed a dramatic issue with broad implications to hold it together. The recall of Mayor Hiram Gill perfectly suited this purpose, because Gill symbolized to the middle class all that was wrong. They were appalled by his decision to support an open-town policy toward prostitution, gambling and liquor, angry over his collusion with downtown businessmen and corporation moguls, and tired of his inefficient, costly administration. On October 8, 1910, the Municipal League and the Public Welfare League (PWL) issued petitions to recall Gill. The PWL, like the Municipal League, was dominated by businessmen and professionals working for morality, honesty, and efficiency in government. It contained, as nearly as can be determined, a greater proportion of lawyers and real estate agents than did the League. These men wanted to abolish the red-light district because it was destroying property values in the south end, where many of them lived. The PWL also differed from the Municipal League in its desire to regulate both public and private morality.

The recall in 1910 was a radical innovation. Conservative Republicans and older capitalists were thoroughly frightened by citizens' challenges, not only in the form of the recall but also in the initiative, the referendum, and Theodore Roosevelt's "new nationalism." A recall was a particularly risky political move for the Municipal League, because it was not as well established as the PWL. Yet, a victory would allow the League, which was less than five months old, to confront a number of issues that required concerted public action.[15]

As a result of Gill's open-town policy in 1910, prostitutes and criminals were venturing into the city's respectable areas. This troubled not only morally minded citizens but also boosters, who feared that outside investors and hard-working, virtuous, industrious individuals would refuse to come to Seattle.[16]

The Municipal League's constituents were disturbed, however, about much more than morality and economic growth. According to the Seattle *Star,* "an afternoon Scripps tabloid which encouraged its readers to take sides without trying to educate them," Gill was collaborating with the privately owned Seattle Electric Company to create a monopoly.[17] Voters had tried to assure competitive electric rates by establishing in 1902 Seattle City Light, a publicly owned and operated utility, but Gill seemed to be undermining this enterprise. Behind Gill, the *Star* asserted, stood "Boss" Jacob Furth, head of the "rich, ravenous and powerful" Seattle Electric. Already Furth had seriously weakened City Light by building an interurban electric and trolley empire and placing Gill and the superintendent of City Light on his payroll. There was some truth to the *Star*'s charges, but there was also a considerable degree of sensationalism.

The Municipal League and the city council investigated. Both reprimanded City Light's superintendent for not competing with Seattle Electric, but neither supplied conclusive documentation of wrongdoing. Presenting irrefutable evidence mattered less to the reformers than destroying the Gill–Seattle Electric ring. They relied upon mass indignation and education to achieve their goal. Extensive canvassing reaped enough signatures to warrant a recall election.[18]

To oppose Gill, the Municipal League and PWL picked George Dilling— a member of both organizations. A successful but not extremely wealthy businessman, Dilling had served one term in the state legislature. There he had gained a reputation as a progressive because he favored stronger laws to curb gambling, prostitution, and the railroad lobby. He had also avoided municipal politics, making the contrast between himself and Gill even more striking.[19]

In the campaign, Dilling reiterated the *Star*'s charges, but the Municipal League also added one of its own, which revealed a great deal about the mentality and composition of Seattle reform in 1910. For the first time the League publicly associated Gill with the established elite, whose economic well-being depended upon extensive property holdings in the already developed center of the city. Its decision to confront the older capitalist class was based on an awareness of Theodore Roosevelt's successful blasts at "intrenched privilege" and "predatory wealth."[20] Also, its members were frustrated by the refusal of the older capitalist class to provide outlying areas, where many League members lived, with adequate service, lower rates, and reduced taxes. To them, the recall represented an opportunity to remove Seattle from the clutches of these prominent citizens. Gill ignored these charges and instead emphasized the great progress the city had made under his leadership. But when the recall was held in early 1911, he was decisively repudiated. The middle class and the more prosperous working class gave Dilling a majority of better than two to one. Gill's support was concentrated in the downtown wards and First Hill, a wealthy precinct.[21]

The hostility between Seattle's old-time elite and the Municipal League did not subside after Gill's defeat. It became more heated when plans were made to construct a new civic center. Voluntary and professional groups considered such a center desirable because of the success of the Alaska-Yukon-Pacific Exposition, a 1909 version of a world's fair, and the concerted drives of many American and European cities to reshape their inner cores for commercial and esthetic reasons. In 1910, the Chamber of Commerce, the Commercial Club, the Seattle Real Estate Association, the Central Labor Council, the Municipal League, the Washington State Chapter of the American Institute of Architects, and the Board of Education formed the Municipal Plans Commission. The Commission secured the services of Virgil Bogue, well known because he had assisted Frederick Law Olmsted, the prominent city planner. Bogue suggested that the civic center be placed in the underdeveloped area south of Lake Union, because it was more accessible and would cost considerably less. Envisioning a hub with arterial highways radiating from it like the spokes of a wheel, he recommended digging tunnels through the hills to the waterfront and to future neighborhoods to the east. He also wanted to construct a funicular railroad to handle traffic up the steep bluff from the shoreline.[22]

The Municipal League and other reform groups believed that the plan would bring cheaper transportation, improved sanitary conditions, better land use, and expanded services and benefits to outlying areas; consequently, they expended time, money, and effort to win community support for the plan. Wealthy property owners of the congested business district claimed that Bogue's plan would discourage outside investors. Publicly they argued that it would substantially increase the burdensome improvement debts incurred during the previous ten years. Privately they raised a sizable war chest and petitioned for the right to construct a civic center in the heart of downtown. To counteract this, Municipal League members visited civic organizations and knocked on doors, attempting to demonstrate that the downtown landlords were concerned with their vested interests.[23]

Why did the League attack such prominent individuals? During the early 1890s these men had achieved wealth and influence from shrewd investments in real estate and businesses when "ground floor" opportunities were extremely promising and aggressiveness won special advantages. Their chances for profit and success had been exceptional because Seattle was then entering a boom stage as a result of basic changes in transportation and accessibility. These changes had resulted from the completion of the transcontinental railroads, spectacular gains in population, heavy capital investments, and the rapid expansion of resource industries. Judge Thomas Burke, James Clise, Jacob Furth, and others had capitalized on the boom by purchasing tidelands at low prices, making bargains with eastern capitalists, and consolidating business investments. As Seattle advanced from frontier to urban metropolis, they rode the tide of progress to the pinnacle of economic, political, and social preeminence.[24] Furth, for example, besides financing and managing local corporations, made and broke aspiring politicians. He "could get on the telephone with a request for money and get it. A politician might run for office without his blessing, but he would not get anywhere."[25]

The claims by Furth and his colleagues that the Bogue plan would raise taxes were to some extent a smokescreen to cover their plan for putting the civic center on property that they owned. The Municipal League admitted that progress was expensive but justified the outlay with their expectations of a Greater Seattle. Beneath this ideological concern for their community, some Leaguers were battling to improve their status and assume a place in the established power structure. Creating a Greater Seattle through reform provided their opportunity to challenge the established elite's refusal to delegate decision making. The elite, on the other hand, feared that any delegation of authority would diffuse effective leadership and clog the governing process with an overabundance of policy-makers and overlapping proposals. They proposed consolidating voluntary groups under the Chamber of Commerce, which would serve as a committee-of-the-whole.[26]

Opposition to the Bogue plan gathered force as the city's major newspapers joined the critics. These papers were not against a planned city, but they were convinced that Bogue was too "radical" and visionary, since he wanted to separate the civic center from the financial center and challenge the long-accepted rectangular grid system with arterial highways.[27] Such overwhelming opposition apparently convinced the voters. The Bogue plan was defeated in 1912 by a majority of two to one.[28]

After the Bogue plan's defeat, the Municipal League found it increasingly difficult to maintain a sense of community. The unbounded confidence that had infused its reform drives dissipated as Seattle-ites discovered that their city was passing from a boom stage into a recession. This transition actually had been underway since 1910, when the pace of economic activity began to slacken. Although population increased by 5,000 persons every year from 1910 to 1913, the rate of economic growth diminished as jobs, payrolls, and manufacturing faltered. Production of lumber mills and manufacturing related to construction diminished; purchases of household furnishings declined from the 1890–1910 level. Food processing increased and small shops expanded, but not enough to offset a recession. Painful and difficult adjustments now seemed necessary because the area was no longer a frontier with rich resources and profitable low-risk opportunities beckoning to potential migrants. Confronted with paying back the millions of dollars they had borrowed when investing in elaborate building programs, Seattle-ites lost their exuberant enthusiasm of the boom years and began seriously to reassess priorities.[29]

One group we shall call "the economizers" argued that retrenchment was the most appropriate response to rising taxes and increased interest rates. Another group, "the spenders," rejected economic cutbacks and stressed the importance of preserving the quality of urban life. Demands from municipal officials for more taxes to cover the rising cost of essential urban services reinforced pleas for austerity from business, professional, and civic groups. At the behest of small homeowners the Chamber of Commerce, the Municipal League, and the Manufacturers Association appeared before the city council to protest high taxes. Drawing a cause-and-effect relationship between tax increases and the "extravagance of a wild boom period," these organizations called for a reduction of public expenditures. Middle-class Seattle-ites were apparently part of a nationwide trend of rebellion at the municipal level against publicly supported programs. Business and professional families were not merely tired of constantly rising taxes; they were contesting how their communities were being managed.[30]

Stunned by the economic turn of events, the majority of the Municipal League decided to cooperate with the prominent businessmen they had opposed between 1910 and 1912. This about-face coincided with a visit from Lincoln Steffens, who encouraged Leaguers to forsake open criticism in favor of cooperative association because civic progress could not be gained without compromise. The economizers agreed and added to their agenda luncheon meetings with the Chamber of Commerce, the Real Estate Association, and the Building Manufacturers Association. The former enemies of the League participated in these conferences to promote greater harmony in a time of trouble.

The proposed shift to economizing produced dissension among reformers. Some thought Seattle was bound to experience another boom period in ten or twenty years and that therefore short-run costs should not assume priority over long-range metropolitan development. To encourage development, they supported further expansion of Seattle City Light. The economizers took issue with them, arguing that this would increase taxes and encourage socialism. Finally, after quarreling among themselves and after extensive lobbying on the part of J. D. Ross, the recently appointed City Light superintendent who had replaced a scandal-ridden predecessor, the majority opted for expansion. The economizers were defeated on this one issue, and some feelings were undoubtedly hurt in the process.

At the same time other Municipal Leaguers became seriously concerned that the impending completion of the Panama Canal would intensify social problems. They concluded that it was necessary to restrict immigration to avoid the additional social disruption that would occur with the influx of thousands of ignorant newcomers upon the completion of the canal. In 1912, these Leaguers had been the prime movers behind a federation of fifty voluntary organizations involved in settlement work. Known as the Central Council of Social Agencies, these bodies ranged from the Women's Christian Temperance Union, the Rotary Club, and the Chamber of Commerce to the Municipal League, the Council of Jewish Women, and the Central Labor Union. At first devoting their attention to eliminating alcoholism, poverty, poor housing, and other social problems, by 1913 they were most concerned about how to cope with the immigrant. Their concern was influenced by general agreement that too many foreigners would produce slums and prostitution. A few were particularly worried that unrestricted immigration would prolong and unduly complicate the economic turmoil caused by closing of the frontier.[31]

In subsequent meetings, the Central Council resolved to pressure the U. S. Congress to create immigrant bureaus in key American ports to keep out undesirables and control the rate of entry. The American Federation of Labor (AFL) and the Central Labor Council asserted that employers were conspiring with large shipping companies to import thousands of immigrants to destroy the competitive position of native American labor. J. Allen Smith, a nationally renowned political scientist at the University of Washington, and Edmund S. Meany, chairman of the history department, suggested that foreigners seeking American citizenship be required to pass a literacy test and "criminal and semi-criminal tests." Smith and Meany assumed, as the AFL did, that this would protect native American workers from being crowded out of their jobs by cheap unskilled labor from abroad. These reformers were more sympathetic to the plight of labor than was the Charity Organization Society of Chicago, but less sympathetic toward the immigrant than were the settlement workers. Some Central Council members, however, reflected the sentiments of the settlement workers. The Reverend Sydney Strong of the Congregational Church, for example, proposed a travelers' protection bureau to safeguard immigrant women from the "nefarious devices employed by white slavers."[32]

Ironically, as Seattle's social reformers tried to control immigration and appease labor, conflict ensued between employers, workers, and more conservative reformers. During the summer and fall of 1913, a number of developments increased the class-consciousness of labor. The closing of lumber mills in and around Seattle produced unemployment and anxiety. An Industrial Workers of the World (IWW) free-speech movement resulted in a city ordinance against street speaking. Finally, the publicity given to the valiant efforts of labor unions across the nation to gain better working conditions contributed to an outbreak of strikes. Employers not only refused to negotiate with strikers but also enlisted thugs and scabs. In numerous issues of the Seattle *Union-Record*, the spokesman for the working class, strikers charged that they had been threatened, beaten, or shot at by company men.

The situation worsened in 1914, when the Employers Association, certain that unionization would lead to collective bargaining and partial ownership of industry by the workers, instituted an open-shop campaign.[33] The Reverend Mark Matthews, pastor of the First Presbyterian Church and a member of the Municipal League, christened the open shop "righteous and American in principle." The *Union-Record* denounced Matthews as antilabor. The Reverend Sydney Strong challenged Matthews and warned that conflict between "labor and capital" was imminent. Strong suggested public debates to clear the air and preserve industrial peace.[34]

These differences sharpened when a new city charter was put before the voters. Following the recall of Gill, Seattle's efficiency-minded reformers had instituted revisions to reduce the high governmental costs, which they felt were considerably "out of line with sister cities of the same population." By 1914 they were determined to strengthen the 1911 revisions. After fifteen freeholders had been selected by the voters and submitted their recommendations, various segments of the community rose up to attack or defend the charter changes. Labor was angry because it had been so poorly represented. Only two of the freeholders were workers. Furthermore, under the new charter "big and special interests" would gain at labor's expense by replacing election of councilmen-at-large with the older, more tainted, precinct-ward system. Most Municipal League members and the older capitalist class, however, were not as concerned with the charter's possibly devastating effects on labor as they were with restoring governmental efficiency in order to realize economic recovery.[35]

The willingness of certain Seattle reformers to accept the ward system distinguishes them from their eastern counterparts in Pittsburgh and elsewhere. Many businessmen and professionals in eastern cities attacked the ward system to promote urban integration and diminish the strength of the labor vote. In Seattle, however, the working class gained political power when wards were eliminated because the workers generally were dispersed throughout the city rather than confined to particular residential districts. This was the major reason that organized labor had worked with reformers only three years earlier to eliminate the ward system. Now it seemed that the reformers were trying to reverse this accomplishment.[36] The proposed charter revision was defeated by a two-to-one majority as workers swamped the polls.

The tactics and defeat of structural reform in Seattle were noteworthy. These reformers, in contrast to most businessmen and professionals of the day, subordinated their drive for centralization to the drive for economy and in the process resurrected a nineteenth-century political form. They could not win, in spite of high governmental costs and the city's homogeneity, because they antagonized a major segment of the voting population.

Although victorious, labor was not assuaged. Unemployment worsened, the state legislature defeated an eight-hour-day bill and then approved prohibition. With the elimination of the liquor industry, more union members were out of work. Workers paraded through the streets calling upon Mayor Gill and the council to provide public works projects. Gill had been returned to office in 1914 after campaigning as a converted reformer who now favored a closed town. The Municipal League and the Central Council of Social Agencies persuaded Gill and the city council to provide food and lodging for the winter, but the unemployed were not satisfied. They demanded $2.75 a day and refused to serve as strikebreakers. Violence flared in November and December, 1914, when unemployed workers raided the Salvation Army and produce stands.[37]

During the winter of 1914/15 progressive movements in New York City, other cities along the Atlantic Coast, and cities in the Midwest were similarly tested by massive unemployment. Progressive mayors in these cities created a variety of emergency committees to raise relief funds and coordinate public and private charities, though for the most part these committees were hamstrung by the lack of sufficient operating funds and the general fear that welfare would be debilitating. In Seattle no such action was even attempted because Mayor Gill was victim of this fear.

The Municipal League's social reformers tried to provide relief and stem labor unrest by proposing a municipal lodging house. They were distraught about the approximately 5,000 homeless, detached males who were loitering around saloons in search of food and drink or drifting from one cheap private rooming house to another. They hoped to supply these men with free room and board and remove them from private rooming houses, which the reformers viewed as "breeding holes of vice and disease." Unfortunately, their chances for success were destroyed by circumstances they could not control.[38]

In late March of 1915, the state legislature passed an antipicketing law. At the same time, public works projects that had been implemented in Seattle and King County in an attempt to mollify labor began proving less than satisfactory. In the *Union-Record,* countless workers claimed that King County commissioners were practicing wage slavery by compelling them to work more than eight hours a day at twenty cents an hour and forcing them to live in contractors' camps that charged six dollars a day for room and board. After protesting for several weeks, the workers petitioned Gill to enforce the city's minimum wage on all public road projects. He summarily refused but reiterated that he was willing to provide food and shelter in exchange for physical labor. According to Gill, it would be immoral to impose further taxes on "good citizens who were struggling to feed and clothe their families" to pay men who were "bums and hoboes dependent on alcohol." The protests continued for approximately six weeks, but Gill did not relent.

Until this point there had been only sporadic violence, but Gill's intransigence fostered a spirit of rebellion in labor ranks. Numerous strikes were called. Employers retaliated with scab labor composed of Japanese sailors and blacks. Gill responded by appointing more than one hundred special policemen to patrol the waterfront, which was the focal point of the conflicts. Daily accounts appeared in the newspapers concerning beatings, assaults, attempted arson, and murders precipitated by strikers' efforts to obstruct the loading and unloading of cargo vessels.

The Chamber of Commerce and more conservatively inclined Municipal Leaguers blamed labor for the violence, while workers blamed employers and the authorities for being overzealous. Businessmen suggested that the violence would end if the strikers were rounded up and driven from the city. The Municipal League, on the other hand, fearing that the port would incur serious economic losses if reconciliation were not achieved quickly, called for mediation and offered concessions to both sides. To appease labor, it supported collective bargaining, with the proviso that arbitration proceedings be administered by a publicly appointed board of citizens. To please businessmen, it tried to convince labor that strikes, lockouts, and the closed shop were contrary to democratic principles because they were based on force. It advised union leaders to abandon forceful methods before the middle class became alienated.

The possibility that such a compromise would work was very small, particularly after the massacre of IWW protesters in nearby Everett one month after the Municipal League had tried to resolve existing differences. Immediately afterward, Seattle's "better elements" organized a Law and Order Society and admonished the community to prepare to defend itself. Labor reasserted its class-consciousness and resorted to economic action to secure its objectives. The Municipal League warned of the dangers of polarization but was unable to patch the fragmentation wrought by recession and labor militancy. There would be a brief hiatus when America entered World War I, but the last embers of cooperation between Seattle's urban middle class and organized labor died out during the latter part of the war and the Red Scare.[39]

Initially the Municipal League adopted the militant stance of publicly challenging the right of the old-time elite to control the city's affairs. Frustrated by their lack of clout in decision-making circles, League members proceeded to organize and lobby to shape the political process more favorably in their direction. Both the League and its opponents were struggling over conflicting interests and the distribution of power, as well as responding to changing social and economic conditions. Residents of the newly annexed outlying areas worried that their environment was becoming uncontrollable and ungovernable. They were also anxious about getting their fair share of the pottage. Against them stood certain prominent citizens who had much to lose because they had achieved wealth and influence through shrewd investments in the downtown area. Their vested interests thus conflicted with those who were still seeking their fortunes in Seattle.[40]

The Municipal League never dislodged these prominent citizens, but it did significantly expand political power by broadening the class origins of Seattle's decision makers. By 1913 Seattle was not exclusively dominated by older capitalists. Their power by then was shared with the rising new middle class. Municipal League members dotted the city council and other public and private posts and controlled many of the city's voluntary associations through the Central Council of Social Agencies. Two had even risen as high as the mayor's office.[41] No longer were League members the "outs." Now they were the "ins."

But their success was offset by a tremendous defeat in the Bogue plan battle and by the arrival shortly thereafter of a major recession, plus the absorption of their ideology by men such as Gill. Leaguers claimed to be building an all-encompassing reform movement, but their organization contained no economic cement as did the downtown business interests, and it offered labor only token representation. They were mistaken in thinking that the sense of community, as they defined it, could be viable in metropolitan Seattle. The main trends were in the opposite direction. Recession and labor militancy were symbols of the increasing fragmentation of the city. Undoubtedly these trends helped shape the League's decision in 1913 to cooperate with, rather than criticize,

Seattle's old-time elite. While cooperation may have been necessary in a time of trouble, it placed the League in a considerably less distinctive position and stretched the city's progressive movement almost to the breaking point. The structural and social reformers of the League had joined together to challenge the older capitalist class. After 1913 this common bond no longer existed.

As a result, the potential for further gains dissolved, reform became rudderless, and existing differences grew more pronounced. Before 1913/1914, prosperous workers had voted with the middle and upper class, but after 1914 these workers no longer responded to rhetoric calling for morality and efficiency in government. This transition was a result of the boom-bust cycle and the changing policy of League members, which sharpened self-interest to the point that it was no longer possible to combine the moral, political, and economic concerns of the working and middle classes.[42] As their world failed to become what they expected, League members lost their confidence and panicked. Slowly but steadily labor militancy, war hysteria, and the Red Scare transformed the Municipal League into an organization supporting reactionary proposals such as the suppression of civil liberties.[43]

AUGUSTUS CERILLO, JR.

5.
THE IMPACT OF REFORM IDEOLOGY:
EARLY TWENTIETH-CENTURY MUNICIPAL
GOVERNMENT IN NEW YORK CITY

The staples of an urban reform program in the Progressive Era—better
utility services and regulation, health, housing and factory laws, zoning
and city planning, the renovation of government and politics, and an improved educational system, among other items—are by now generally
well known. One influential interpretation of these "reforms" views them
as the hallmarks of a city modernizing and centralizing its institutions
and politics in response to the realities of urban physical and industrial
growth and the needs of an influential business and professional class.
Because municipal support was needed for many of these progressive
programs, city government itself underwent a transformation. As sketched
by historians Robert H. Wiebe, Samuel P. Hays, Otis A. Pease and others,
modern municipal governments were characterized by expanding responsibilities, more bureaucratic and systematized procedures, increasingly
centralized decision making and organization, a growing dependence
on professional specialists, and a pattern of continuous interaction
between citizens and government. This transformation, in Wiebe's words,
"separates the progressive years from the nineteenth century and points
toward modern political behavior."[1]

Progressives in New York City were at least partially successful in their
efforts to restructure and modernize the government of the nation's
largest metropolis. Before 1900 city hall had been ruled, except for an
occasional reform triumph, by Tammany men whose political ethics and
behavior had changed little from the notorious Tweed days. New York's
government was largely untouched by innovations in business, financial,
and administrative procedures. After five decades of agitation, housing
studies, sanitary surveys, and tenement house legislation, two-thirds of

Gotham's inhabitants continued to live in overcrowded and filthy apartments, and New York's government was unequipped to deal with the problem. The situation was much the same with respect to gas, electric, and rapid transit services. By the first decade of the twentieth century, America's preeminent city had little more control over the development and quality of its transportation facilities than it had had in 1875, when New York's first rapid transit act was passed; and as late as 1905, New Yorkers were entirely at the mercy of private gas and electric companies.

In contrast, by about 1916 the contours of a modern city government were visible. More of New York's day-to-day municipal operations were in the hands of bureaucrats, and the government was continuously involved in the city's health, housing, and utility problems through an enlarged and scientifically oriented board of health, a new tenement house department, a more stringent housing law, and a public service commission—all subdivided into bureaus and divisions and part of an expanding municipal structure. Experts in and out of government, in organizations such as the Bureau of Municipal Research, offered professional advice and helped fashion programs for Tammany politicians as well as reformers. Thus the bureaucratic management of a growing number of urban problems was becoming a permanent feature of New York City's politics.

These progressive innovations and programs, however piecemeal and rudimentary by the First World War, were more than just responses to obvious needs. They also derived from certain assumptions about municipal administration—a philosophy of urban political reform that had at its heart a modern conception of society, government, and political leadership. The interaction of ideology and reform is sharply focused in the thoughts and activities of several influential New York progressives—Lawrence Veiller, Hermann M. Biggs, Charles Evans Hughes, Henry Bruère, William H. Allen, Frederick A. Cleveland, and John Purroy Mitchel—and in the several pieces of new municipal machinery they created. This essay will focus on these men and their ideas and reform efforts to improve housing and health, streamline the government, and regulate utilities. Whatever the reform specialty, they all shared a common faith in administered progress.

Of all the problems facing New Yorkers, none touched more lives so continuously and directly as housing and disease. Since the early nineteenth century, housing reform and the public health movement had been closely related causes, centering on Manhattan's slums.[2] Both movements during the progressive years owed much of whatever success they achieved to two ambitious, hardworking, and brilliant young men:

Lawrence Veiller and Dr. Hermann M. Biggs. They combined a passion for the facts and a scientific study of municipal problems with an evangelistically zealous faith in the potential use of government power to right city wrongs.

Lawrence Veiller, a self-confident, aggressive young man, articulated a modern view of the necessity for continuous and broader participation of government in maintaining the social and physical health of the community. After graduating from the City College of New York in 1890, he plunged into social work on Manhattan's Lower East Side. Observing tenement life at its worst, especially during the depression that began in 1893, the twenty-year-old Veiller concluded that improved housing for the poor was "the starting point of everything."[3] Thus, housing reform became the central, although not exclusive, concern of his professional career.

Not impressed or satisfied with the work of several previous New York State legislative housing investigations (1856, 1884, 1894), and convinced that existing laws—the tenement house acts of 1867, 1879, 1887, and 1895—were neither enforced nor adequate, Veiller, in 1898, "conceived the idea of starting a movement which ... would continually seek to improve the conditions of the tenement house."[4] A series of quick triumphs established the ambitious reformer as one of the more creative forces behind progressivism's answer to slum housing evils. He organized a tenement house committee within the Charity Organization Society (COS) and, in 1900, impressed and educated uptown New Yorkers with a tenement house exhibit of cardboard models, photographs, maps, charts, and diagrams of existing blocks of slum houses. The same year, with Governor Theodore Roosevelt's support, Veiller wrote and helped get through the state legislature a bill creating New York's Tenement House Commission. Serving as secretary, Veiller brilliantly and systematically directed its work and wrote most of the commission's final reports. In addition, he drafted the important new tenement house law of 1901 and planned New York City's and the nation's, first permanent municipal Tenement House Department.[5]

Between 1901 and 1916, Veiller stamped his image on what became a national urban housing movement by combining traditional values and goals with innovative and modern techniques. In an essay entitled "The Housing Problem in American Cities," possibly the single best summary statement of a progressive understanding of the nature of slum housing and the social causes of poverty, Veiller catalogued what he believed were the major moral, industrial, and social effects of overcrowded housing. Moral standards were lowered, he thought, because home life was destroyed, parental and religious influence weakened, and privacy nonexistent.

"The street, the dance hall and the saloon," he feared, were replacing the home and church as the center of social life; he also was convinced that immigrant workers depressed wages and encouraged female and child labor and tenement sweat shops. "Democracy," Veiller wrote in his handbook of housing reform, "was not predicated upon a country made up of tenement dwellers, nor can it so survive."[6] The redistribution of city dwellers to rural or at least suburban communities was, in Veiller's view, the ideal, long-range solution to congestion.

Yet, Veiller realized the majority of New York's working people were trapped in the core city. Over two-thirds lived in tenement houses, many of which were six-story double-decker buildings occupying 75 percent of a twenty-five-foot lot and housing four families to a floor. Veiller's tenement law of 1901 sought to alleviate their plight through restrictive housing codes regulating the fireproofing, sanitation and ventilation of tenements. For example, new houses were required to have large courts proportionate in size to the height of the buildings, bathrooms in every apartment, and completely fireproofed stairs and public halls. Landlords were required to remodel old tenements to provide some fresh air and light in dark, interior rooms, modern water closets on each floor of the house, and better fire escapes. In other words, this law sought to prevent bad housing in the future and correct tenement evils of the past.[7]

In his creation of effective restrictive housing legislation, Veiller also worked out the bureaucratic techniques of meaningful government regulation. A complicated problem like slum housing required expert and scientific study and "constant and continuous attention," he insisted. "The mere passage of some piece of remedial legislation will be of little value, unless such legislation is properly enforced."[8] Thus he created for New York City a separate tenement house department, "charged with no duty except the supervision of the tenement houses—a department of such size as to adequately fulfill such functions."[9] Roy Lubove suggests this innovation illustrates Veiller's modern belief that using the coercive power of government was a more effective reform technique than relying on moral suasion or people's good intentions. "It is clearly the duty of the state to see that conditions shall not arise under which citizens shall be denied the ordinary conveniences of living," Veiller wrote in his analysis of urban housing problems.[10]

A practical-minded man, Veiller placed limits on the functions he assigned to the state in regard to housing. While he opposed unregulated private development, he also opposed what for him was the other extreme, the municipal ownership and operation of tenement houses. "I must confess," he wrote, "that I can not see why the municipality should go into the business of providing housing accommodations any more than it should go into the business of providing food for the poorer members of the community, or clothes, or fuel, or in fact, not only the necessaries of life, but even the conveniences."[11] Moreover, he frequently claimed that if the city entered the low-cost housing market, private entrepreneurs would be driven out and the municipality would inherit a housing burden too massive for its financial resources and managerial competency. The regulation of tenements, an exercise of the police power of the state, was Veiller's preferred solution to the housing question; it represented a moderate position somewhere between municipal socialism and laissez-faire capitalism.

The Tenement House Department owed much of whatever success it achieved to the continued interest and vigilance of Veiller and his friends in the Charity Organization Soceity. During its first two years of operation, Veiller, as first deputy commissioner, organized the new municipal agency and outlined the duties of the buildings, inspection, and records division. In addition, he saw that apartment houses were inspected and violations corrected. Over the years after 1903, under both Tammany Hall and reform control of New York's government, Veiller and the COS's tenement house committee, as unofficial watchdogs, remained the guiding force behind the Tenement House Department. They had a corrupt and incompetent Tammany department head fired; fought off amendments to weaken the housing law pushed by various builders, real estate men, bankers, and landlords; and secured new language explicitly stating that apartments with up-to-date facilities fell within the meaning of "tenement house" in the law of 1901. By 1916, Veiller saw his municipal creation grow to a bureaucracy of more than five hundred employees. Between 1902 and 1914 the department had answered over 500,000 tenant complaints, filed violations against 193,000 of them, and supervised the construction of over 24,000 new tenements. "On balance," writes Roy Lubove, "the idea of a separate housing department paid off in terms of a cleaner and healthier New York."

Nevertheless, bureaucratically enforced restrictive legislation was an essentially negative approach that could only insure against poor housing below a minimum standard. It did not provide for the construction of enough decent low-cost housing to satisfy the needs of New York's poor, and, ironically, had the potential to reduce the private building of such housing due to cuts in the profit margin. Thus, by the First World War some housing economists and architects had begun advocating government-subsidized or government-built cheap housing to supply the need. Although Veiller fought such suggestions as socialistic, by the 1930s a new generation of reformers had begun moving beyond restrictive housing legislation to more direct government involvement.[12]

Housing reformers benefited by developments in the closely related public health movement. Before the 1870s, most doctors assumed infectious diseases were caused by unsanitary conditions and naturally centered their attention on cleaning up tenement slums as part of a more general campaign for municipal cleanliness.[13] Those physicians who "viewed public health as a specialized responsibility of government" helped convince the New York state legislature to create the Metropolitan Board of Health in 1866. Not surprisingly, the following year, when New York's first tenement house law was enacted, the new Board of Health was given the task of enforcing its provisions.[14]

In 1870, due to the municipal charter revision secured by Tammany boss William Marcy Tweed, the state-controlled health board became the New York City Board of Health. For the balance of the century, the department built up its administrative machinery, partially professionalized its staff, and increased its activities and budget, thus firmly establishing public health as a municipal responsibility. Perhaps even more significant for public health in the progressive years was the discovery of the germ theory of disease, which, beginning in the 1890s, was to revolutionize American medicine and establish the New York City Health Department "as the preeminent American center for bacteriological research and for its application to public health problems."[15] In part this was due to the leadership of Dr. Hermann M. Biggs.

A precocious student, Biggs began studying medicine at Bellevue Hospital Medical College while still an undergraduate at Cornell University. Cramming a usual seven years of college and professional work into three and a half, he earned an M. D. in 1883. Both at Bellevue and in postgraduate work in Germany, Biggs had been exposed to the new science of bacteriology. In 1887, he and Dr. T. Mitchell Prudden, working at the recently built Carnegie Laboratory, made use of the new scientific insights into the germ theory of disease to isolate by biological procedure the cholera vibrio from Italian passengers on an immigrant ship. Not until five years later, however, when the city was threatened by an Asiatic cholera epidemic, were Biggs and his colleagues able to convince the Health Department to create a Division of Pathology, Bacteriology, and Disinfection. Placed under Biggs's charge, the division organized a diagnostic laboratory which, Charles-Edward A. Winslow notes, became the "first health department laboratory in the world for the application of this new science to the routine diagnosis of disease."

From the time the laboratory was created in 1892, the Health Department was able to move boldly and more scientifically against such disabling and killer diseases as cholera, smallpox, diphtheria, and tuberculosis. Under Biggs's leadership, the laboratory expanded its facilities and personnel, subdivided along functional lines, and began producing antitoxins and vaccines. As the Health Department's activities expanded, the department greatly improved its methods for collecting vital statistics on births, marriages, and deaths, which, tabulated on a ward basis, proved especially valuable to all sorts of reformers concerned with slum living.[16]

For Biggs, Prudden, Dr. William H. Park (Biggs's laboratory assistant and a specialist in bacteriological diagnosis), and their associates, the establishment of a municipal laboratory and the widening of the scope of the Health Department's activities reflected not only a commitment to the new medicine but a commitment to continuous, professionally led, bureaucratic management of the health care needs of New Yorkers. "Everything which is detrimental to health or dangerous to life," Biggs optimistically told the British Medical Association in 1897, "is regarded as coming within the province of the Health Department." He further explained what for most doctors was a revolutionary view of the government's responsibility to maintain the community's health. "So broad is the construction of the law," he said, "that everything which improperly or unnecessarily interferes with the comfort or enjoyment of life, as well as those things which are, strictly speaking, detrimental to health or dangerous to life, may become the subject of action on the part of the Board of Health."[17] By the time, then, that Mayor Seth Low appointed Biggs general medical officer of New York City in 1902, his public health philosophy had evolved from a negative focus on the municipal and scientific control of disease to a more positive and potentially expansive promotion of health. "He started on conventional lines of police power with isolation of the acutely contagious case," Winslow writes, "and step by step, he visualized a wider type of activity in which every resource of medical science should be utilized in the prevention of preventable disease."[18]

As general medical officer of New York City, Biggs played a major role in formulating Health Department policies. Over a decade or so, the department expanded its activities while it grew in size and personnel and went through several managerial and administrative reorganizations. Its annual budget increased from about $1 million in 1900 to an estimated $3,882,000 for 1913. Along with the general renovation, the department also improved its methods of operation and standardized procedures for buying supplies. The department's efforts to control and cure tuberculosis, begun so successfully on Biggs's initiative during the 1890s, continued after 1902. In addition to the already established policies that provided for the assignment of inspectors to investigate the disease, routine bacteriological examinations for diagnostic purposes, and physicians' reports on all cases, the department opened a tuberculosis dispensary and hospital, sent nurses to visit homes struck by the disease, and pioneered in the establishment of a sanitarium.

A good deal of the Health Department's effort was directed toward the young, as it pioneered in school and child health care services. In 1902, at the urging of Lillian D. Wald, the department appointed this country's first school nurses and established an eye hospital and clinic. To centralize responsibility for child health services, and hopefully cut the high mortality rate among New York's youngsters, Dr. S. Josephine Baker successfully crusaded for the creation, in 1908, of a Division of Child Hygiene, which firmly committed the Health Department to a program of preventive medicine. Under her direction the new agency was given charge of midwives, the sanitary supervision of day nurseries, and the medical examination of school children. She quickly increased the division's number of school nurses and systematized and expanded its activities to include dental clinics and health care centers. By 1914 this new division had become a bureau with 697 employees. Further to protect the young, the Board of Health fought for pasteurized milk and the establishment of infant milk stations.[19]

After 1913 Biggs worked to revolutionize New York State's health department, but city health commissioners Dr. Sigismund S. Goldwater and his successor, Dr. Haven Emerson, continued during reform mayor John Purroy Mitchel's administration to expand the scope of the Health Department's activities in the direction of the maintenance of community health. Goldwater reorganized the Health Department, completely rewrote the city's Sanitary Code, created new bureaus, including a novel Bureau of Health Education, and experimented with a district health center plan, which was extended to larger portions of the city by Dr. Emerson. After Emerson took over, he continued Goldwater's policies, mobilized the medical resources of the city to fight a major polio epidemic in 1916, and renamed the infant milk stations "baby health stations," to reflect their broader concerns with child care education.[20]

In 1918 Tammany Hall again controlled New York's government and, according to public health historian John Duffy, ended an extremely innovative era in the Health Department's history. Nevertheless, for most of the years between 1900 and 1917, the Health Department enjoyed Tammany's support and remained relatively free of politics. Inevitably Tammany appointed a number of political hacks to the department's many divisions and bureaus, some of which became more interested in graft than health; but probably the department's effectiveness over the years was hindered more by inadequate funds, personnel, and facilities. In addition, the department faced frequent opposition by private doctors to any enlargement of municipal preventive medicine. Perhaps more significant than the department's shortcomings during a seminal era in the development of public health is what Duffy suggests about the legacy of progressive doctors such as Hermann Biggs and his allies. In the Tammany-controlled years that followed, Duffy writes, "the Health Department survived largely because of its solid bureaucratic structure, its excellent public image, and the work of a large number of dedicated professional health workers."[21] He also could have included the impact of those doctor-reformers' revolutionary view of the municipality's responsibility for the community's health.

Along with health care and housing, the quality of utility services—gas, electricity, and public transportation—also greatly affected the living and working conditions of all New Yorkers. Like housing and most health care, utility services were private enterprises. For several decades businessmen had dominated the politics of utility promotion, largely confining city and state involvement to a few legislative investigations, some franchise stipulations, and a series of business-controlled rapid transit boards. By 1905 local government still did not have the capability to plan, promote, and manage in the public interest a comprehensive utility system. Yet, most agreed that the city's privately owned and operated streetcars, noisy elevated lines, and one subway—financed and owned by the city but privately built and operated—were inadequate. Likewise, residents chronically complained about poor gas and electric service and high rates charged by the monopoly Consolidated Gas Company.[22]

For a variety of political reasons, and in response to pressure from numerous civic and commercial organizations led by the Merchants' Association, the Republican-dominated state legislature in 1905 appointed a joint committee, headed by Senator Frederick C. Stevens, to investigate the entire gas and electric issue in the metropolis. Charles Evans Hughes, by reputation a lawyer's lawyer and a man with no political ambition, was chosen chief counsel to the Stevens Committee. With a brilliant display of research and investigatory skills, Hughes pieced together a sordid tale of corporate greed, profiteering, overcapitalization, high rates, and poor service. At the end of the hearings, much like Lawrence Veiller after the tenement house investigation of 1901, Hughes shaped the data into a legislative report that resulted in the creation of New York's first permanent, continuously functioning gas and electricity commission.[23]

Hughes emerged from the gas investigation, and a subsequent life insurance investigation, "as a public figure of outstanding prominence."[24] His reputation as a tough, brilliant, and honest lawyer was exploited in 1906 by President Theodore Roosevelt, who forced a corrupt and faction-ridden state Republican party to nominate Hughes for governor. In a hard-fought campaign against Democratic candidate William Randolph Hearst, Hughes began developing his political philosophy. To counteract Hearst's enormous popularity among workers, Hughes expressed sympathy for labor's right to organize and urged the eight-hour day for public construction workers, child labor legislation, and a better state employer liability system. Against Hearst's call for public ownership of utilities, Hughes advocated government regulation, an approach he had used in his gas and electric commission bill. "I believe there should be effective governmental control of all great enterprises in which the public is interested and which depend upon the public for their right to be and to do," he told a Glens Falls campaign audience. Hughes defeated Hearst by about 75,000 votes, and the new governor quickly became the political embodiment of progressive reform in New York.[25]

Generally, Hughes believed that the American people were much more interdependent than in the past with respect to health, housing, education, utilities, labor conditions, and natural resources. Such interdependence required "intelligent cooperation . . . a constant extension of governmental activity," he explained at his first inaugural. That same year, he warned a group of Cornell University graduates that "the time was coming when individual enterprise would be restricted and that, in the course of time, producer and consumer, the businessman and the workingman, would all welcome interference by the Government." A few years later, in his *Conditions of Progress in Democratic Government*, Hughes generalized that in a modern society "the interests of the community" increasingly had to take priority over extreme individualism and the quest for private gain and opportunity. The governor further clearly revealed his kinship with fellow progressives in New York City in his concern for the conduct and procedures of a government of expanding scope and function. "Public enterprise," he wrote, "requires managerial capacity of a high order."[26]

Robert Wesser has written that Governor Hughes emerged "as one of those exceptional public servants who functioned as an agent for the reform of political, economic, and social disorder."[27] In his years as chief executive, Hughes helped numerous urban social progressives—Lawrence Veiller, social workers Homer Folks, Lillian Wald, and others—and the scores of social welfare organizations they represented to push through the legislature woman and child labor laws, a workmen's compensation act, measures improving the inferior court and probation systems, and public health bills. Similar to political reforms, these laws expanded bureaucratic supervision over social and economic aspects of life.[28]

Hughes even more directly translated his concern for the public good into achievement in the areas of administrative and political reform. Ignoring the machine politicians of his own party, he investigated the efficiency of executive departments, replaced incompetent officials, and generally centralized his authority over state government. Probably the most important reform law of Hughes's governorship was his utility measure, which created two five-member public service commissions, one for New York City and one for the rest of the state. This statute central-ized in a single state commission regulatory authority over New York City's subways, street surface lines, elevated roads, and gas and electric companies and granted authority to plan, build and, if need be, operate elevated or subway lines.[29] In his struggle to get the public service com-mission bill enacted, and in subsequent speeches and writings on the utility issue, Hughes compiled a progressive document for effective ad-ministrative control of public service corporations and revealed the broader ideological underpinning of his reform program.

One theme he constantly reiterated was the obligation of a concerned government that served the public. In reviewing New York City's trans-portation situation after his election Hughes told the legislators, "all the existing lines, surface, elevated, and subway, are overburdened and the people suffer in mind, body and estate." Besides new facilities, he explained, there was an "urgent necessity for more strict supervision to secure better service on existing lines."[30] In arguments over ways to deal with the question of amount and quality of service, Hughes explicated another popular progressive theme, the necessity for coercive admin-istrative power. Certainly he felt it was a matter of practical necessity for the legislature "to confer proper power upon a subordinate adminis-trative body." He told the Utica Chamber of Commerce that the legislature just was not equipped to deal continuously, flexibly, and ef-ficiently with the extraordinary number and variety of utility questions constantly arising. Only an administrative board with "full power to conduct investigations and to make whatever orders in relation to operation may be necessary," he suggested, "could secure the performance of public obligation."[31]

To be effective and just, the very administrative structure of bureau-cratic power had to be made harmonious, economical, and efficient. It was to implement this third theme of good government that Hughes concentrated in a single utility commission power over gas, electric, and transportation facilities in Greater New York. Moreover, it was his goal, he told audiences, to have "a commission of dignity, of force, of ability, representing the best intelligence of the State," and possessing "equip-ment and such technical assistance as will enable it to deal with the matters before it thoroughly and expertly." A year after the passage of the public service commission bill, reformer Henry Bruère expressed the belief of many progressives that the commission had "adopted the principle of basing its actions not on guesses or expediency, but on facts secured through scientific inquiry."[32]

The Public Service Commission quickly settled into a routine of work and attacked some of the more obvious and long-standing utility abuses. The product both of experience and ideology, it carried on its supervisory and planning functions through a number of bureaus and divisions, which employed engineers, accountants, lawyers, and other professionals. Its bureau of statistics and accounts devised and installed in utility corporations a system of accounts and records that became the basis for many of the commission's published reports. While its franchise bureau classified all existing utility franchises, the Public Service Commission, over several years, ordered a number of improvements in transportation service, equipment, and safety devices. Consumer complaints about poor gas and electricity service, faulty equipment, and unfair rates were investigated and usually settled informally. Most notably, the commission systematically inspected and tested all new and repaired gas and electric meters —over one million by 1910.[33]

While of unquestioned value, much of this early work, especially that which buried the Public Service Commission in statistics, projected the agency not as a dynamic regulatory body but as something of an information center. Bogged down in the routine details of its work, the commission rarely showed the imagination or the will to take the initiative in formulating public utility policy. Generally reluctant to wield a big stick, the commission envisioned itself as a forum through which consumers and companies could adjust their differences, and preferred settling most utility service matters informally—by letter, telephone, or personal consultation. While congenial to corporate executives and well-suited to bureaucratic management, such easy, flexible procedures made little public impact. Utility consumers expected their commission to function as an advocate, not an impartial judge; as a governing agency, not an information bureau. Predictably, then, an overexpectant citizenry scarcely appreciated the Public Service Commission's real though modest accomplishments or understood the commission's inexperience with public regulation of a giant industry.[34]

This public feeling that New York's regulatory commission generally fell short of reform expectations was reinforced by a conjunction of two developments that led to a legislative investigation of the regulatory system. The Public Service Commission joined the majority of the city's Board of Estimate and Apportionment in 1913 in signing the dual subway contracts, labeled by then president of the Board of Aldermen, and future progressive mayor of New York, John Purroy Mitchel, as "a bad business bargain for the city." These contracts with the Interborough Rapid Transit Company and the Brooklyn Rapid Transit Company called for the two private corporations to expand New York's elevated and subway lines with the city sharing the costs of construction, and included other financial and technical agreements advantageous to the companies.[35]

Moreover, shortly after Governor Hughes left Albany for the United States Supreme Court in 1911, Tammany Democrats, in control of the state government, stacked the Public Service Commission with their men, several of whom had close ties with the local transit companies. "What the governors of the State of New York since Hughes have done to the public service commission," lamented utility reform theorist Delos Wilcox, "is enough to make the angels weep." More down to earth, by 1914 many New Yorkers were upset over "the crisis in public service regulation."[36]

The joint legislative committee appointed to investigate the Public Service Commission pronounced "the whole scheme of regulation" a failure, and the Tammany commissioners incompetent. Most of the specific criticisms centered not on the bureaucratic approach itself, but on how the bureaucrats in office behaved. The committee did suggest that combining utility regulation with transportation construction was a mistake and recommended that these functions be handled in separate agencies.[37] However, the committee understood that "while the experiment of regulation and supervision tried has not justified expectations the policy of regulation and supervision has not had a fair trial, and it is hoped that the scheme of revision and reorganization submitted comprehends such changes in the law as are desirable."[38]

None of the legislative committee's recommendations for reorganizing and improving public utility regulation suggested going back to a pre-1907 arrangement. The progressive espousal and creation of bureaucratic means to manage a large portion of New York City's economy was not rejected in the reorganization of the public service commissions but was bequeathed to the next generation. Although new commissions were organized and new men ran them, the progressive method, so well described by Charles Evans Hughes back in 1907, remained intact.[39]

Reformers fighting for better tenements, health care, and utility services—whatever their precise individual motives—generally shared a desire to control the effects of industrialism and improve the conditions of living for New York's citizens. They also moved beyond their private professional and associational reform activities to demand government intervention, and in the process greatly expanded the scope of municipal administration. Inevitably this raised to a new intensity the old problem of the managerial competency and honesty of public officials.

For years in New York, various citizens' associations and reform clubs had hoped to get effective government through charter, ballot, and civil service reform and by electing "good" men to office. Even when occasionally successful against Tammany Hall at the polls, these reformers failed to achieve much because the municipal administrative and business system was chaotic and obsolete. For example, executive decision-making power was fragmented among a score of city officials and elected bodies, greatly reducing the mayor's ability to govern effectively and responsibly. And New York lacked a budget system and scientific accounting and data collection procedures.[40]

Three young progressives, William H. Allen, Henry Bruère, and Frederick Cleveland, and their brainchild, the Bureau of Municipal Research (BMR), along with political and civic reform allies such as John Purroy Mitchel, George McAneny, and William Prendergast, spearheaded a drive to reform New York's business methods and managerial techniques. Both Allen, an expert in social work management, and Cleveland, a professor of finance at New York University and a municipal accounting consultant, had earned Ph.D.'s at the University of Pennsylvania, where they had imbibed Simon Patten's passion for efficiency and economy in government. Together with Bruère, a social worker with a Harvard University law degree, and the financial backing of R. Fulton Cutting, Andrew Carnegie, and John D. Rockefeller, they created the nation's first municipal research bureau. The nonpartisan BMR, staffed with experts, was to "apply the processes of research, and the disinterestedness of research, and the techniques of business management, to public affairs and civic problems."[41]

An examination of these research bureau reformers' writings, as well as their work for and within the mayoral administrations of Democrats George B. McClellan (1903-1909) and William J. Gaynor (1909-1913) and the progressive-fusionist Mitchel (1913-1917), reveals a great deal about the values behind and the history of the modernization of New York City's government during the Progressive Era. Going beyond nineteenth-century crusaders for honest but rather limited government, these men believed that government was "the indispensable instrument of effective community cooperation" and should concern itself more with the day-to-day problems and needs of its citizens. "We are beginning to see that city government has a social purpose and that *laissez-faire* should no longer dominate our politics," wrote Cleveland. A progressive government, in the thinking of Cleveland, Bruère, and their colleagues, took "cognizance of the new social spirit that places public welfare above all other aims of human effort"; it provided "leadership in filling every ascertained community want."[42]

In their published books and articles, all of these reformers suggested the kinds of services and concerns they considered necessary twentieth-century municipal functions. In his *The New City Government*, Henry Bruère argued a progressive welfare program should guarantee urban dwellers:

personal and community healthfulness; equitable taxation for community benefits; purposive education; protection from exploitation by tradesmen, landlords and employers; prevention of injury to persons or property; adequate housing at reasonable rents; clean, well-paved, well-lighted streets; efficient and adequate public utility service; abundant provision for recreation; prevention of destitution caused by death, sickness, unemployment or other misfortune; publicity of facts regarding government's program, acts and results.[43]

Even more radical for the time, William Allen claimed city children, and by implication all city dwellers, possessed, in addition to the usual inalienable political rights—free speech, freedom of the press, right to trial by jury, etc.—certain rights with respect to "every day comforts, necessities and pleasures." He claimed many children were denied "the right to health, the right to schooling that educates, the right to industrial efficiency, the right to a body capable of enjoying life's battle and efficiency's reward."[44]

These reformers, at least in their published statements, seemed to recognize, to quote Bruère's apt statement, "the people of a municipality do not live by asphalt and pure water alone." They expected city government "to further the health, intelligence and economic capacity of its citizens."[45] Moreover, they recognized that in New York and elsewhere, as municipal governments expanded their scope and functions, they had not improved their methods of operation. Public affairs, unfortunately, were not "managed by public servants with efficiency and economy."[46]

To be progressive, then, a city government also had to be efficient, which meant it intelligently planned social services to meet actual needs, created the necessary bureaucratic organization to carry out its policies, introduced business techniques in administration such as accounting and budget systems, appointed and carefully supervised trained employees, and was staffed with public officials who cooperated with a knowledgeable and factually informed citizenry.[47] Not conceived of as a "penny-pinching proposition at all," as Cleveland later recalled, the movement for a progressively efficient government was, in Bruère's words, an "effort to develop the potential forces of city government for harnessing to the work of social betterment." Elsewhere, Henry Bruère labeled such an effort "the task of modernizing the methods of . . . governments."[48]

For over a decade after they organized the BMR in 1906, "the ABC's," as Allen, Bruère, and Cleveland came to be called, and their staff of lawyers, accountants, engineers, and other experts, reformed New York's administration, created a literature of public administration and a Training School for Public Service (1911), and helped in the establishment of a municipal reference library (1913). Beginning under Democratic mayor McClellan and reaching a climax under progressive mayor Mitchel, whose closest advisor was Henry Bruère, the Bureau reformers forced incompetent officials from office and encouraged the appointment of professionally trained experts as department heads. They worked with Comptrollers Hermann A. Metz (1905-1909) and William Prendergast (1909–1917) and other public officials to install in the finance and other departments of government cost and efficiency records, an accounting system, the nation's first municipal budget system that provided for line-by-line itemization of expenses, and other such techniques of business management. In addition, they conducted various studies of the operations of government that became the basis for several administrative reorganizations, the establishment of a central purchasing plan and payroll division, and the creation of a number of specialized advisory staff agencies within the government.[49]

The bureau men publicized their philosophy of reform as well as their specific achievements through a variety of publications that included printed reports of departmental studies and *Municipal Research,* a magazine, each issue of which was devoted to a specific topic of public administration. In addition, the bureau published handbooks on accounting and other municipal business methods, and Allen, Bruère, and Cleveland each authored numerous articles and books. In 1911, the BMR founded the first school in the nation "dedicated solely to preparing young men for work in government."[50] In the Training School for Public Service, university graduates read intensively in the literature of scientific management, budget-making, and the like, and spent hours in city agencies observing and doing research for senior staff members. By 1921, when the school and Bureau were reorganized as the National Institute of Public Administration, over one hundred graduates filled either public service jobs or headed research bureaus in cities across the country. The school's program also inspired a growing number of universities to develop graduate training in public administration.[51]

In their writings, Bruère and the other research bureau theorists and reformers stressed the compatibility, even necessity, of combining the virtues of efficiency and community welfare, which together they believed produced a progressive government. They vehemently denied being overly concerned with the "means and methods of government rather than its programs and objectives."[52] Yet, an examination of the bureau's contributions to reform, especially during the administration of John Purroy Mitchel, when bureau-influenced reformers controlled the major offices of government, reveals a lopsided concern with the structural details of research and administration and too little real thought about people and the common purposes of government. "There was too much emphasis on economy and too little attention devoted to the needs of a growing city" during the Mitchel administration, suggests Edwin R. Lewinson, the mayor's biographer. The reformers became enamored with a "pay-as-you-go" fiscal plan to finance non-self-sustaining city improvements. By paying for such improvements out of current revenue, the reformers hoped to decrease the city's debt, save interest, reduce the budget, and perhaps cut taxes. That "it would hamper future municipal improvements" never entered their calculations.

In his study of Mitchel's mayoralty, Lewinson further demonstrates how welfare and education services too often were sacrificed on the altar of efficiency and economy. John A. Kingsbury, commissioner of the Department of Public Charities, brought about several needed improvements in municipal child care institutions but also displayed an excessive zeal for economy when he sent home to their families hundreds of feeble-minded and other dependent children in charitable institutions to save the city money. In fact, the commissioner favored private over public charity. Yearly, the Board of Estimate appropriated less money for the city's schools than the school board demanded; the operation of evening high schools and summer schools and the construction of new buildings were curtailed because of insufficient funding. Public school teachers, accused by Comptroller Prendergast of laziness, feared pay cuts if the state legislature granted the mayor control over salaries. Mayor Mitchel and the Board of Estimate even experimented with double sessions in the more crowded city schools to save building and teaching service costs.[53]

To the extent that Mayor Mitchel and his administration reflected the BMR's political philosophy, it was repudiated by the people in 1917, when Tammany's candidate for mayor, Judge John F. Hylan, overwhelmingly defeated Mitchel, 313,956 votes to 155,497.[54] Preoccupied with economy, Robert Caro writes, Mitchel "did not want to do anything with the money thus saved, but save it. His boasts were not of what was being done to meet the city's needs but of what was being done to save the city's money."[55] Budget and accounting systems, purchasing plans, and new bureaus of efficiency institutionalized a measure of honesty in government but could not be eaten, used, or enjoyed by the public. These municipal reformers expanded the city's bureaucracy, not its services. In other words, they failed to distinguish means from ends and never resolved the conflicting twin tendencies inherent in the political philosophy of men such as Bruère, Cleveland, and Allen: better administration as a necessary precondition for social betterment or merely a penny-pinching affair. Nevertheless, the legacy of these progressive good-government reformers resided in New York City's modernized administration. It was left to others to tip the scale on the side of service and welfare.

Whatever the limitations of progressive achievements, the theoretical, legislative, and administrative legacy of New York's progressives was reform with a modern ring. Increasingly, government was looked to for answers, and municipal programs were implemented through administrative agencies. Experts more frequently shared in the decision-making process, and a growing, permanent administrative bureaucracy provided an alternative channel to the legislature for suggestions to continuously modify laws, policies, and government. In other words, government, in a structured way, was permanently involved more than previously in the lives of New Yorkers. To the extent that ideas shape events, this striking change in New York's government and politics reflected changed perceptions about the role of government in a modern urban society.

MICHAEL H. EBNER

6. REDEFINING THE SUCCESS ETHIC FOR URBAN REFORM MAYORS:
FRED R. LOW OF PASSAIC, 1908-1909

For urban reform politicians who aspire to a more exalted elective position, the mayoralty is a perilous way station. Unlike the presidency and governorships, it has been engulfed in historical uncertainty. Originally the mayoralty was not filled by popular election, although by 1850 it had attained legal if not functional recognition as the pinnacle of attainment in municipal government. Twenty years later the growth of executive power was apparent, culminating, at least in larger cities, with its supremacy and a resultant diminution in the authority of councilmen. But as the search for a successful formula of urban governance expanded to intermediate and smaller-sized cities, the so-called strong-mayor concept itself was eclipsed by such adaptive innovations as the commission plan, beginning in 1901, and the city manager format in 1912. Both generally purported to reform municipal administration by infusing executive leadership with business-oriented, professionalized techniques of modern management.[1]

Theoretical interest in urban government during the late nineteenth and early twentieth centuries was not coincidental. The years 1877 to 1917, or thereabout, are regarded as a continuum during which human and institutional patterns of organization and behavior were undergoing a process of modernization spawned by the industrialization and urbanization of American society. Within the rapidly changing urban polity, authority and decision making were subjugated by the integrative process of centralization, thereby imposing a more rational (and, ideally, conflict-free) system of governance upon the citizenry.[2]

Political success—if "success" is defined by reelection or ascent to higher office—long has eluded urban reform mayors.[3] Focusing on the single-term administration of Frederick R. Low, the reform mayor of Passaic, New Jersey, 1908/1909, this study will reexamine the success ethic in urban politics. Conventional political wisdom might suggest that Low failed miserably to address himself to the issues stemming from the city's urban-industrial expansion. Indeed, he possessed the ironic distinction of being both Passaic's first modern reform chief executive and the first incumbent to be denied renomination. Still, more than sixty years after his political demise, physical evidence remains of Fred Low's vision of Passaic as "The Ideal City." Even his foremost journalistic detractor, the *Passaic Daily Herald,* in commenting on his defeat, allowed that "the future will take a much more charitable view of his schemes and ambitions than the present. His appeal to the fanciful rather than the real has had an influence for good and not for evil."[4]

Although the mayoralty remained a position of civic honor in Passaic at the onset of the twentieth century, the office possessed limited executive power and administrative responsibility. Reflecting historic misgivings over the investiture of broad administrative authority in a single executive, local government was decentralized. The council was elected by wards, and its committee system accorded members quasi-administrative power to cope with such municipal services as public safety and sanitation. Moreover, the council drafted the annual budget, although the mayor could recommend alterations prior to its adoption. City-wide elections of tax assessor and collector also detracted from the executive's role; the creation of the elective position of councilman-at-large, whose duty was to preside over council sessions, established what amounted to a rival for the mayor's statutory authority. Finally, until Fred Low changed the arrangement by advocating mayoral appointment of the school board, trustees had been elected by wards on a partisan basis.[5]

The city Fred Low governed was a post–Civil War phenomenon. Its estimated population in 1870 was 2,567, whereas New Jersey's principal pre-war cities—Camden, Elizabeth, Jersey City, Newark, Paterson, and Trenton—all had populations exceeding 10,000 by 1860. Passaic was not even incorporated as a village until 1869. Four years later, when it was incorporated as a city, it was developing rapidly into a small industrial center specializing in the manufacture of textile-related goods; in 1900 the city would rank fourth nationally in production of worsteds. The population tripled in the decade 1870–1880 to 6,532, and doubled in each of the three successive ten-year periods. In 1910 only 13.8 percent of Passaic's 54,773 inhabitants were native-born whites of native parentage, 33.2 percent were second-generation Americans, and 52 percent were foreign-born; another 1 percent were black. The city's foreign-born population that year was, in fact, the highest proportionally in the nation.

"New" immigrants from Russia, Austria-Hungary, and Italy made up nearly four of every five among the foreign-born; the principal groups of "old" immigrants were Irish, English, Scotch, Dutch, and German. Passaic's textile mills, which by 1912 employed nearly three-fourths of its total labor force, obviously attracted the city's immigrant-stock inhabitants.[6]

When Mayor Low is measured against his predecessors, dating back to 1869, he clearly differs from the established mayoral typology. Save for a single-term Democrat in 1885/1886, all were Republicans; Low was aligned with the progressive wing of the Republican party, known in New Jersey as the "New Idea." The previous mayors had lived on the west side, either in the Second or Third Wards, which included the city's affluent neighborhoods; Low lived on the east side in the Fourth Ward, the city's "zone of emergence" for offspring of the immigrants. Previous mayors had been Protestant, of native or "old" ethnic stock; Low's Unitarian affiliation set him apart from those members of the more conventional denominations. Occupationally, the earlier mayors fell into the usual range of entrepreneurial, industrial, or professional endeavors; here too the exception was Low, who edited a trade publication for steam engineers. Finally, Low's vocational activity, which was no less "progressive" than his politics, further distinguished him as a man whose ideology, unlike that of his predecessors, did not reflect the predilections of the business and industrial sectors.[7]

Frederick Rollins Low prided himself on being a self-made individual who confronted the forces of modernization and coped with them creatively. Born in 1860 in Chelsea, a suburb of Boston, he left school at age fourteen to work as a telegrapher and stenographer for Western Union. His lifelong vocation commenced in 1880, when he joined a Boston textile trade publication and developed an abiding interest in the technology of steam engineering. Although his knowledge of the field was largely acquired informally, Low also sought the aid of professionally trained experts. He was credited with several inventions, and for a brief time in the eighties was engaged in an engineering partnership. He flourished, however, as a journalist. The Boston apprenticeship ended in 1888, when Low was retained by a fledgling New York City publisher (ultimately, McGraw-Hill) to edit *Power,* a journal for steam engineers founded four years earlier—a position he held until his retirement in 1929. In an era when engineering was being transformed into a highly complex field struggling to remain abreast of the onrush of innovation, he took special pains to advocate the responsibility of engineers to society.[8]

As much as Low endeavored to distinguish between, if not separate altogether, vocational and civic pursuits, his ideas on engineering and politics were inextricably linked. While Low the "editor" refrained from overt references to "Mayor" Low, the experiences he encountered in Passaic were implicit in his editorial commentaries. When he debated public ownership of utilities with a reader in 1909, for example, Low prefaced his emphatic defense of the concept with the disclaimer, *"Power's* subject is engineering and not political economy." At almost the same time, in carrying out his civic duties, he told an audience of local mail carriers that government ownership of utilities was comparable to federal control of the postal service.[9] Despite avowing the separation of technology from politics, therefore, Low's editorials during his most intense involvement in Passaic underscored the unity of his thinking.[10]

Fred Low's engagement in public affairs prior to his election as mayor affords insight into his preparation for subsequent urban leadership. Following service on the board of health, he was elected a Fourth Ward councilman in 1900 on the Republican ticket. Regarded as a "fair man" by opposition factions, his devotion to municipal ownership of the water supply also gained favorable notice. Low was denied renomination in 1903, however, because he had advocated a public park for his ward in the face of express opposition from neighborhood property owners. Yet, during that very year, his stature in both the party and community was heightened by his election as chairman of the Republican municipal committee and president of the prestigious Passaic Club.[11]

Heretofore a well-intentioned, civic-minded citizen, Low underwent an ideological transformation in 1905-1906. After returning to elective office in 1905 as councilman-at-large, he broke with the Republican "regulars" for the "New Idea" wing of the party. This change into an "issue-oriented mass educator" committed to social and economic democracy coincided with Low's opposition to the Public Service Corporation, a statewide utility conglomerate and the bête noire of political reformers.[12] In 1905 and 1906 the utility's local contract was being renegotiated. Because citizens had been voicing mounting criticism over high rates and inadequate service since 1900, in 1906 the issue was politically exploitable. Eventually Public Service won renewal, but only after inordinate legal encounters and excessive rancor within the city council had forced a short-term contract favorable to the public's interest. A tax agent of the utility, Bird W. Spencer, three times the mayor of Passaic (1879-1885) and long active in the Republican leadership, reputedly had wielded enormous influence lobbying among some councilmen. Indeed, when Fred Low was denied renomination as councilman-at-large in 1906—being defeated in the Republican city convention after having carried the primary for delegates with 56.9 percent—it was widely assumed that his defeat was the product of Spencer's malign influence.[13]

Actually, Low had been in the mainstream of New Idea activities even before he was denied renomination, serving as chairman of its municipal organization. The objective of this movement was to capture the apparatus of the Republican party from the regulars. It had been germinating since 1901, when Mark M. Fagan was elected mayor of Jersey City, and by 1905 it had spread across the urban-industrial region of northeastern New Jersey. Its leading theoretician was George L. Record, Fagan's corporation counsel, a firm adherent of Henry George's Single Tax. New Idea proponents favored such political reforms as direct nominating primaries, campaign practices legislation, and popular election of United States senators, as well as a host of economic proposals such as equal taxation and franchise limitation.[14]

Although the New Idea movement ebbed elsewhere after 1906, the intraparty dispute intensified in Passaic. The immediate issue in 1907 was the mayoral nomination. The primary pitted Fred Low, the vanquished councilman-at-large, against Bird Spencer, who was seeking a return to the mayoralty after a twenty-three-year interlude. Manifest in this contest was the Public Service contract dispute of 1905-1906. "The acknowledged representative" of the utility was the label attached to Spencer by a leading reformer, who added that the mayor cannot serve two masters —the people and Public Service. Another proponent of Low's nomination observed, "There is a class of men who represent corporate control in public affairs and Mr. Low is pitted against a man who represents just that." Likewise, Dr. Charles M. Howe, four times the mayor of Passaic (1887-1889 and 1899-1901) and still active as well as highly regarded in civic circles, documented how Spencer had opposed the interest of the public in an 1899 controversy over "dollar gas."[15] Low swept the contest for the nomination with 63.8 percent of the ballots and subsequently carried the general election with 59.6 percent.[16]

The campaign of 1907 was significant because it included aspersions on the ability of Low to govern effectively—charges heard repeatedly during the next two years. This attack was initiated by Spencer and subsequently taken up by the Democratic mayoral candidate. Foremost was the contention that Low's prior record in elective offices predestined him to be a lavish spender bent on draining the public treasury of the hard-earned funds contributed by taxpayers. A second anti-Low thrust played on his well-established reputation as a reformer. His vaunted integrity, it was suggested, had been blemished by political deals with a Republican "syndicate" dominated by George P. Rust, publisher of the *Passaic Daily News*, that was using him as an unwitting foil to thwart Spencer. "Low's hunger for office has eaten out his heart and intelligence" asserted the Democratic *Passaic Daily Herald*. The third anti-Low stroke highlighted his relatively recent involvement in public affairs. Charging that Low's responsibilities at *Power* necessitated his daily presence in Manhattan, Spencer averred Low's proclivity for excessive spending resulted from his lack of intimate acquaintance with the city's administration.[17]

Obviously sensitive to these allegations, Low declared he would be an "all day mayor . . . accessible to all citizens at all times." No deals or promises had been consummated on his behalf, he added; economy in

TABLE 6-1. Electoral Analysis, Passaic, 1904-1909

1910 Demographic Profile	W-1	W-2	W-3	W-4	City
% of total population (T.P.)[a]	40.7	14.1	9.9	35.4	54,773
% of foreign-born white (FBW)	53.5	8.1	4.2	34.2	28,255
% of FBW in ward's T.P.	*68.0*	*29.5*	*21.8*	*49.9*	*52.0*
% of "old" FBW	10.5	27.5	15.5	46.4	6,013
% of "old" FBW in ward's T.P.	*2.8*	*21.4*	*17.2*	*14.4*	*11.0*
% of "new" FBW	65.2	2.8	1.1	30.9	22,242
% of "new" FBW in ward's T.P.	*65.2*	*8.0*	*4.5*	*35.4*	*40.6*
% of second-generation white	37.0	15.1	8.8	39.1	18,209
% of SGW in ward's T.P.	*30.3*	*35.6*	*29.7*	*36.7*	*33.2*
% of nat.-born white/nat. par.	3.3	31.0	33.5	32.3	7,536
% of NBW/NP in ward's T.P.	*1.1*	*30.3*	*46.6*	*12.5*	*13.8*
% of Afro-Americans (AA)	17.0	60.9	9.0	13.1	535
% of AA in ward's T.P.	*0.4*	*4.2*	*0.9*	*0.4*	*1.0*
Persons per city lot[b]	7.0	1.7	0.5	4.0	3.3
Homes built before 1899[c]	26.3	16.7	16.1	40.9	100.0
Homes built 1900-1919	25.7	24.0	14.9	35.3	100.0
Political Data					
% of registered voters, 1907[d]	20.1	23.9	18.6	37.4	4,963
Votes for—					
FRL—Councilman-at-large 1904[e]	48.5	79.7	80.7	60.6	64.3
FRL—Counc.-at-lge, primary 1906	25.9	71.2	74.7	43.8	56.9
FRL—Mayoralty primary 1907	49.1	63.1	74.7	62.8	63.8
FRL—Mayoralty 1907	48.2	68.8	80.4	49.4	59.6
FRL—Mayoralty primary 1909	16.3	32.5	49.3	35.3	35.8
Spencer—Mayoralty 1909	53.3	69.5	72.4	61.5	63.4
School Bd. Ref. 1908—YES	19.9	56.6	68.9	53.0	53.3
Public Safety Ref. 1908—YES	20.9	38.1	48.6	32.5	33.6

[a]*Thirteenth Census of the U. S., 1910,* vol. 3, *Population* (Washington, 1913), 153. An additional 238 foreign-born persons are classified as miscellaneous and thus not included in this table except for the purpose of calculating the total population and foreign-born population.

[b]*Passaic Daily News,* February 21, 1911.

[c]*Sixteenth Census of the U.S., 1940, Housing* (Washington, 1942). Suppl. to 1st series, *Passaic Block Statistics,* 5.

[d]*Passaic Daily News,* October 23, 1907.

[e]Election contest data has been culled from press reports on the day immediately following the contest.

government was his highest priority. What he did not say was that money saved through honest, professional, and efficient administration would be applied, as his critics surmised, to upgrade existing municipal services and facilities as well as to launch some new ones.[18]

Although Low cautiously mentioned a few specific programmatic ideas during the campaign, he burst forth with an expansive agenda soon after his installation on January 1, 1908. Dwelling on rising agitation for building a new high school—a by-product of Passaic's 97.2 percent population increase between 1900 and 1910—he advocated "speedy completion" of the project. He further spoke of the "congested" districts on the east side, especially the immigrant-populated First Ward. A "pressing need" for public parks existed there, he said, in advocating the expenditure of "not less" than $100,000 to create a city-wide network. In addition, he advocated the depression and roofing of the Erie Railroad tracks traversing the heart of Passaic's central business district, to be followed by renewal of the downtown and construction of a civic center "the equal of any in the state."[19] Despite opposition from Passaic's volunteer fire fighters, Low also stressed the necessity for their gradual replacement by a paid, professionalized department.[20] Other items emphasized by the mayor included improved street sanitation and the construction of public baths—both of which were aimed primarily at improving life in the First Ward.[21]

The final feature of Low's initial program was a proposal to alter the structure of local government to achieve the goals of the new administration. Two proposals aimed explicitly at reducing the quasi-administrative power of the council. His highest priority was creation of a police commission appointed by the mayor to eliminate partisanship "as far as possible" from the department's affairs; Low tied this to specific suggestions for remedying existing deficiencies in police administration. He also called for reinstitution of a liquor excise board, partly to relieve the council of its duties in this patronage-laden realm. The final alteration concerned the board of education. Low proposed replacement of the elective board with an appointive body designated by the mayor and not subject to council confirmation. This, the mayor asserted, would attract "a high class of executive ability" to oversee effectively the proliferating system of public education.[22]

Almost immediately following his election, and well before he assumed office, bitter and protracted controversies plagued Low. The *Passaic Daily Herald* exercised a critical, and sometimes irresponsible, role in fostering opposition among councilmen and the public. In a highly publicized battle of wills with the council majority that extended five months into his term, Low was ultimately thwarted in his attempt to designate his choices as city attorney and municipal surveyor. He was forced, instead, to accept holdover appointees from his predecessor.[23]

This defeat was compounded by a controversy over public ownership of the water supply. The issue offered Low a superb opportunity to expand his electoral base among Passaic's immigrant and second-generation citizens, who fervently advocated municipal control. (Low's mean support on the ethnic-dominated east side in the balloting for mayor had been only 49 percent.) Furthermore, his reputation as a foe of privatism on this and related issues was well established. But in spite of incessant editorial pressure by the *Daily Herald* to declare himself categorically in favor of terminating the private arrangement, the mayor momentarily delayed. At an emotion-pitched public meeting in March 1908, he courageously raised questions as to the fiscal and legal ramifications of an immediate condemnation of the facilities owned by the Acquackanonk Water Company. Councilman Joseph Spitz, a Fourth Ward Democrat whose election in 1904 marked the first time a "new" ethnic had sat on the governing body, then capitalized on the situation by assuming an uncompromising pro-condemnation stance. Although Low eventually joined Spitz, he had denied himself a chance to add popular momentum to his administration. Ironically, advocacy of a municipally owned water supply caused George P. Rust, the publisher of the *Passaic Daily News* and his patron in the campaign of 1907, to eventually withdraw editorial support of his administration. Yet, in the end Low's own early misgivings about rapid conversion to municipal control were proven correct, and his reluctance saved the city from excessive litigation expenses that surely would have resulted had his decision been dictated by political expedience. Indeed, when he left office in December 1909, a permanent solution still had not been achieved.[24]

Simultaneously, Low was further stymied in his attempt to consolidate executive power. Twice in 1908 the mayor sponsored referenda—on June 2 for the institution of independent police and fire commissions, and in the November general election for the adoption of an appointive board of education. The former was rejected by 66.4 percent of the voters, and the latter carried with 53.3 percent.[25]

Both of these proposed reforms were plausible efforts to achieve modernization in essential public service realms, given Passaic's rapid growth. The mayor argued that the dual public safety departments had expanded to the point that the respective standing committees of the council could no longer oversee their administration. "I will select men who are competent of managing big things," he declared.[26] The appointive school board, which was to supplant one elected from the wards on a partisan basis, was a favorite of reformers nationally who sought to centralize decision making in their quest to upgrade public education. Low perceived the schools as instrumental in transforming Passaic's "heterogeneous population" into "staunch and true American citizens." (Eight months later, in fact, when the Russell Sage Foundation's Ayres Report, *Laggards in Our Schools,* was issued, considerable controversy ensued because of the abysmal statistical ranking of Passaic's schools.) The central theme articulated on behalf of this proposition, however, as expressed by a board member from the Third Ward, emphasized the role of the executive branch: "We have always had good mayors in Passaic and by leaving the naming of trustees to the mayor I believe we shall get better boards."[27] Whatever the soundness of Mayor Low's design for reform of public safety, his strategy in the referendum campaign precluded any chance for its implementation. As interest in the issue intensified in April, the mayor took the offensive by authorizing a gambling raid on the saloon of Councilman John J. Welch, a First Ward Democrat and political fixture. This was followed by an exposé of beer drinking and a resultant brawl, again involving a councilman, in a firehouse on Easter morning. Clearly ploys to dramatize the necessity for reform, this tactic, so reminiscent of Mugwumpish attitudes toward morality, fueled existing criticism of the commission as elitist and intrusive on personal standards of behavior.[28] Indeed, the incident contributed to the coalescence of an opposition composed of the *Passaic Daily Herald*, the self-proclaimed guardian of democracy and liberty, the volunteer firemen, and Bird Spencer.[29]

Low's problem with the school board proposition came in the aftermath of its approval. The foremost opponent of the appointive concept had been Edward J. Levendusky, a First Ward Democrat. Elected in 1906 to the board, his ascent marked the first time that a citizen of Slavonic heritage had won a municipal office. Voters in Levendusky's ward had opposed the change by 80.1 percent. In appointing the new school board, which remained well balanced ethnically and geographically, Low had bypassed Levendusky, though he appointed several other current members of the elective body. In what must be construed as an implicit rebuke to Low, the First Ward electorate subsequently selected Levendusky as a councilman, making him the first Slav to hold that position.[30]

Granted the significance in Low's mind of expanding mayoral power through the structural alteration of government, this concern was overshadowed by the issue of fiscal responsibility. Because economy was the byword in Passaic, and because he needed the prospective savings to sustain his ambitious program, he duly focused on this issue. Along with other early twentieth-century mayors who assumed the role of "reformer," Low very often found himself in an especially complex dilemma —seeking to govern efficiently while simultaneously engaging in programs to enhance the ambience of urban life.[31] In Fred Low's case, this dilemma would prove his eventual undoing.

In June 1908, in the aftermath of his defeats on executive appointments and on the commission referendum, Low dealt prudently with the budget for the new fiscal year. He found reinforcement from the *Passaic Daily Herald*, which commented that only by practicing "strictest economy" would the mayor be fulfilling his campaign promises. Indeed, when the city council's version of the new budget called for an increase of 13.4 percent over 1907/1908, Low trimmed it 4.2 percent and threatened to veto any effort to restore the cuts. Subsequently, the municipal tax rate was set at $1.46 per $100 of assessed property value, a rise of just five cents. Passaic's mean per capita expenditure for aggregate municipal services other than utilities, $8.60 in fiscal 1908/1909, actually compared most favorably both nationally and statewide. Little wonder that the *Daily Herald*, which earlier had forecast a tax rate in the $1.55–$1.60 range, congratulated Mayor Low.[32]

TABLE 6-2. Fiscal Analysis

	Per Capita Expenditures 1908/9	Per Capita Expenditures 1909/10	% of Change in Tax Levy, 1908/9–1909/10	Total Expenditures 1909/10
All U.S. Cities[a] 30,000 (mean)	$16.07	$16.45	− 6.1	$2,583,255
All N.J. Cities 30,000+ (mean)	12.17	12.50	− 4.5	1,193,877
All U.S. Cities[b] 50,000–100,000 (mean)	10.80	11.07	+ 4.7	612,939
All N.J. Cities 50,000–100,000 (mean)	10.50	10.60	+12.7	5,862,905
Passaic 54,773[c]	8.60	8.44	+27.0	365,220
Newark 347,469	19.06	19.03	+ 5.7	5,862,905
Jersey City 267,779	11.28	11.77	+ 6.4	3,048,766
Paterson 125,600	10.77	10.52	− 4.1	1,102,742
Trenton 98,915	10.33	10.68	+10.8	743,484
Camden 94,538	10.90	10.81	+ 3.1	713,397
Elizabeth 73,409	8.61	8.86	+10.2	573,104
Hoboken 70,324	12.89	12.95	+17.7	698,139
Bayonne 55,545	11.69	11.67	+12.6	584,295
Atlantic City 46,150	20.02	21.97	+15.2	959,556
W. Hoboken 35,403	9.72	9.59	+13.2	189,400
E. Orange 34,371	−	17.38	−	496,042
Perth Amboy 32,121	−	9.33	−	183,351

[a]The total number of cities in this category increased from 138 in 1909 to 184 in 1910.

[b]The total number of cities in this category was fifty-eight.

[c]Population data based on 1910 report.

Source: See below fn. 32, 35, and 37.

Despite the short-lived political benefits, the mayor probably derived little or no satisfaction from this encounter. Unlike those urban progressives for whom efficiency was the quintessence of their civic involvement, Low was primarily interested in the resultant budgetary flexibility that allowed him to introduce improved or altogether new public services.[33] Over the next year he advanced several of the key items on his agenda, including the new high school and the city-wide network of parks, gradual replacement of the volunteer fire fighters with a paid department and chief, and programs to upgrade public health services. In an editorial series, the *Daily Herald* gloomily warned that Low's ambitious goals would affect the tax rate adversely, as they indeed did.

The municipal budget for fiscal 1909/1910 increased 11.3 percent, the new tax rate being set at $1.70 per $100, a twenty-four-cent advance. Low's critics gleefully pointed to nearby Paterson, with a population nearly two and a half times as large, where the new tax rate of $1.71 reflected a rise of only five cents.[34]

Actually, the budget for fiscal 1909/1910 proved a paradox. On the basis of per capita expenditures, Passaic's situation had remained favorable. Of the nation's eighty-eight cities in the 50,000–100,000 population category, the aggregate expenditure was $11.07, a twenty-seven-cent increase over 1908/1909. The figure for Passaic declined sixteen cents to $8.44, the lowest among the thirteen cities in New Jersey with at least 30,000 inhabitants. Less favorable, however, was the comparative data on the tax levy. Passaic's increased 27 percent, whereas the state's six cities in the 50,000–100,000 group had a mean increase of just 12.7 percent; only Hoboken's 17.7 percent jump approached that of Passaic. The *Daily Herald* played on Paterson's case, of course, where the tax levy actually decreased 4.1 percent. Lost, however, was the fact that among the six cities in New Jersey with similar population sizes, Passaic's tax levy was the lowest, 36.2 percent below that of Elizabeth, which ranked fifth, and 50.9 percent off Trenton's, which placed highest.[35]

Passaic's untoward situation resulted from a policy decision on tax reform by Mayor Low. In his first message to the council he had pledged to collect a state-mandated levy on personalty holdings, a provision of the tax code consciously ignored by his predecessors. Allowing that he did not favor the intent of this tax, which New Idea Republicans in the legislature had struggled gallantly, albeit unsuccessfully, to alter in 1905, the mayor nevertheless insisted that henceforth this levy must be paid into the municipal treasury. This tax, as might be expected, was greeted with skepticism, if not outright opposition. While owners of realty, whatever its size, tacitly had tolerated the long-standing "property tax," if for no other reason than force of habit, innovations—whether a tax on net income or sudden compliance with the personalty levy—constituted a threat to the stability of the political economy.[36]

The objective of the mayor was to increase the assessed valuation on the textile mills, which employed well over half of the industrial labor force, in order to support the physical and programmatic improvements on his agenda. Of the more than $3.8 million in new tax ratables added to the 1909/1910 assessments, 76.9 percent were estimated derived from mill property. Although individual property parcels had been assessed at 75 percent of true value heretofore, mill holdings were at only 25 percent until the mayor's action brought at least some industries up to 60 percent. Total valuation rose 11.8 percent, while in comparison the six cities in

New Jersey in the 50,000-100,000 population category had a mean increase of just 6 percent, with only Bayonne's 16.1 percent advance exceeding Passaic's. By contrast, nearby Paterson's total valuation went up a mere 2.9 percent.[37]

Low's fervent desire to achieve equalization was virtually destined to end with a negative political impact. Despite warnings, he failed to forsee that by unilaterally advancing the valuations disproportionately to those of other municipalities in the taxation unit, he had concocted an unhappy situation wherein the county and state tax bill levied on the city would be inequitable. Hence, even if fixed costs remained at virtually the same level as the preceding year, a greater burden would still be placed on the local taxpayers.[38]

Local reaction to Low's policy was mixed. Predictably, a representative of one of the mills could only view the tax reform program with exasperation. Alluding to the presence of "socialistic ideas" in the city, he mourned the fact that the industrial complex no longer was perceived as a constructive force, but instead as "an evil and nuisance." Similarly, a letter-to-the-editor signed "Rubber Foreman" observed: "I see because we have an extravagant administration the industries of the city are to be made to pay. . . . When I go to the boss for a raise I do not want him to tell me that taxes and overhead are increasing so much that I am more likely to get a cut." Assessor William A. Reid, the lone Democrat elected city-wide and a long-time clerk in a textile mill, sided with Mayor Low, sarcastically stating, "I am told someone is passing around a petition to the mill owners to sign their protest. If that is true, pass around a petition to every taxpayer. . . ." Councilman Robert D. Benson, a Second Ward Republican who was the foremost advocate of the public park project, also recognized the necessity for the tax increase, observing that "Passaic has the poorest labor of any city its size in the country." But Councilman Spitz, the Fourth Ward Democrat, accurately claimed that Low's plan would only bring about a tax rise for all property owners, not just industry.[39]

Granted that Low's program for tax reform was ill-conceived from the perspective of practical, traditional politics, the idealism that motivated him requires analysis. His public statements revealed an intense concern over achieving equalization on behalf of the individual taxpayer. His most complete expression was an address in late April 1909 to a meeting of Single Tax advocates in New York City. Like many of his fellow progressives, Low acknowledged the influence of Henry George's *Progress and Poverty,* and his invitation to share the platform with Oregon's William S. U'Ren resulted from his conscious decision to appoint an avowed "single taxer" to the board of assessors the preceding January.[40]

Low's speech began with an unequivocal plea on behalf of the Single Tax. All citizens, he observed, had an obligation to pay rent for the ground that they occupied within the community as a "contribution toward the benefits provided at the common expense." Then, in what was clearly the key statement, he proclaimed that, "Most of the inequality and imposition of oppression of the past has been based on private ownership of the soil." While not advocating the abolition of private property, Low noted that the evolution of "our highly civilized system" had been characterized by particular emphasis on "privilege." It was essential, he said, to develop an "intelligent public interest" to reformulate the political economy and recapture the "stolen government" in the name of the people. To accomplish this, he pointed to the rise of progressives such as Governor Charles Evans Hughes of New York, who he believed were indicative of "a growing determination to shake off the reactionary agents of the system upon the reigns of government." Actually, Low's advocacy of the Single Tax distinguished him from progressives like Hughes and placed him in the ideological company of such nationally acclaimed reform mayors as Jersey City's Mark Fagan, Detroit's Hazen S. Pingree, Toledo's Samuel "Golden Rule" Jones and Brand Whitlock, and Cleveland's Tom L. Johnson.[41]

The controversy over taxation coincided with the events leading up to the mayoralty election of November 1909. On August 13, former mayor Spencer, Low's rival in the primary of 1907, announced his candidacy for a fourth term on an "economy" platform. This declaration came amid charges of excessive commissions on the sale of private property to the city for the park development project, and it included a strong, if oblique, condemnation of "graft." After initially professing disinterest in a second term unless a suitable reform successor could not be found, Mayor Low filed one month later. In doing so he issued an elaborate statement of his achievements, fended off claims of "extravagance," and candidly observed that his own and Spencer's ideology reflected "the extremes of present day political thought, policies, and interests."[42]

Although neither Low nor Councilman Benson was in any way implicated in the so-called parks scandal, this question dominated the press for six weeks preceding the primary. The incumbent's prospects were hindered, moreover, when the supposedly neutral *Passaic Daily News* concluded that the city-wide network of parks, unlike the new high school, was financially imprudent. Meanwhile Spencer, the seasoned politician, capitalized on the harping about Low's excessive spending in the Democratic press by adopting the rhetoric of efficiency so popular among taxpayers. On election day Low failed to capture a single ward and garnered just 35.8 percent of the Republican ballots, a falling off of

28 percent from the contest against Spencer two years earlier. (The biggest drop, 32.8 percent, occurred in the First Ward, followed by 30.6 percent in the Second Ward, 27.5 in the Fourth Ward, and 25.4 percent in the Third Ward; the mean west side decrease, 28 percent, was 2.2 percent lower than the east side figure.) Spencer then won the general election with 61 percent of the votes against a totally ineffectual Democrat and a Socialist who drew only minimal support.[43]

Low's mishandling of the fiscal issue does not altogether explain Spencer's landslide victory. The incumbent's behavior had been largely symptomatic of his attitude toward the polity in which he functioned. His words as well as deeds were imbued with a perception of what Roy Lubove has labeled an "organic city," wherein continued deterioration would be stymied by the distinctively progressive concept of an urban panorama that was "socially integrated and physically beautiful." In a speech to the Monday Afternoon Club, an organization of socially concerned Protestant women, Low had offered an exhaustive analysis of Passaic as "The Ideal City"; asking citizens to "dream a little," he portrayed an architecturally unified city with a new civic center in its commercial district as an integrative symbol of human endeavor. Similarly, in a Fourth of July address, the mayor had expressed a compelling concern for the future: "There are two ways of using a heritage—one is to use its opportunity, and the other is to improve its advantage . . . so that those who come after us may enjoy it more abundantly." Notwithstanding the prophetic nature of such statements, they contributed significantly to the demise of politicians in the reform mold. "Progressive municipal reform failed, not so much because it lacked a philosophy," it has been argued, "but because it wove a reform program around the fragile possibility that men could transcend their 'superficial' differences and cooperate in the building of an organic city devoted to the deliberate 'culture of urban life.'"[44]

Frequently masterful in articulating his agenda, all too often Low was mistaken in the tactics he used to achieve his goals. Accustomed as an editor to expressing opinions in *Power* that were initially unpopular but whose validity he ultimately could prove, his experience as mayor probably was disconcerting in that every expression and action was subject to instantaneous public scrutiny and evaluation. When Low voiced misgivings, in May 1908, over the performance of the board of health in dealing with hospital facilities for tuberculars, to take one instance, he was lambasted as a "man who does not know which way he is going." On another occasion, late in July 1908, he visited Councilman Welch at his saloon—the site of the infamous gambling raid—to solicit support for a policy decision regarding police affairs. When the press publicized

Low's presence there, he angrily reacted with words described as "sulphuric." Finally, in the bitter primary race of 1909, Low sought to fend off Spencer's intemperate spending charges by releasing three highly sophisticated mathematical tables dealing with taxation. Here he shared a failing of many progressives whose faith in humanity was rooted in science, technology, and devotion to empirical evidence and data. Naïvely, he believed that if citizens reviewed carefully the information therein all such allegations would be disproved.[45]

Could it have been different? There has been a tendency to answer affirmatively, pointing to isolated instances of success in the ranks of urban reformers. "The work of reform," Theodore Roosevelt told the first National Conference for Good Government in 1894, "has got to be done by actual, hard, stubborn, long-continued service in the field of practical politics itself."[46] Hazen Pingree, four times elected mayor of Detroit (1889-1895) and twice the governor of Michigan (1896-1901), is the best example of this dictum. The broad-based support he fostered locally by combining attractive social and economic policies with patronage contributed significantly to his statewide successes. Victory beyond the municipal level, however, was an exception for reform mayors. Jersey City's Fagan and Cleveland's Johnson, to take two notable examples, were rejected by their local electorates despite heroic efforts to govern in the Pingree tradition.[47] Indeed, the most successful reform mayor in American history, Grover Cleveland, who served successive terms as chief executive of Buffalo (1881-1882), governor of New York (1882-1884), and president of the United States (1885-1889 and 1893-1897), clearly fits into the older, moralistic Mugwump cast. Aside from proving "ugly honest," Allan Nevins observed, his campaign lacked programmatic plans for improving Buffalo. Rather, he became known as the "veto mayor," a characteristic that extended to his gubernatorial and presidential administrations as well.[48]

Clearly Fred Low was not the equal of Hazen Pingree in mastering "practical politics," to borrow T. R.'s words. To be sure, he recognized in theory the complexity of modern urban society, and he was committed to improving it by means of participation in the political process. "System based on order," he wrote in *Power*, "is the underlying principle of true progress [in] every line of human endeavor."[49] He was unable, however, to translate this rather mechanical notion into a workable formula for politically induced social change beyond his initial two-year term as mayor.[50] No matter how earnestly he tried—and there were indeed visible results of his stewardship, e.g., the new high school, the city-wide park system, a professionalized fire department, upgraded public health and sanitation services, and tax reform—Low's understanding of the political process, despite a decade of experience in lesser offices, proved inadequate for the challenges he encountered. But to argue that he failed because he did not achieve reaffirmation from the electorate suggests a very narrow conception of success for urban reform politicians. Rather, the case of Mayor Low belies the conventional axiom that political *survival* dictates the definition of *success*.

MARTIN J. SCHIESL

7. POLITICIANS IN DISGUISE:
THE CHANGING ROLE OF PUBLIC ADMINISTRATORS IN LOS ANGELES, 1900-1920

In recent years historians, such as Samuel P. Hays, Melvin G. Holli, and James Weinstein, have made a thorough and critical analysis of urban progressivism. The movement was led by agents of special privilege who sought to destroy democracy as expressed through machine politics and transform city government into an efficient businesslike operation. It was administration by municipal experts serving primarily business and professional interests.[1] But the reformist dedication to bureaucratic efficiency did not mean just the reconstruction of governmental machinery to fit the needs of the corporate world. Ernest S. Griffith provides a more balanced perspective: "Morality, efficiency, and humanity in government were the objectives; structural reform improved the tools for their accomplishment."[2]

In this context, an examination of Los Angeles progressivism reveals the dangers of romanticizing the old party boss and treating too lightly the improvements in city management. The political machine, organized initially to assure regional support for the Southern Pacific Railroad, dominated the local Democratic and Republican parties. Winning elections meant jobs for a host of party hacks. Public utility interests and agents of the Southern Pacific worked hand in glove with the bosses, buying up profitable franchises, city contracts, and monopolies on water, electricity, gas, and transportation.[3] The recurrent bribery and corruption, the ill-functioning municipal bureaucracy, and the debasement of politics led finally to the campaign of reformers from the middle and upper classes to reorganize urban administration along the lines of authority and responsibility. They worked to replace the periodic and discretionary assistance of the machine with a modern system of decision making and security for all Los Angeles residents.

The municipalization of public utilities provided an important enlargement of administrative authority. In 1900 several commercial and civic organizations protested against the high charges and irregular service of utilities, especially the water business. They formed a Citizen Committee to persuade city authorities to municipalize the water facilities. In response, the council authorized a $2 million bond issue in 1901 for the reacquisition of the waterworks, which had been leased to a private company. The voters, wanting better service at lower costs, approved the issue by a wide margin, and the city assumed ownership in 1902. The council established a five-man Board of Water Commissioners, appointed by the mayor, to manage the plant.[4] To the surprise of the board, much of the flow of the Los Angeles River was being wasted and per capita use was excessive. The commission improved distribution facilities and installed meters to regulate consumer demand. It also acquired the city's other water companies.[5]

In conjunction with this development, the Los Angeles Municipal League pressed for the application of the civil service system to appointive offices. Composed of native-American business and professional people who demanded that public affairs be conducted in accordance with principles of community interest apart from party loyalties and needs, the League objected to the bosses' practice of filling posts in municipal administration with ill-educated and partially qualified persons. Without the attraction of spoils, the League reasoned, partisan incompetents would not seek public office and city officials would have no reason to create jobs to reward the party faithful. Administrative authorities could then run their departments in a more efficient and economical manner. After investigating Chicago's merit system, which had been functioning for six years, the League drafted a civil service amendment and persuaded the council to place it on a general election ballot in 1902. The voters endorsed the proposition that created the Los Angeles Board of Civil Service Commissioners. The five-man commission was authorized to classify offices under merit regulations, select candidates for appointive posts by competitive examination, and remove civil service employees only for incompetence.[6]

Mayor Meredith P. Snyder, a reform-minded Democrat, disregarded political affiliations and based his selections for the civil service board on ability and merit. The commission included such high-minded persons as Henry W. O'Melveny, a prominent lawyer who had served on charter revision boards, and Dr. John R. Haynes, a wealthy physician and close observer of urban public employment. Though only one-third of the city positions were under the new regulations, these appointments meant new standards of performance in Los Angeles' government. "It was hardly to be expected that the Civil Service System, involving radical changes in the methods of appointment and discharge of a large number of city employees, could be established without some friction," reported the commission in 1903, "but we are glad to state that there has been very little opposition to the new system, and nearly every department of the City Government has given its cordial acquiescence and cooperation from the outset."[7] Especially responsive was the new Board of Water Commissioners. It rightly saw merit rules as the stimulus to better service. Mayor Snyder informed the council in 1904 that "in no city department has the operation of civil service rules been more advantageous than in the water department ... where new employees have obtained ... high efficiency because of the careful examination conducted by the civil service commission."[8]

This effort to reform public employment was not an unmixed blessing. Persons who might have been excluded from municipal jobs because of economic or social disqualifications had continually entered the lower levels of city government under the cover of machine patronage. In this way spoils politics had facilitated the sharing of political power among disparate groups. On the other hand, the civil service commission, along with its progressive supporters, did not lose sight of the oppressive nature of spoils. They saw in this system the relentless pressure on city employees to supplement their official activity with outside political work. "Their right to vote at primaries and elections is free from attack," declared the president of the board in 1904. "Inasmuch, however, as Civil Service employees are relieved from the effects of partisanship, both as to appointment and tenure of office, it is a proper regulation of the system that they should be inhibited from engaging in active, partisan political work." Accordingly, the commission prohibited classified employees from assisting in election campaigns. It also stipulated that violators of the rule would be dismissed from office.[9] Both regulations represented a new view of municipal service, in which performance was less a matter of the traditional obsession with party fealty and more a consideration of the community obligations of administrative personnel. The civil service commission sought to replace the restrictive influence of machine partisanship on department operations with a system designed to expand the capacity for more integrity and responsiveness in the city government.

But partisanship did not disappear from municipal adminstration. In 1904 and 1905, departmental chiefs filed charges with the civil service

board against several employees for "pernicious activity in politics."
The commission closely investigated the accusations and removed some of
the employees from office.[10] More important, it appeared that one administrative board might come under the direction of the machine. In 1905
the voters approved a charter amendment that created the Los Angeles
Board of Public Works. Appointed by the mayor, the three-man commission received all work handled by the council and mayor in connection with contracts on public improvements. It was in charge of the
construction and maintenance of streets, sewers, municipal buildings,
disposal of garbage and sewage refuse, and all utilities owned or operated
by the city.[11] Such responsibilities made the department a rich pasture
for greedy politicians. Furthermore, the electorate had approved a $1.5
million bond issue to purchase water-bearing lands in the Owens Valley
for the construction of a 225-mile aqueduct that would cost nearly $23
million. Fearing that considerable amounts of public revenue might flow
to the parties, the Municipal League and the Chamber of Commerce
vigorously resisted the bosses' effort to gain control of the public works
board and formed a committee in 1905 to select honest and able men for
the commission. The committee persuaded Mayor Owen McAleer to
accept its nominees, and the council grudgingly confirmed the appointments.[12]

Los Angeles' government, however, was still embroiled in party politics.
Although the progressives gained some seats in the council in the elections of 1906, the bosses retained control of the legislature and secured
the election of Democrat Arthur C. Harper to the mayoralty.[13] Machine
councilmen, less concerned with administrative efficiency than with
political loyalty, rewarded the party faithful with jobs without regard to
need. In the health department, for example, political hacks became
inspectors and performed few useful functions. Mayor Harper was also
receptive to the appeals of the bosses: he appointed regular Democrats
to the police, public works, and water boards. Reformers vigorously protested this action, warning that the mayor might use his office to
strengthen the old machine or possibly create a new one.[14] Even the
civil service board was not immune from the virus of spoilsmanship. Two
members of the commission, Dr. David H. Edelman and Milton K. Young,
were active in the Democratic organization. They pressured the board
to discharge, without reason, Dr. T. Perceval Gerson as medical examiner
of the commission and to replace him with two appointees who had close
association with the Democratic party. George B. Anderson, editor of the
progressive *Pacific Outlook,* charged that the commission had "set a
vicious example to other municipal bodies."[15]

Such practices aroused the progressives. They shared the conviction of upper-middle-class reformers in other cities that efforts to reorganize municipal authority had to be complemented by practical schemes to gain and keep power.[16] In 1908 Meyer Lissner and Marshall Stimson, two prominent attorneys, and Edward A. Dickson, associate editor of the Los Angeles *Express*, formed a Good Government League devoted to structural reform. So effective was this civic organization that by 1909 it constituted a powerful force in city politics. The League, drawing support from the city's growing native middle classes, secured the passage of charter amendments abolishing the ward system and establishing nonpartisan elections.[17] These reforms undermined the traditional parochialism of local politics and intensified the metropolitan thrust of the progressive movement. In the process, the city's political structure was moving away from what Samuel Hays sees in the American city as a local focus with personal relationships and toward a new integrative system based on a cosmopolitan perspective and reflecting impersonal, bureaucratic procedures. Reform members of the upper class sought formal power to maintain a political environment conducive to the rationalized management of urban affairs.[18]

Lax law enforcement provided the opportunity for progressives in Los Angeles to gain control of the government. In 1908 Thomas L. Woolwine, assistant prosecuting attorney, launched a campaign against the liquor and vice traffic and uncovered evidence of graft that appeared to involve the mayor, members of the police department, and prominent businessmen. Enraged by Woolwine's refusal to stop his investigation, Mayor Harper removed him from office. The Los Angeles *Herald* took up the gauntlet and revealed that Harper and some business associates from the utilities industry had established many joint-stock companies, and that they, along with some members of the police department, continually extorted money from saloons, gambling establishments, and prostitution houses by forcing them to purchase the stock as "certificates for protection."[19] In response, a group of progressives representing the Chamber of Commerce, the City Club, and the Municipal League circulated a recall petition that condemned the mayor for failing to "enforce impartially the laws and ordinances of the city." They gathered enough signatures for an election in March 1909 and nominated George Alexander, former county supervisor who had opposed the machine, as the Good Government candidate.[20] Meantime, the Socialist party nominated Fred C. Wheeler, a prominent labor leader. Wheeler conducted a vigorous campaign, in which he stressed Socialist dedication to improved conditions for the working classes and promised more public welfare services. Shortly before the election Harper, declaring that the bosses had deserted him, resigned from office. Alexander won the election by a narrow margin of votes.[21]

The progressives, accustomed to a mayor who had appointed people on the basis of political loyalty rather than general competence, anxiously awaited Alexander's selections for the administrative boards. "I believe it is due me that the commissioners should tender their resignations," Alexander announced, "and I will reappoint such of them as I see fit."[22] However, the civil service, public works, and water commissioners saw this request as a partisan maneuver and refused to resign their posts. The civil service board declared that Alexander and his progressive supporters were seeking to gain control of the commission so that they could then place their followers throughout the government. Alexander, however, reminded the commission that it had violated civil service principles under Mayor Harper and declared he wanted to provide the citizenry with more responsible service. At the same time, members of the fire, parks, police, and health boards, upon which the mayor served ex officio as chairman, recognized the impropriety of staying in office under a man who had not appointed them and resigned within a short time after Alexander took office. The mayor persuaded young business and professional men who had been active in the recall movement to serve on the boards with him.[23]

These actions encountered severe criticism from the Los Angeles *Times.* Supporting the conservative wing of the Republican party, the *Times* charged that the real motive of administrative reorganization was to establish a coalition for the regular elections.[24] As expected, the progressives denied the allegation and reiterated their commitment to nonpartisanship. But the actions of the mayor showed otherwise. Seeing political machinery as essential to anyone who hoped to keep office, Alexander was using patronage power to build an organization that could compete on equal terms with the machine. Supported by the Good Government organization, he easily defeated the regular Republican candidate in the December election, and all the other offices went to the progressives.[25]

The main thrust of Alexander's mayoralty was to replace the shoddy machine-created bureaucracy with more effective means of serving the wants and needs of the city's rapidly growing population. Los Angeles, with its congenial climate, varied landscape, and spacious layout, drew large numbers of migrants from the Midwest. The population of the city grew from 102,000 in 1900 to 319,000 by 1910.[26] Determined to provide all residents with better services and efficient administration, Mayor Alexander dismissed several commissioners for alleged incompetence and replaced them with persons who had professional experience in their areas of service. Eager to establish their authority, these officials specified employee duties and responsibilities and assured their staff that appointments and promotions depended solely on personal merit. In this system, civil servants were not required to supplement their work with political services or protect their jobs by making contributions to the machine. They thus identified more with a department and accepted its values and obligations. "The impatient layman who paid the taxes was apt to put down the expansive nature of a department or bureau to its desire for greater power, higher salaries, and more spoils," writes Ernest Griffith. "He overlooked the fact that the more professional and more dedicated a civil servant was, the more he would believe in his job and would want to expand its scope and effectiveness."[27] This perspective led administrative authorities to secure more appropriations and expand departmental functions. By the end of 1912, the government had built new fire and police stations, reequipped the fire department, and carried out street-paving and sewer-constructing projects. It also expanded the park and playground system, corrected through a new housing commission unhealthy conditions in house courts and tenement districts, and succeeded in keeping the city on a sound financial basis.[28]

Bolder improvements occurred in law enforcement. Under Edward Kern, who served as police chief from 1905 to 1909, policemen had not seriously pursued criminals who had close ties with party bosses. Factional disputes within the department reflected partisan feuds outside the government, and promotion usually depended on the favor of those commissioners with more political influence.[29] In cooperation with the reform-minded police board, Chief Charles E. Sebastian introduced greater discipline and supervision, discouraged intradepartmental factionalism, and assured personnel that promotions depended mainly on efficient service. The department also established a municipal farm to care for alcoholics and secured new ordinances to better regulate public conduct. By 1913 detectives and patrolmen were vigorously enforcing laws against gambling, vice, and liquor.[30]

Complementing this reform of police work was the campaign to curtail the influence of the utility corporations on the government. The city council exercised authority over charges and services. Few progressives, however, trusted the legislature to regulate private utilities. They believed that some legislators would submit to the pressure of utility interests and that others lacked the administrative machinery to supervise them. Therefore the reformers, led by the Municipal League, drafted an initiative petition proposing the formation of a Board of Public Utilities to be appointed by the mayor. Passed by the electorate in December 1909, the ordinance created a three-man commission empowered to examine earnings and propose rates, investigate complaints, and provide recommendations on all applications for franchises.[31]

The utilities commission, however, worked under severe handicaps. It could be pressured by the companies and overruled by the council. In 1911 engineers on the board's staff closely investigated the properties of electric companies and suggested an upward adjustment of their rates. The utilities commission accepted the proposals and submitted them to the council for approval. The legislators, backed by Mayor Alexander, rejected the recommendations. After further conflict with the council and the mayor over utility rates, members of the public utilities board resigned in June 1911.[32] "The Board is nothing but a Court standing between the people and the big corporations and endeavoring to do, if possible, exact justice to each and therein lies the trouble," declared a new appointee to the commission.[33]

Mayor Alexander disagreed. He protested against the tendency of some appointive officials to submit to the pressure of utility firms for sympathetic consideration.[34] To alleviate this deplorable situation, Alexander joined forces with the council to municipalize all public utilities in Los Angeles. The Owens Valley aqueduct presented the best opportunity to extend municipal ownership. In 1909 the electorate approved a charter amendment that entrusted responsibility for a public power project to the Bureau of Aqueduct Power in the public works department. The board of public works then persuaded the council to authorize a $3.5 million bond issue for building generators along the aqueduct route, and the legislature submitted the proposition to the electorate. As expected, local power companies vigorously opposed the bond issue. The voters, however, did not want this crucial source of energy to be wasted and endorsed the proposition by a majority of more than seven to one in 1910. One year later, Alexander and the progressives sponsored the transformation of the water commission to the Board of Public Service, to operate municipal water and electricity systems. The board, aided by engineers from the public works department, proceeded to build the generating plants. Meanwhile, the utilities offered to buy and market the city's power. By a majority of ten to one, however, the electorate rejected this proposal to lease aqueduct power for distribution.[35]

The public service board promptly advised the council to authorize a $6.5 million bond issue to acquire or erect a distribution system. This issue encountered opposition from business-minded administrators in the public works and utilities departments. Convinced that employees of the utility corporations could better manage the distribution of electricity, these officials endorsed the campaign of the companies to market the public power and resisted the mayor's effort to establish a city-owned electrical distributing system.[36] The public service board assumed a different position: "Any scheme for selling the power to the companies for a term of years . . . would afford the greatest possible inducements on the part of the companies to interfere with the city's politics as is evident at this time. . . ."[37] It helped the progressives to organize a Power Bond Campaign Committee in 1913 to promote the bond issue for the distribution network. Unfortunately for the public service commissioners, the electric companies marshalled considerable opposition to the power bonds. The electorate, faced with other issues totalling nearly $11 million, refused to vote the bonds the necessary two-thirds majority.[38]

This struggle over municipal ownership contradicted the progressives' basic assumptions about the political process. It had stimulated rather than eliminated conflict in city administration and brought out divergent views of civic welfare among appointive officials. Furthermore, municipalization had intensified rather than depressed partisan politics in Los Angeles. Nevertheless, the contest reflected the inner dynamics of progressive political reform: municipal ownership was an issue that cut across parochial interests. The protagonists were politically active professionals and businessmen who sought to convert the metropolitan community to their definition of enlightened public service. Their opportunity came in the 1913 election.

Frightened by the renewed threat of the Socialists, Meyer Lissner and Marshall Stimson accepted an invitation of conservative reformers to join forces with businessmen and regular Republicans in a Municipal Conference.[39] Lissner and Stimson recommended that William Mulholland, who had built the Owens River Aqueduct, be nominated for mayor. The conference, however, ignored the engineer and nominated John W. Shenk, former city attorney, on a nonpartisan ticket of business-minded legislators. Enraged over not being consulted before the formation of the conference, Edwin T. Earl, publisher of the Los Angeles *Express,* organized other reformers into a People's Campaign Committee, which endorsed Shenk but nominated a separate ticket for the council. In backing the committee's slate, the *Express* charged that there was no commitment in the platform of the Municipal Conference to the eventual public ownership of all utilities.[40] Lissner ignored this accusation and told conference members to campaign for the nonpartisan ticket because the candidate stood for the "development of . . . public utilities . . . on a sound business basis" and would "represent all sections of the city faithfully and well." In the primary, Shenk won a plurality, while Harry H. Rose, an independent, defeated the Socialist candidate, Job Harriman, for second position. Many businessmen, with the Socialist threat removed, abandoned the conference. In the runoff, Rose secured their votes and carried enough of Harriman's supporters to soundly defeat Shenk, 46,045 votes to 38,109. Moreover, only five of the eleven councilmen-elect were affiliated with the Municipal Conference.[41]

Contrary to the view of one historian of Los Angeles, however, political progressivism did not lose its "momentum." True, the outside progressives had lost control of local government and remained divided over the main goals of political reform.[42] But now the prime impetus for the renovation of administration and public programs came from reform-minded employees on various levels of the government. Mayor Rose fully supported the efforts of administrative officers to modernize further departmental operations and provide improved services.[43] More importantly, charter amendments and civil service reform had dismantled the machine-created bureaucracy and destroyed the traditional methods of political organization. In the process, the center of administrative control had shifted dramatically; it now rested not outside the municipal departments, but with appointive officials who derived their authority from city-wide constituencies. This transference of power enabled civil servants to be what one authority on public administration sees as semi-administrators and semipoliticians with considerable influence over both policy formation and execution. In this system, bureaucratic power becomes the dominant expression of an "officially based partisanship" as opposed to the "spoils-based partisanship" of a party-run polity.[44] Municipal administrators were a new political force in Los Angeles.

Some city officials and civic associations suffered misgivings about this realignment of municipal decision making. They were disturbed about the tendency of a department chief to move in his own direction and turn his bailiwick into a fraternity of tolerance. The civil service board often encountered criticism from other city commissions and heads of departments for refusing "to make exceptions and grant privileges which are not in accordance with the spirit of the merit system." It asked for the power to remove inefficient employees on the grounds that appointive authorities were "loath to make dismissals until forced to do so."[45] Less critical but equally dissatisfied with governmental operations, the efficiency committee of the Municipal League declared that the "defects of our city government arise from conditions over which the departments have had little control." Accordingly, the League sponsored an ordinance that created an Efficiency Commission in 1913. After a close investigation of city government, the commission, which included the city auditor, chairman of the council's efficiency committee, and vice-president of the civil service board, pointed out that the separation of powers among the mayor, council, and department chiefs obscured official responsibility and contributed to municipal mismanagement. It called for charter revision that would emphasize administrative centralization and professional expertise.[46]

The city manager form of government, which concentrated executive functions in an appointive officer, well filled this prescription as well as the progressive faith in nonpartisan experts. In 1914 the efficiency commission drafted a set of charter amendments, which included the application of civil service regulations to all administrative officers and a city manager, who would appoint a director to head each department. "Perhaps the most insidious criticism will be that the political 'machine' will be built up under the proposed plan, which will make it possible for a few men to exercise overwhelming power," wrote Dr. Jesse D. Burks, director of the efficiency department. "A machine is indeed provided for—a simple machine with direct drive and few parts, properly constructed, manned, and efficiently managed...."[47] The proposals, however, encountered opposition from a few officials who contended that the replacement of boards with individual commissioners answerable to a nonelective official would undermine representative democracy in Los Angeles.[48] The council, in response, decided not to submit the proposals to the electorate and instead authorized an elected Board of Freeholders in 1915 to draft a new charter.

Dominated by professionals who assumed that the voters shared their desire for more efficiency in municipal administration, the board dismissed the radical manager plan and incorporated more conservative provisions into the document. The charter retained the mayor and council and extended their terms to four years. It divided the government into five "humanitarian" departments headed by amateur commissioners and seven "business" departments headed by professional administrators. The board also included alternatives for more political provisions, such as councilmanic districts, proportional representation, and department managers. In campaigning for the document, the Citizens' New Charter Committee proclaimed that it would secure a "great advance" in efficient administration and not "raise political questions and disputes."[49]

Unfortunately for the freeholders, the Citizens' New Charter Committee could not reassure defenders of the existing governmental structure, who criticized the charter on both political and administrative grounds. Some charged that the changes would encourage bureaucratic partisanship, while others claimed that the substitution of managers for commissioners would undermine the reformed bureaucracy. The voters, less dissatisfied with public management than were the freeholders and the citizens' committee, rejected the document.[50]

The defeat of the 1916 charter left Mayor Frederic T. Woodman in a precarious position. Appointed to the mayoralty after the resignation of Charles E. Sebastian, Woodman, a reform lawyer and former member of the harbor commission, promoted various administrative improvements, especially in the police and utility departments. He advanced the progressive notion of positive government and won the mayoralty election in 1917.[51] His appointees to the municipal commissions, however, experienced some difficulty in maintaining close supervision of government activities. The commissioners were not able to reconcile departmental obligations with mayoral directives and identified more with the growing city bureaucracy. Further, the civil service board had amended its certification rules so as to increase the number of names eligible for various appointive posts in Los Angeles' government. This made it possible for a person with some "influence" among department authorities to be selected over a more qualified candidate.[52] Mayor Woodman saw these conditions as a deterrent to executive leadership and endorsed the campaign of the Efficiency Commission for more centralized administration.

Armed with broad investigatory powers, the commission's staff of accountants and trained administrators had closely examined departmental policies and procedures and recommended measures to improve the efficiency of the government's operations. It helped the heads of departments consolidate several bureaus and provided the council with more accurate data in formulating the city budget. At the same time, the agency could not avoid alienating leading officials. Some resented the commission's powers, while others were reluctant to adopt various proposals. They sought to abolish the Efficiency Commission and its activities. However, the Municipal League and the Chamber of Commerce prevailed upon the council to save the commission. Woodman then recommended a new plan of organization, whereby the mayor would be president and would appoint two experienced administrators with council confirmation. The legislators accepted the proposal and passed an ordinance in October 1916 that reorganized the commission.[53]

The Efficiency Commission quickly established better working relations with city officials. "We assume that heads of the various departments must accept responsibility for the success or failure of any change in the organization or management of their several departments," the agency asserted. "The function of the Efficiency Commission, as we conceive it, is to cooperate with administrative officers in locating defects in organization and management; to discover how these defects may best be corrected; to submit to the heads of the departments, and to the Council, plans for improving the public service; and to cooperate with the proper officers in putting into effect any plans that may be agreed upon."[54] City authorities, in turn, welcomed the recommendations of the commission's staff because they advocated increasing the power of department heads, furnishing them with more information, and tightening the lines of control within their agencies. The efficiency department assisted the civil service board in standardizing jobs and salaries so that administrative officers could supervise their personnel more closely. It helped the city auditor devise budget classifications to determine estimates of expenditure and extend uniform accounts to all departments. In addition, the efficiency department drafted new license ordinances, established a system of records for the health department's nursing division, devised employee efficiency records, and modernized the municipal industrial bureau.[55]

Such work brought about to some extent the reconciliation of popular government with the renovation of city management. To be sure, progressive structural reform, as Melvin G. Holli points out, meant the enshrinement of middle- and upper-class notions of efficiency and morality in municipal government.[56] However, the old machine system in Los Angeles, with its lack of formal administrative leadership, made it difficult for concerned citizens in residential areas of the growing metropolis to know who was mainly responsible for carrying out public policy. Los Angeles' population, consisting of increasing numbers of foreign-born migrants, doubled in the 1910s.[57] The reformed bureaucracy permitted closer coordination of department programs and greater public visibility for top appointive officials. The government could then perform an expanding range of services for all residents.

Police reform met this challenge. Especially important were changes in department procedure and a more humanitarian treatment of the underprivileged and unfortunate. Chief John L. Butler organized a school to train patrolmen in law enforcement, instituted a central filing and records system, established a bureau of statistics, and made available to other departments and local newspapers records on crime and police procedures. In cooperation with the police commission, which included the mayor, he curtailed indiscriminate arrests for minor infractions, expanded municipal farms to assist the rehabilitation of criminals, and established a traffic bureau, an arson squad, and social agencies such as a lost persons bureau. The department could now provide community services as well as improve its crime-fighting capabilities.[58]

Other administrators sought to provide more direct aid to both native workers and impoverished ethnic minorities. In 1916 the city council replaced the municipal charities bureau with a Social Service Commission, to organize private charity on a more systematic and constructive basis. The council passed an ordinance requiring charitable agencies to register with the Social Service Commission and authorized the commission to examine records and personnel, suggest certain procedural changes, and approve applications for endorsement. The commission investigated various agencies and endorsed those that met the "actual needs of the community" and displayed a "reasonable standard of efficiency." In the process, charitable and philanthropic institutions, such as orphan asylums, old-age homes, relief agencies, and hospitals, filed their records with the municipal agency to avoid conflicts of policy and adopted proposals for improving operations.[59]

More important was the work of public-spirited professionals who staffed the new bureaucracy under Mayor Woodman and administered the vital health and welfare functions of the city from 1917 to 1919. Unlike the neighborhood-based machine bureaucracy, these civil servants dealt with problems that cut across provincial community lines. They helped senior officials improve the physical environment so that the government could meet the social needs of the metropolis. There was an expansion of services that benefited all classes, such as street improvements, aggressive public health services, and effective regulation of utilities. Furthermore, the needs of lower-income groups were not ignored. In the various city departments, public health physicians and nurses, legal officers, social workers, playground directors, and other experts provided humanitarian services to the working-class sectors of the city, such as low-cost clinics, free legal aid, tenement inspection, and recreation areas.[60] Especially active was the health department's housing commission. Composed of eight assistant health commissioners and several inspectors with police powers, the bureau centralized its inspection procedures and vigorously enforced municipal building codes that set minimum structural and sanitary standards. It also instructed landlords on the prevention of bad tenement conditions and helped state legislators draft better housing laws.[61]

This emphasis on social engineering revealed a consensus among appointive officers about the appropriate role of the municipal bureaucracy. They rightly believed that the government could effectively meet the continued demand of all classes for better service with more administrative regulation of urban development. The acquisition of an electrical distribution system was the most dramatic achievement. In 1919 the public service board, having secured earlier approval of the $6.5 million proposition and the right to buy existing private facilities, persuaded the council to authorize a $13.5 million bond issue for the purchase of Southern California Edison's distributing system. To get popular support for the proposition, the board appealed to civic organizations and metropolitan newspapers. In response, the Chamber of Commerce, Municipal League, and Central Labor Council, backed by the Los Angeles

Examiner, joined forces with the public service commissioners to promote
the issue. Los Angeles Gas and Electric, supported by some commercial
groups and the Los Angeles *Times,* vehemently opposed the bonds. The
voters, however, endorsed the issue. Litigation initiated by Los Angeles
Gas and Electric delayed the transfer of the system until May 1922.
The public service board paid the Edison Company and acquired power
distribution facilities.[62]

Public administration in Los Angeles, however, had diverged sharply
from the progressives' aspirations in 1900. After all, civil servants were
actively enlisting the support of efficiency-minded legislators and outside political allies and had campaigned in bond issue elections. More
importantly, politics had not been exorcised from civic management;
only its form had changed. The reformed bureaucracy emerged in 1920
as the new center of municipal authority and was more entrenched than
the power blocs of the old local machine. Accordingly, career administrators would be less preoccupied with community responsibilities and
more concerned with advancing their own prestige and status in government. The progressive mayors and appointive officials, on the other
hand, had replaced the exploitative arrangements of machine patronage
with a more equitable and innovative service system. In doing so, they
had modernized public employment, established new forms of official
leadership, and extended considerably the social welfare duties of the
metropolitan government. Such a situation was not, of course, limited
to Los Angeles, but existed as well in other reformed American cities.
The loyalties and values derived from employment in municipal administration determined, to a large extent, the quality and scope of governmental operations and services.

JOHN F. BAUMAN

8. DISINFECTING THE INDUSTRIAL CITY:
THE PHILADELPHIA HOUSING COMMISSION AND SCIENTIFIC EFFICIENCY, 1909-1916

Housing reform in Philadelphia during the years 1909-1916 illustrates the scientific and technical orientation of the Progressive Era. In the nineteenth century, housing reformers, while linking their concern for poor housing with epidemiology and the control of public health, usually stressed the pathos and moral degradation of the slum environment. By 1909, however, housing reformers had discarded their plaintive descriptions of unkempt tenement children for trenchant discussions of underdrainage, tuberculosis, and the abatement of sanitary nuisances.

Identified, therefore, with the physician-based public health movement of the nineteenth century and receptive to scientific argument, housing reform in the early twentieth century offers a case study of the degree to which science and efficiency influenced progressive urban reform. This essay focuses on the Philadelphia Housing Commission (PHC), which after 1909 became the Quaker City's principal agency for housing reform. It examines the origin of the PHC as an outgrowth of the concern that the city's bureaucratic-minded business, social work, and civic leaders evinced in sanitary control and scientific management. By looking at the activities of the PHC between 1909 and 1916, the year the commission was renamed the Philadelphia Housing Association and by studying the philosophy of its executive secretary, Bernard Newman, this study demonstrates how the PHC vividly mirrored the nexus between scientific efficiency and urban progressivism. It suggests also that scientism afforded a weak scaffolding for reform.

A number of historians have identified the reform impulse of the early twentieth century with the ripening of interest in technical efficiency generated by forces of secularization and modernization. Samuel P. Hays has noted the link between "conservation and the gospel of efficiency," while Robert H. Wiebe has emphasized a broad stream of "bureaucratic-mindedness." Roy Lubove, James H. Timberlake, and John D. Buenker have isolated the vein of scientific efficiency in social work, prohibition, and political reform.[1]

In addition to connecting housing reform to scientific efficiency, this study underscores the relationship between the sanitary and the efficiency strains of housing reform. In *The Progressives and the Slums,* Lubove explains how Lawrence Veiller introduced into New York City an "ideal of scientific housing based on expert knowledge and strong centralized organization."[2] He especially emphasizes Veiller's obsession with expertise. Indeed, housing reformers in Philadelphia owed much of their inspiration to Veiller. However, as this investigation also suggests, the PHC coupled an affinity for scientific efficiency with traditional campaigns against privy vaults, poor ventilation, and overcrowding, swirling the city's housing movement into the vortex of the sanitary sciences. After 1911, when the "sanitarian" Bernard Newman became the PHC's executive secretary, housing reform in Philadelphia fused with sanitary reform, and the commission hoisted the standard of hygienic efficiency.[3]

Housing reformers in nineteenth-century Philadelphia had responded to the philanthropic impulse. In the 1890s the Octavia Hill Society (OHS) and the Whittier Center Housing Corporation endeavored to uplift the city's working-class poor by offering decent housing at reasonable rates. By the turn of the century the society was managing more than 400 properties in the most congested sections and still paying its philanthropic subscribers 5 percent interest on their charitable investment.

Both the OHS and the Whittier Center Housing Corporation linked bad housing to human degradation. According to Helen Parrish of the OHS, human virtue withered in the city's loathsome courts, where the stench of refuse mingled with the noxious exhalations of overflowing privy vaults. However, the members of the OHS did more than resettle the deserving poor in freshly scrubbed and painted houses. Friendly rent collectors regularly visited the tenants and preached cleanliness, thrift, and sobriety. The society hoped by example to persuade landlords to either refurbish their wretched tenements or demolish them and build attractive low-rent housing. Once decently housed, the dangerous classes would be regenerated and the chasm between the rich and poor bridged.[4]

But by 1911, the Dickenesque imagery of huddled masses and tenement rogues was passé. While housers* occasionally warned of the rift between the classes, they discarded the passionate rhetoric of Dickens, Charles Booth, and Thomas Carlyle for the glossary of the social and bacteriological sciences. America in the late nineteenth and early twentieth centuries experienced the paroxysms of dynamic change. Sociologist Gino Germani has described the period as the culmination of an initial stage of modernization and the dawn of a second, or "definitive," stage. In the latter, industrial values were diffused throughout the culture. The 1890s marked the close of the "root, hog, or die" industrialism, and the appearance of the highly structured modern corporation. As the scale of modern industrialism enlarged, so did the size and complexity of the city. The labor force of European immigrants and migrants from rural America intensified both the density and heterogeneity of the city, and helped create the modern metropolis.[5]

The onset of modernization nurtured considerable gestation and precipitated a new social orientation. Old values and norms were shaken or shattered, leaving many people adrift searching for order in what Robert Wiebe calls the "distended society." Violent strikes, nativism, and racism were among the symptoms of the heaving and rupturing of a society in the throes of great change. Cities became steadily differentiated, and change increasingly manifested itself in institutional forms. Finally, and most significant for this study, instrumental rationality, or the concern for the most efficient means to achieve ends, became the criterion for choice in the social, economic, and technological spheres of urban life.[6]

An important consequence of this process of modernization was the emergence of the expert who professed mastery over the complex social and economic interrelationships of the new society. Urban imagery replete with congested streets, tottering slums, and the quilted work of immigrant enclaves, epitomized to university-educated engineers, sanitarians, and social workers the inequities of a malfunctioning competitive process governed by a fickle marketplace.[7]

Experts and laymen alike decried the evil of the tenement. Since the 1890s, the reformer-journalist Jacob A. Riis had upbraided the tenement as the scourge of America. But the dreary tenement regions Riis denounced in *How The Other Half Lives* were generally unique to New York City.[8] When Philadelphia investigators failed to uncover counterparts

---

*In the twentieth century individuals in Europe and America who professed expertise in housing usually spoke of themselves as "housers."

to New York's Mullberry Bend, they concluded that fortuitously Philadelphia was a "city of homes"—not tenements. Not until the joining of housing reform with public health did the public recognize the enormity of its housing problem; and at least in Philadelphia the scions of scientific management directed the merger.[9]

In many ways the PHC represented the culmination of certain social and structural reform tendencies. Philadelphia, with its textile mills, locomotive works, and metal-fabricating plants, was an important industrial center at the turn of the century. Although dirty, acrid, congested, and boss-ruled, the city was fully abreast of the forces of modernization. Industrialization and an expanding transit system had produced a diverse society, which in turn spawned a class of individuals highly conscious of their special skills. Well organized, these people strived to shape the city according to their perceptions of the future. During the panic of 1893, for example, social workers, through the Citizens Permanent Relief Committee and the Society for Organizing Charity (SOC), systematized relief into a coordinated professional operation. By 1901 the SOC was headed by Mary Richmond, credited with establishing the principles of modern social casework. Richmond insisted that social workers be professionally trained and helped establish the Pennsylvania School of Social Work as a center for scientific education. Moreover, the research of the University of Pennsylvania's Phipps Institute into the bacteriological origins of tuberculosis and other disease reinforced the interest of social workers in the relationship between sanitation and social welfare.[10]

In addition to organized social workers and associations of businessmen such as the Board of Trade, Philadelphia boasted a number of civic organizations, such as the Committee of Seventy, the City Club, and the Municipal League. These groups expressed the interest of the business community in a more efficient and therefore more economically prosperous metropolis. Professional, business, and civic organizations championed the City Beautiful, especially the Fairmount Parkway (now the Benjamin Franklin Parkway), which promoters intended not only to beautify the city but also, by cutting a diagonal artery west, to facilitate the growth of the suburbs. Both social reformers and businessmen were motivated by efficiency to transform Philadelphia into a place where nonpartisan, enlightened leadership would guide the city in the direction of economy.[11]

The presence of the father of scientific management, Frederick Winslow Taylor, who performed his time-and-motion studies at the North Philadelphia Midvale Steel plant, strengthened this fascination for efficiency. A number of prominent city businessmen, such as Samuel P. Fels, soap king and Single Tax advocate, and the reformer Rudolph Blankenburg, were attracted by Taylor's ideas. When Blankenburg was elected mayor of Philadelphia in 1912, he sought Taylor to head the Department of Public Works. Taylor refused but recommended a protégé from Philadelphia, Morris L. Cooke, a socially conscious mechanical engineer. In Cooke's eyes engineers were shaping the new civilization, leading society into a promised land of efficiency and social justice.[12]

As a result of challenges and clashes in the city's political arena, the strain of scientific efficiency was infused into the housing movement. In 1905 the Philadelphia reformer George W. Norris, an investment banker and advocate of efficient government, formed an independent City Party and entered the mayoralty campaign against Boies Penrose, Edwin Vare, and the Republican machine. The City Party, composed of Democrats like Norris and independent Republicans, lost. Like structural reform movements in Pittsburgh, Detroit and elsewhere, the party's support came exclusively from the city's business aristocracy and residents of affluent in-city suburbs like Oak Lane, West Philadelphia, and Chestnut Hill. The enormous immigrant and working-class populations of the core and industrialized zones remained beyond the concerns of Norris's charter-tinkering brand of anti-machine reform. However, the City Party challenge blurred the image of Philadelphia as "corrupt and contented." More significantly, the reform crusade against bossism chastened Penrose into making some important concessions. Penrose had the state legislature enact several structural reforms, including a uniform primary law, the abolition of the notorious assessor's list of voters (with its padding of some 75,000 fictitious names), and the establishment of a Civil Service Commission. At the same time, Penrose gestured to the proponents of social efficiency; in 1907 the state legislature created a Division of Tenement House Inspection, staffed by two experts.[13]

Unquestionably, the two tenement house inspectors, Carol Manning and Arthur Buchholz, faced a Herculean task. Between 1907 and 1909, the city's Department of Public Health and Charities licensed more than 2,000 tenements; but while each dwelling was subject to inspection, the undermanned division inspected very few. In fact, the Tenement House Act creating the division applied only to buildings defined as dwellings in which three or more families slept and cooked on the premises. Gustavus Weber, the secretary of the Octavia Hill Society, observed that the vast number of two- and three-story houses moldering in narrow courts and alleys escaped coverage. According to Weber, the city's most conspicuous evil was not the tenement but insanitation, particularly "the presence of privy vaults and surface drainage."[14]

By 1909 the tide of interest in efficiency flowed strongly in Philadelphia, and housing reform benefited. A year earlier George W. Norris had helped found the Bureau of Municipal Research (BMR), whose board of directors included Dr. George Woodward, Samuel Fels, and George Burnham, Jr., all distinguished business and civic leaders who stood for efficiency and favored a government administrated by either a commission or a city manager. The BMR worked closely with social agencies. In 1909 these agencies argued that the city's squalid housing made effective social work impossible. That fall the SOC, Children's Aid, and the Tuberculosis Society, among others, joined Weber in declaring that housing was a sanitary and not a tenement problem. At this juncture the OHS called a conference of housing, health, and social work organizations including the Child Welfare Society, the SOC, the Phipps Institute, and the BMR. Appropriately enough, the group met in the City Hall office of Dr. Joseph Neff, the physician-director of the Department of Public Health and Charities. The delegates aimed to create a housing commission, "to consist in part of citizens interested in improving the housing conditions of Philadelphia and in part of *experts having the direction* of such welfare institutions that come in close touch with housing conditions."[15]

Evidence of the technical and sanitary orientation of the new housing movement abounded. The conference was especially concerned about the city's death rate and the causes of preventable disease. Delegates listened to such speakers as Edwin Solenberger, Secretary of the Children's Aid Society and member of the Pennsylvania Conference on Charities and Correction, and J. Prentice Murphy, also of the Children's Aid Society, discuss impure air, defective plumbing, insufficient light, overcrowding, and the effect of insanitation on the city at large.[16]

The deliberations produced the Philadelphia Housing Commission (PHC), which aimed to enforce existing housing laws by using the agents of cooperating organizations to report insanitary conditions. The commission was conceived as an agency that would systematically gather and analyze data to be used in rationalizing control over housing and sanitation. Clearly the organization fulfilled the aspirations of social workers, businessmen, and health experts. In fact, of the eighteen names closely identified with the PHC, seven were trained social workers, seven belonged to the medical community, and three were efficiency-minded businessmen.

Sketching the background of a few commission members suggests more fully their bureaucratic interests. Dr. Joseph Neff was the first president of the PHC. As director of the city's Department of Public Health and Charities, he had worked to educate the public in "sanitary matters" and had marshalled a sizable campaign to reduce the infant mortality rate. Porter Lee, general secretary of the SOC, chaired the commission's

Committee on Investigations, while Edwin Solenberger, secretary of the Children's Aid Society headed the commission's publicity drive. Both were environmentalists who argued that efficient social work was impossible where clients lacked a "sanitary place in which to sleep, play and study."[17]

Board members like Dr. George Woodward had earned impeccable credentials for efficiency in the ranks of the BMR and the City Club. Others, like Drs. Charles Hatfield and H. R. M. Landis, had won their stripes in the service of the famed Phipps Institute. In addition to Samuel Fels of Fels Naptha Soap and the BMR, George W. Norris was the most prominent business member of the PHC. Norris was best known as the banker-lawyer who had battled the Penrose-Vare machine in 1905. In 1911 he presided over the commission, was vice-president of the City Club, director of the SOC, and under newly elected Mayor Blankenburg directed the Department of Wharves, Docks, and Ferries.[18]

The PHC predicated its success on cementing close cooperative relationships with the city's numerous social welfare organizations. Utilizing the neighborhood workers of such agencies as the Union Benevolent Association and the Juvenile Protective Society, the commission collected data on conditions for use in strengthening and enforcing housing laws. The commission issued statistical cards enabling cooperating workers to easily report dangerous conditions, including "foul" or "absent" sewer drainage, "inadequate toilet accommodations," the existence of "noxious trades," and "overcrowding." Despite considerable cooperation from social and health organizations, the PHC in its first two years failed to excite full-fledged housing reform. Gustavus Weber, the commission's first volunteer secretary, left after one year. Without his leadership the commission and housing reform drifted sluggishly until 1911.[19]

In December 1910, Neff and two other board members of the PHC, Porter Lee and Helen Parrish, called a meeting on "Health and Housing" in the office of Mayor John E. Reyburn. Neff sensed an "unmistakable interest in . . . housing. . . ." With the approaching session of the state legislature in mind, he considered the time "ripe for an impressive step forward." Therefore, he had the commission assemble an audience of "men of money and influence" to hear Lawrence Veiller, among others, preach on the necessity for stricter housing laws. Veiller declared that the law must police not only the tenement but all dwellings, and be vigorously enforced by a large corps of inspectors. He also emphasized the need to educate tenants in the science of urban living, a job he felt "best performed by sanitary inspectors preferably women." The public, stressed Veiller, must learn "the effect of bad housing on other social conditions;

the relation of ventilation to TB; of defective plumbing to diphtheria; and of defective sewage to typhoid fever."[20]

The conference proved successful. The PHC budget was increased enough to employ a full-time executive secretary. Against Veiller's advice that the young man was an "unknown" in the guild of American housers, the PHC hired Bernard Newman. Veiller's opinion notwithstanding, Newman quickly established himself as the dominant personality in the Philadelphia housing movement. His background lay primarily in the scientific-bureaucratic tradition. A Unitarian minister who had engaged in postgraduate studies at the New York School of Philanthropy, Newman had served an institutional church in Brooklyn before coming to Philadelphia. But he evinced negligible interest in theology and declined use of the appellation "reverend" in applying for the Housing Commission job. At the School of Philanthropy he had specialized in financial management and then had pursued an avid interest in housing by visiting Europe to inspect modern dwellings in London, Liverpool, Manchester, Glasgow, and Edinburgh. On his return, he studied American and European housing law and lectured on housing reform before church and civic groups. In the five years following his appointment to the PHC, Newman took courses in engineering and public health at Harvard and the University of Pennsylvania, thereafter referring to himself as a "sanitarian."[21]

Within days after he took over as executive secretary, Newman instituted a regimen of order and efficiency. His administration harmonized with his pragmatic philosophy of reform. As a Unitarian, Newman nourished the hope for a world of justice but harbored little hope of attaining the Kingdom of God on Earth. Shortly after taking the commission position, he wrote a friend that his job was simply "looking out for the houses of the people to improve them in a structural and sanitary way." His greatest hope lay in employing scientific methods to uncover causes of social misery. In Newman's view the task required the talents of the "social engineer." But, "[w]e do not have to be a social engineer," argued Newman, "to know that the difficulties of life grow more acute as men come together in towns and cities." Newman believed that the right kind of engineer could reduce those problems to a minimum and guarantee the essential human needs of sunlight, air circulation, ample water, and efficient drainage. In concert with Morris Cooke he called for a comprehensive plan that "looked forward to the development of the town as the highest point of efficiency as a home center."[22]

Newman attributed the cause of most urban ills to bad planning, which he traced to the nineteenth century's solicitude for property rights and ignorance of the "economic efficiency of human rights." The scars of blight betrayed the failure to assay the social costs of streetcar lines, utility extensions, and new housing construction. Bad planning ultimately produced poor housing, and to Newman:

> The importance of the home cannot be overestimated. If the house is good, the residents therein are able to exercise their best ability in every sphere of life. The home will not make a scholar out of a dunce . . . , but a bad home may cause . . . a normal lad to become immoral; a baby in full health to sicken and die. . . . I do not think we can place too much emphasis upon the importance of a good home, and by that I mean a good home . . . giving to the individual members the privacy they need, protecting them against all the evils of overcrowding, thoroughly sanitary in every way.[23]

Like structural reformers, Newman bemoaned that cities were not run by people prepared to expose the inefficiency of municipal departments, campaign for stricter laws, and "protect these laws from the assaults of selfish interests."[24] He also joined many contemporaries in blaming waste and injustice on a popular ignorance of the facts. "The most pitiful thing in the city," sighed Newman, "is the cry of little children for a decent place to live and play. Such conditions . . . would not stand a minute before an enlightened public opinion."[25]

The reform activities of the PHC reflected the fusion of the philosophy of the social gospel with the issue-oriented, popularly based educational concerns of the progressive expert. The philosophy, however, did not posit a goal, but a process, which involved the collection, interpolation, and publication of data and the promotion of legislation. To educate the city, the PHC took its facts, lavishly illustrated with pictures, charts, and lantern slides, before church, business, and civic organizations. Moreover, whenever it could be arranged, Newman led concerned citizens on tours through the slums.[26]

Not only was Newman versed in the science of sanitation and housing, but he also understood the principles of agency administration. Newman systematically structured the board of the PHC to include both an architect and a sanitary engineer. He reorganized the staff of two paid workers and several volunteers to enhance research capabilities and expedite the handling of housing complaints. At the same time Newman determined to enlarge the PHC's universe of cooperating agencies. Thirty-five organizations attended the 1912 annual meeting. By 1915, forty-two agencies cooperated with the commission, a number of them social service departments of city hospitals, which assisted by correlating patient health records with the reported insanitation of home environments.[27]

Building code modernization and improved sanitary inspection constituted the principal achievements of the PHC. It was strongly technical and scientific—not humanistic. Convinced that progress happened not through human perfectibility but through the massing of facts against recalcitrant legislators, the PHC focused on hard data to make a case for reform. As such it was not the personal tragedy of slum life but the statistics on the social and economic costs of blight that preoccupied sanitarians like Newman.

The statistics on Philadelphia's moldering slums bulked large as a case for reform. In the ancient river wards, block after block lacked sewer drainage, leaving the seepage to form brackish rivulets and pools in the penumbra of courts and alleys. Frequently, two or three inches of stagnant water collected in the cellars of alley dwellings. A 1911 study of almost 6,000 of these structures discovered 1,600 overflowing privy vaults.[28]

The effluence from obnoxious trades added to the vile stench of uncovered vaults and belied any claim the city made to modernity. "Pig men," in defiance of the health code, kept 40,000 swine penned and slopping on the city garbage. The reeking odor from the steam and stench of milling swine blended with the nauseating wafts from "dog pure" lofts. A single block in South Philadelphia had ten "dog pure" merchants brazenly purveying their product (which was used commercially as a tanning agent). But horse stables and manure bins also contributed to the stinking murk, and even the Children's Hospital stored a six-by-fifteen-foot pile of dung in its rear yard.

According to the PHC, more than 200,000 people dwelt amidst these vile surroundings, and too frequently conditions inside rivaled the noisome muddle outside. Rooms were dark, unventilated, and in one case, at least, shared with a host of pigeons, dogs, cats, insects, and vermin. Few homes boasted indoor plumbing, and ordinarily a hydrant in a garbage-strewn court supplied the water for five or six families.[29]

Amidst such dreadful surroundings, disease played havoc with the city's health. The PHC cited cases of several members of a family succumbing to tuberculosis in one month. Understandably, scientific reformers denounced this relationship of preventable disease to housing insanitation. Newman pointed out that diphtheria, scarlet fever, and tuberculosis failed to discriminate among victims. Nor, he affirmed, did contagion "confine itself to any particular section of the city." He protested that housing was the prime factor in such contagions as tuberculosis and that quarantining was no longer a viable solution. "In these days of germs," argued Newman, "a perfect quarantine cannot be established, while the perosity of the average slum house makes any attempt through disinfection merely a form. . . ."[30]

In addition to disease, housing reformers espied the virus of immorality and criminality vitiating the frail body of the slum society.

To Newman both the prostitute and the thief owed their fates to overcrowded housing, where family life was fractured by the presence of boarders. The Housing Commission noted families where twelve to fifteen people, mostly boarders, shared one bedroom. But while Newman deplored the immorality of overcrowding, he lashed out vehemently at the burden of inefficiency that it forced upon the city. He railed at the tremendous toll that congested areas levied in police, health, and fire costs. Furthermore, a PHC study established a positive correlation between wards having population congestion and the incidence of election fraud; corruption, therefore, was traceable, at least in part, to congestion. "Make it impossible for an insanitary building to be inhabited, or for insanitary areas to exist," asserted Newman, "and you are going to tone up the people and get a better grade of citizenship."[31]

The PHC, then, worked to modernize the city and make it aware that the twentieth-century metropolis could no longer afford the inefficiencies of congestion, poorly drained back alleys, pig sties, and dog pure lofts. But while publicity alerted Philadelphians to the shame of stench and the health dangers of raw sewage, the bureaucratic solution to the problem lay in the slow, tedious process of rational planning and the enactment of enforceable laws. To that end Newman called for "the coordination of all community projects, *public and private,* so that the maximum of public good may be obtained with a minimum of public injury...."[32]

The campaign for a new housing law embodied the commission's single effort to make Philadelphia a modern and "useful" city. In 1911 the new Blankenburg administration sanctioned a PHC proposal to revise the ineffective 1907 housing law. Following two years of meetings and consultations with outside experts (including Veiller), the state legislature in 1913 passed the Heidinger housing act, which embraced most of the PHC recommendations.

The new law was a magnificent piece of "Tayloresque" legislation. It streamlined the process of inspection and code enforcement by merging the jobs of housing, sanitary, and safety inspector into one agency, the Division of Housing and Sanitation, to be lodged in the Department of Health and Charities. The new division was empowered to prohibit cellar occupancy, require indoor water closets in all new tenements, and enforce all laws against overcrowding. In addition, the code forbade manufacturing in tenements and prohibited the keeping and slaughtering of animals, as well as the storage of manure within city limits.[33]

It was the machinery of enforcement that made the housing law an exemplar of bureaucratic efficiency, on the one hand, and stirred the wrath of politicians and real estate interests on the other. The statute established a corps of one hundred sanitary inspectors authorized to demand entry into any dwelling (tenement or not) suspected of concealing unfit conditions. After declaring a house unfit, inspectors could condemn the property and evict its tenants. Since the division possessed awesome legal responsibility for sanitary order, the PHC charged that it should be headed by a "sanitary engineer who had gone into the hygiene side of his profession" and "is a graduate of a larger technical school."[34] As envisioned by the PHC, the Division of Housing and Sanitation would exert "administrative control" over the law and erect an efficient system to collect, analyze, and summarize information. The division, in fact, would function as a punitive instrument to enforce modern standards of sanitation. Naturally, the PHC perceived the division as a milestone in the transformation of the inefficient city into a "useful" modern environment.[35]

Business organizations like the Chamber of Commerce and the Board of Trade joined the PHC in endorsing the sanitary objectives of the new law. The Board of Trade, like the BMR, pictured a useful city equipped with broad, attractive boulevards, gleaming waterfronts, and harbors with deep, wide channels. In the view of business, commerce flourished not only amidst a sound tax structure but where the city presented an appearance of prosperity. Congested slum districts impressed a Packard Motor Car Company executive as a "tremendous waste of energy and money." He inveighed against the stagnant surface drainage, the "criminal negligence" of unprotected vaults, and the crime of families' using open hydrants for drinking water. But, "as a businessman," he condemned in particular the wasting of "the dynamic energy of the inhabitants of these districts. . . . In order to obtain the maximum efficiency from any workman," argued Packard's M. T. Rogers, "he must have good conditions under which to live and work. . . . Health makes life and life creates property and property is the wealth of the world. If you destory your health, you decrease the wealth and the world and civilization are the losers."[36] Businessmen viewed the efficient city as vital to their interests. Slums threatened not only people but profits, a point on which, no matter how crassly twisted, Bernard Newman and his PHC colleagues agreed.

Unfortunately, neither the scientific-minded social reformers of the PHC nor the supportive business community considered enlisting the slum dwellers in the crusade for a useful city. While investigators revealed an understanding of the complex ecology of the modern city, none fathomed the subtle economics of the boarder problem, nor wrestled with the fates of tenants forced to vacate uninhabitable dwellings. Despite Newman's protestations of concern for justice, that concern required a humanistic sensitivity lacking in the empirically oriented votaries of scientific efficiency.[37]

But while technical experts seemed oblivious to the inequitable benefits of the city useful, people like boss Edwin Vare were not. The machine's simple operating maxim that "the boss knows what is good for his people and gives it to them" proved an unbreachable ideological wall in 1915 and 1916. The PHC got its housing law, but no funds to implement it. According to the loophole in the law, only the city councils could appropriate funds to hire inspectors, and, alas, the councils were "bossed" and intractable. In 1915 the state enacted a compromise housing bill that yanked the teeth from the Heidinger legislation. This latest act eliminated all but five of the one hundred inspectors, muddied the definition of a tenement, and diffused the power of the Division of Housing and Sanitation by returning the authority to condemn unfit dwellings to the Department of Safety.[38]

In reality, the commission's housing law toppled with the Blankenburg administration. PHC became the Philadelphia Housing Association in 1916. Its confrontation with the realities of city politics tempered its more stringent demands, but it continued to press for efficient and impartial housing law enforcement.[39]

The PHC marked a significant change in the direction of housing policy. Under it reform lost its philanthropic identity and adopted the methodology and rhetoric of science and efficiency. In its stress on community-wide coordination, interagency cooperation, and the key role of the expert, the PHC epitomized the bureaucratic reform organization that appeared with the arrival of twentieth-century modernization. To reformers like Bernard Newman, the socially heterogeneous metropolis demanded coordination to restore needed integration between its fragmented parts. Professional social workers, physicians, housers, and other social engineers argued that only the trained expert possessed the knowledge and vision to orchestrate the needs of the metropolis. Social reformers condemned the provincialism of ward politicians, who ordinarily spurned expertise and stymied efforts at city-wide planning. But while structural reformers like Norris and members of the BMR waged war on bossism and sought to combat fragmentation through the city manager concept, the short ballot, and stricter election laws, the PHC, no friend of the boss, avoided open confrontation with the machine. Newman believed that battling the machine jeopardized the passage and enforcement of housing laws. Moreover, the PHC regarded publicity and restrictive legislation as better means of meshing the fragmented parts of urban society. A public fully aware of the cost and danger of insanitation would, reasoned Newman, compel the passage of zoning and housing laws. Social harmony would follow the establishment of these middle-class standards of social and sanitary order.

Clearly, then, the PHC epitomized bureaucratic standards of social and sanitary order. It utilized principles of scientific and technical efficiency to establish criteria for a modern urban environment. As an archetype of bureaucratization, the PHC collected a massive body of factual data on housing dilapidation and insanitation, and so armed, erected a legal edifice of housing ordinances and sanitary codes aimed at disinfecting the environment.

However, the commission's initial thrust in the direction of modernization through sanitary efficiency was blunted. Its goal of social betterment became tangled in a webbing of procedure. The PHC busied itself with numerous investigations, produced countless news releases on the squalor of the city, and in effect, after 1915 monitored and assisted the undermanned Division of Housing and Sanitation. But despite the efforts of the PHC, Philadelphia, like New York and other cities, confronted enormous problems of slum growth and blight in the 1920s. The next decade found the city's thousands of unfit bandbox tenements, court, and back alley dwellings horribly overcrowded and the acrid stench of overflowing privy vaults still befouling the air.

While an examination of the values and methods of the PHC illustrates that the agency helped spearhead modernization, it also shows that the PHC failed to appreciably improve the housing environment of the slum. The scientific values of the PHC were embedded in a thin layer of urban society—represented by engineers, technicians, and social workers. Beneath this mantle, in the ethnic and working class neighborhoods where its policies had to be implemented, the unscientific, inefficient, but effective personal politics of the boss remained impervious to the allure of both the PHC and modernization.[40]

WAYNE J. URBAN

9. PROGRESSIVE EDUCATION IN THE URBAN SOUTH:
THE REFORM OF THE ATLANTA SCHOOLS, 1914-1918

Lawrence Cremin's classic 1961 study of progressive education, *The Transformation of the School,* profiled the thought of reform intellectuals such as John Dewey, Jane Addams, and Francis Parker. Cremin concluded that progressive ideas were a basically humane and democratic attempt to come to terms with a new, urban-industrial society.[1] Within three years of Cremin's study, two works appeared which, though covering the same time span, differed dramatically in interpretation. In a monumental study of the high school from 1890 to 1920, Edward Krug depicted the social efficiency movement that had captivated secondary educators; the movement envisioned the schools as a means of adjusting individual students to the values and realities of modern society through the three-pronged program of vocational training, education for social service, and education for social control.[2] Raymond Callahan studied educational administration between 1900 and 1920 and described how the business value of efficiency had captured school administrators, resulting in a mentality that sought to control spending as its prime objective.[3] Neither of these studies found reform to be particularly humane or democratic.

This chapter looks closely at the schools in one city to see the local relationships among the versions of reform studied in a national context by Cremin, Krug, and Callahan. In Atlanta, social efficiency and business efficiency emerge as the predominant reform goals, though accompanied by frequent and often insincere democratic rhetoric. Close consideration of the backgrounds, ideas, and proposals of Atlanta reformers leads to the conclusion that progressive education was the product of a self-conscious reform elite that imposed change on a largely reluctant populace.

The reluctance of many Atlanta citizens to accept the "benefits" offered by progressive school reformers caused both groups to look for political help at the state level in achieving their goals.[4] Educational reformers allied themselves with the progressive wing of the Georgia Democratic party, while opponents tied themselves to the conservatives. Close analysis of these alliances suggests that Georgia's progressive movement in politics, just as in education, was not particularly democratic in leadership, composition, or goals.

The prime mover in the reform of the Atlanta schools was Robert J. Guinn. He was chosen as school board member and elected board president in 1914; he oversaw the introduction of extensive changes in the Atlanta schools until he resigned from the board in 1918. A look at Guinn's experience before assuming the board presidency is important in understanding progressive education as practiced in Atlanta.

Guinn was born in Conyers, Georgia, a small town about fifty miles east of Atlanta, where he was educated by his father and pursued the dual careers of newspaper editor and teacher. From the beginning, Guinn astutely blended education and politics, with acquired family connections, to advance himself in the state educational hierarchy. In 1895 he was appointed assistant to the state school commissioner and later became president of the Georgia Education Association.[5] He then was chosen school superintendent in Fulton County, the area surrounding but not including the city of Atlanta. Evidently frustrated by the low salaries received by even the top school officials, Guinn left the profession in 1900 to enter the insurance business. This did not signal a total abandonment of school affairs, however, since he was chosen as a board member in Fulton County, and later served on the boards of the State Normal School at Athens and Emory College. While involved as a businessman and school board member, Guinn did not neglect his long-time interest in politics; he actively supported a businessman reformer in the 1908 Atlanta mayoral race and managed the campaign of a United States Senate candidate in 1914.[6] Guinn was a businessman who sought to mold city and state politics in ways supportive of business. He would attempt to implement similar values in the Atlanta schools.

Guinn's major drawback as an educational reformer was his dearth of formal schooling and credentials. He overcame this shortcoming by quickly introducing to Atlanta public school reform four individuals who possessed extensive educational backgrounds. M. L. Brittain, Celeste Parrish, Joseph Wardlaw and Laura Smith all had been affiliated with and/or educated at the most prominent national and Georgia institutions of educational reform: the University of Chicago and the State Normal

School in Athens. In 1914 Brittain was state superintendent of instruction in Georgia, and Parrish was one of his assistants. When Guinn sought a survey of Atlanta's schools that would serve as a basis for reform, he consulted with Brittain and then appointed Miss Parrish to conduct the investigation. Later, during his tenure as board president, Guinn appointed Wardlaw as superintendent and Miss Smith as elementary supervisor in the Atlanta schools.[7]

Because of their connection with the University of Chicago, all four of these reformers were familiar with the ideas of the "new education" as made famous by John Dewey at that institution. New or progressive education involved linking the activities of the school with the life of the larger society, grounding classroom practice in the science of psychology, and using the interests of the child as a starting point for school work while simultaneously adjusting the curriculum to the new kinds of students who enrolled after the passing of compulsory attendance laws. Guinn and his fellow reformers sought to introduce progressive educational practices throughout the schools of Georgia. Celeste Parrish, for example, while serving on the faculty of the state normal school, urged her students to abandon textbooks and traditional subjects and concentrate instead on developing "units" of work that would interest the children and relate to their community life.[8]

Applying this orientation to her 1914 survey of the Atlanta schools, she was especially critical of teaching methods and curriculum in the elementary schools. Existing instruction was abstract, rigid, formal, and too devoted to drill and repetition at the expense of the subject matter itself. Teaching could be improved by hiring a supervisor to help experienced teachers learn the new methods. Normal classes should be shifted from Girls' High School to one of the existing elementary schools, thereby ensuring that teachers in training would learn the new ideas in a laboratory setting. The elementary curriculum, much too traditional, needed to be broadened in order to seek "closer connections with the experience of the children and with home and civic conditions."[9] Parrish's proposals, Deweyan in many of their particulars, exemplify well the humane and democratic aspects of a progressive education that sought to help children liberate themselves from the shackles of an outdated curriculum and a constricting teaching method.

The democratic, liberating progressivism that permeated Parrish's elementary proposals included a social-efficiency strain most evident in her proposals for Girls' High School. She sought to replace the economically unrealistic college preparatory curriculum with a broader course of study that included science, the arts, and commercial and household subjects. The major objective of this effort was to prepare students realistically for their future life, at home or in the working place. This goal was also prominent in several of her other proposals, particularly vocational training and vocational guidance.[10] Whether these programs served needs that students and their parents saw as meaningful is problematic, since school officials relied on their own determination of student interest and abilities, as well as society's needs.

The disparity between the ideas of reformers and of the public surfaced in 1916 during a debate over the establishment of a Bureau of Research and Guidance in the schools. This agency would build on already existing vocational innovations in school curricula by ensuring that vocational training was geared to the needs of the city's employers. The Guinn board, after an unsuccessful attempt to obtain funds for the bureau from the city council, turned to private sources and received money from a prominent businessman.[11] This suggests that school reformers and business interests were more than willing to override the wishes of elected representatives. to provide for an agency that acted in the interests of the city's employers.

The issue of consolidating Atlanta's high schools also shows that reformers were determined to implement their programs over the objections of citizens most affected by the changes. Consolidation, a major goal of social-efficiency educators throughout the country, was sought by Guinn and Superintendent Wardlaw over the vocal opposition of many high school students and their parents. Reformers wanted consolidated high schools, not to accomplish any equalitarian goals, but rather to provide differentiated curricula for students of different social classes. Thus, high school administrators would gain centralized control over the vocational decisions of all students, ensuring that these decisions were made realistically, under the direction of educational experts.[12]

The business-efficiency aspect of progressive education in Atlanta was apparent in several reform policies, each of which indicated the priority of curtailing expenses in the reform agenda. When Guinn implemented a merit system of pay in the schools, teachers found that a major outcome was a marked reduction in the total payroll. Similarly, when Guinn required teachers to teach summers in his newly established vacation schools, he changed contracts from a ten- to a twelve-month period without significantly increasing total pay. Still another innovation with similar results was the institution of double sessions in the schools. This lowered average class size to approximately forty students but forced many teachers to teach both sessions without a proportionate pay increase.[13]

In short, the totality of educational reform as practiced in Atlanta exhibited in its social and business efficiency aspects what Michael Katz has called the "darker side of progressivism."[14] Though reformers claimed to be meeting citizens' needs, they made clear that school officials would define these needs; that students would be trained in public schools for jobs in private business; and that reform would be accomplished with public funds doled out in a penurious manner by cost-conscious officials. None of this seems particularly humane or democratic.

The unrepresentativeness of Atlanta's school reforms is further illustrated by the opposition to school reform. Already mentioned in this regard has been the objections of teachers to double sessions. Joining teachers in this opposition was an organized group of vocal, affluent mothers, the Women's School Improvement Association.[15] Though neither teachers nor parents took an explicit anti-Guinn stance on this issue, their subsequent participation in moves against the board president indicates their unhappiness with his policies. Overt opposition to the Guinn reforms first surfaced in 1914, when he indicated his intention to replace Superintendent William M. Slaton with a man more "progressive" and sympathetic to a thoroughgoing reform of the schools. Strenuous objection to the Slaton firing came from the *Journal of Labor,* official newspaper of the Atlanta Federation of Trades, as well as from the powerful morning daily, the *Atlanta Constitution.* Both papers defended Slaton's conservative educational philosophy, which stressed basic skills, formal discipline, and improvement through an increase in school facilities. Labor's newspaper remarked that under Guinn changes had been introduced that seemed to be nothing more than "fads." The *Constitution* stressed its agreement with Superintendent Slaton's suspicion of curricular innovations.[16] Shortly after dismissing Slaton, Guinn gave teachers further reason to fear him when he removed the former president of the teachers' association, Theodore Toepel, from his position as Director of Physical Culture.[17]

Guinn's adversaries were suspicious of educational reformers who assumed that the schools were fundamentally unsound. What these conservatives sought was not progressive innovation but an increase in school funding to build more buildings and increase teachers' salaries. In an effort to bulwark their claim that little popular support existed for Guinn's policies, conservatives gathered 10,000 signatures on petitions favoring the retention of Superintendent Slaton. In addition to their conservative pedagogical views, Slaton supporters had strong local loyalties. They were offended that an outsider, Guinn, would fire a man who had worked his way through the teaching ranks and succeeded his father as superintendent. In spite of this opposition, Guinn went ahead and fired Slaton, replacing him with an interim appointee after State Superintendent Brittain turned down the job. Guinn's ultimate choice as superintendent was Joseph Wardlaw, whom he brought in initially as assistant superintendent.[18]

Guinn and Wardlaw presided over Atlanta's schools until 1918, when the *Constitution* published a lengthy criticism of reform by W. F. Dykes, principal of Boys' High School.[19] Dykes's major target was Guinn's proposed consolidation of the high schools. This issue aroused the feelings of both the affluent parents of Boys' High School students and parents of the students at the other high schools, none of whom wanted to see the high schools lose their separate identity. In response to the Dykes criticism, the city council investigated the schools. Many reform opponents, including teachers and parents, offered anti-Guinn testimony to the council's investigating committee. Teachers complained of the economic penalties suffered under the merit system, and parents testified to the harm done their children by double sessions and other Guinn policies. Perhaps most damaging was the testimony of the president of the Women's School Improvement Association that Guinn had defended double sessions as an intermediate step toward his ultimate goal of bringing the platoon school, or Gary system, to Atlanta.[20] This system, which involved curricular innovation and day-long use of every inch of school space, was recognized throughout the country as the embodiment of reformers' dreams; however, attempts to introduce it in other cities, such as New York, had created a bitter controversy. A Gary system for Atlanta aroused opposition from several groups: well-to-do parents feared any plan that originated in a grubby factory city like Gary; organized workers were suspicious of any reform that originated in a "company town"; and teachers were suspicious of any organizational scheme that fundamentally altered familiar working conditions. Thus, Guinn opponents in 1918 took the same position that they had three years earlier over the Slaton controversy: the schools were fundamentally sound and Guinn's reforms were both unnecessary and dangerous.[21]

The opposition to Guinn was not based solely on a conflict in educational philosophy; opponents charged at the time of the Slaton firing that Guinn was using the schools for political purposes. The superintendent's brother was John Slaton, governor of Georgia. The governor charged that his brother's removal was an extension of Guinn's anti-Slaton political activities. Earlier in 1914, the year before the firing, Guinn had managed the campaign of one of Governor Slaton's opponents in a race for the U. S. Senate. The governor charged that Guinn was using the Atlanta schools, as he had formerly used the State Normal School, to build a political base.[22] The political differences between Guinn and the Slatons were part of a larger rivalry between the two leading factions of Georgia Democrats, the only party of consequence in the state. The leader of one faction was Senator Hoke Smith, and Guinn's candidate in the 1914 senatorial race was supported by this faction. The ideas of Smith's faction were publicized in Atlanta's afternoon daily, the *Journal*, the only local paper to defend Guinn's right to replace Slaton as superintendent. Links between Smith and Guinn were educational as well as political. The senator was a major force in the movement for federal aid to vocational education and had pushed for vocational policies such as manual training as a member of the Atlanta school board at the turn of the century. He also frequently shared a speaker's platform with Celeste Parrish during the campaign for federal aid to vocational education.[23]

The acknowledged leader of the faction opposed to Hoke Smith was Clark Howell, editor of the *Atlanta Constitution*. The involvement of the Howell faction in the opposition to Guinn is evident from the frequent criticism of Guinn's handling of the Slaton affair in the pages of the *Constitution*. Howell was a long-time friend of organized labor, and the support of Slaton by labor's own newspaper is testimony to the Howell-labor alliance in school affairs. Equally noteworthy is the prominent membership of Howell's wife in the Women's School Improvement Association during that organization's opposition to Guinn's policies in 1915 and 1918.[24] In the latter year, the anti-Guinn charges of W. F. Dykes were displayed on the front page of the *Constitution*, which publicized the subsequent investigation of Guinn with obvious relish.

The political orientations of the two factions differed as did their positions on educational issues. Smith's faction bore the label "progressive" because of its support for various reforms, the most famous of which was state regulation of railroads. Smith had made reform and railroad regulation two important planks in his successful 1906 race for the governorship. Howell and his faction defended the railroads and were generally suspicious of reform and reformers; they thus sought and were granted the label of "conservatives." Yet, the labels were misleading in several ways. Hoke Smith's biographer, Dewey W. Grantham, sees the governor's reform period as a progressive interlude in an otherwise flexibly conservative career. Smith had served in the 1890s as Secretary of the Interior in the cabinet of conservative Democrat Grover Cleveland, and his orientation in the Senate from 1911 to 1921 was generally conservative. Even in opposing railroads, Smith was operating as much in terms of his earlier experience of serving anti-railroad clients to build up a law practice as he was acting from any deep-seated commitment to anti-business reform. Grantham does not find a distinction between the Smith progressives and the Howell conservatives based on any consistent articulation of issues such as reform. The struggle between the two factions of the party was more for power and control of patronage than it was a battle between two well-defined approaches to government. The Howell group represented an older, Bourbon elite, while the Smith faction spoke for the newer urban commercial interests that had surfaced with changes in the region's economy.[25]

Given this lack of fundamental conflict on issues, it is not surprising that the factions often resorted to the skillful manipulation of voters' emotions to gain political victory. Smith used fear of blacks to help himself gain the governor's office in 1906 and in turn was confronted in 1918 with the charge that he and his ally Senator Thomas Hardwick were pro-German, since they took an anti-British position in defense of Georgia cotton farmers.[26] The pro-German charge also surfaced in Atlanta city politics in 1918; at that time, Guinn's opponents charged that he and Superintendent Wardlaw had conspired to place a German sympathizer on the Boys' High School faculty. A pro-Guinn board member who ran for mayor faced the identical charge from his opponent. Guinn's critics argued that under him the schools were being Prussianized, while Senator Smith's foes argued that he had expressed sentiments that favored the "Hun."[27] The existence of the emotional German issue during the World War I period was crucial to Guinn's opponents, since it brought about his resignation from the school board, an outcome his foes had sought unsuccessfully since the Slaton firing three years earlier.

Not content with getting rid of Guinn, opponents moved to change the method by which he had been chosen a school board member. They pushed through the legislature a law that called for the popular election of board members as a substitute for the system of council selection. After this change, voters proved their antipathy to progressive education by electing a board that was vociferously anti-reform.[28]

What does not emerge in the politics of reform is any clear-cut relationship between progressivism and popular democracy. If Atlanta and Georgia progressives are to be described as democratic, it can be only for their advocacy of policies that they themselves defined as democratic. The opposition to reform by parents, teachers, and labor seems to indicate that most citizens were suspicious of such self-styled progressives.

In his study of Wisconsin reform in the 1890s, David P. Thelen has argued that an authentic "democratic" progressivism arose as a consumer coalition united to control the evils of big business and quasi-public utilities. This "democratic" progressivism degenerated, according to Thelen, into producer-oriented interest groups that pursued their own welfare instead of the common interest. This special interest reform, which prevailed in the first two decades of the twentieth century, was an "undemocratic" progressivism that repudiated the representative goals of earlier reformers.[29] Guinn-Smith reform fails on both particulars in Thelen's picture of democratic progressivism: a reform coalition was absent in Atlanta school affairs—in fact, the reforms aroused a coalition of opponents; and neither Guinn, the insurance man, nor Hoke Smith, the lawyer and advocate of vocational education, can be seen as anti-business. Atlanta reform seems to be a good example of Thelen's interest-oriented progressivism; the educational policies served the interests of employers and the professional school reformers who developed them.

The rise and fall of Robert Guinn as reformer points to several conclusions about the nature of progressivism in urban education and politics. Guinn's reform was long on efficiency and short on representative democracy. The curricular policies of Parrish that sought to liberate children from outdated, rote learning became the Wardlaw reforms that sought to harness children to the values and needs of a new economy. Similarly, the major goal of progressives in Georgia politics was to win control of the Democratic party, rather than to advance the principles of democratic reform. Representative proposals such as the direct election of senators would be advocated when they fit the major objective of progressives; but such undemocratic policies as the white primary and special-interest, pro-business opposition to child labor amendments were advocated when they fit the larger goal of attaining or retaining political power. Cremin's picture of political and educational progressivism as humane and democratic may fit the ideas of the intellectuals described in his study, but it is a poor description of the institutionalization of these ideas in Atlanta's schools. The dominant reality in Atlanta reform was an ideology of social and business efficiency that cared little for the concerns of students, parents, teachers, or workers.

This reality was not untypical of urban reform in other cities during this period. David B. Tyack, in his recent study of city schools between 1890 and 1940, delineates the development of an "administrative progressivism" as the dominant ideology among schoolmen. This ideology blended social and business efficiency into a single point of view that sought to remake the children of the city according to progressive ideas of what they should be.[30] This is precisely what seems to have occurred in Atlanta. Samuel P. Hays has seen the efforts of urban school reformers as part of a general urban reform movement that sought to take various aspects of city government out of the hands of elected politicians and shift control of city affairs to appointed experts. The experts, though claiming to represent no interest, turn out in Hays's analysis to embody a point of view much more in agreement with that of business interests than of the general population.[31] Again, this seems representative of the Atlanta experience.

Yet, the actual political activities in any city will seldom be regular enough to completely fit any generalization such as that of Hays or

Tyack. The role of organized labor in Atlanta school affairs in 1914 and again in 1918 is testimony to the complexity of city politics. Labor, as previously mentioned, could usually be counted on as a supporter of political conservatives, both locally and in the state legislature. A close look at educational politics in Atlanta leads to a qualification in this generalization. Already mentioned in this essay was labor's alliance with the anti-Guinn conservatives on the issue of the Slaton firing in 1914; but when the city council investigated the Guinn board in 1918, labor was strangely silent. The explanation for this silence is found when labor's role in the 1918 mayoral race is considered. The unions supported James L. Key in this election because he had taken a vigorous pro-union position in the 1916 Atlanta street railway strike and maintained that stance for two years. In school affairs, Key was a pro-Guinn member of the school board who took a strong stand in favor of reform.[32] Key's support on the crucial street railway issue must have been more important to labor than his advocacy of school reform; thus, the unions muted their opposition to the Guinn educational programs in order to sustain their alliance with Key on street railways. This situation is an excellent example of John D. Buenker's characterization of urban reform politics in the Progressive Era as a process involving shifting coalitions of various interest groups. It also, of course, reinforces David Thelen's earlier mentioned description of interest-oriented reformers.[33] The absence of consistent ideological and issue orientations in Atlanta and Georgia politics supports Buenker's general description of reform as the result of a coalition of various interests, not an ideological crusade for democracy.

Having shown how the Guinn reforms relate to much of the historical analysis done on urban progressivism, it remains important to comment briefly on the way in which the Atlanta situation was unique and ungeneralizable. In studying Atlanta, the politics of educational reform does not become clear until the situation is analyzed in terms of state-level political differences. Reform in the city was never frequent or cohesive enough for a recognizable reform faction or set of issues to emerge. City politics seem confused and confusing; the numerous mayoral candidates and vocal council members spoke with forceful personalities but in a bewildering babble of voices on the issues. This was, no doubt, true to some extent in every city, but Atlanta, lacking even a local political machine for reformers to oppose, had political activity of such variety that the city has heretofore escaped the comprehensive political analysis that historians have applied to other cities such as Chicago, Memphis, or Baltimore.[34] When the Guinn reforms are looked at from a background of state politics, however, the picture becomes much clearer. Guinn was directly tied to one of the factions in state politics, and thus Atlanta educational reform was related to educational and political activity at the state level. Many crucial decisions that affected the city of Atlanta were made by the legislature and governor. City government was present and necessary, but not as important for municipal affairs as was state government. Nowhere in the existing studies of Atlanta during this period has evidence surfaced that city residents were concerned about this situation. The total lack of home-rule agitation in Atlanta stands in stark contrast to events in other cities during the Progressive Era.[35]

A plausible explanation for this phenomenon of undisputed state control of city politics would be twofold. First, Atlanta was the state capital: legislators met in the city, knew it, and had more understanding of and less antipathy toward the city than legislators in other states had toward their biggest cities. Second, the factions of the Democratic party that were represented by the two local newspapers were both city and state factions. Control of the city and the state were not seen as separate issues by the competing elites; the newspapers were voices of both the city and the state.[36] The rural-urban differences that plagued many cities and states in the Progressive Era were muted in Georgia, where control of the capital city was coexistent with political control of the state. This political situation made the battle for urban school reform in Atlanta unique in one respect; it was primarily a contest between opposing state political factions and only incidentally involved the various segments of the city itself. Given this structural uniqueness, however, it should be restated that the content of school reform in Atlanta was quite similar to that in other cities.

EUGENE M. TOBIN

10. "ENGINES OF SALVATION" OR "SMOKING BLACK DEVILS":
JERSEY CITY REFORMERS AND THE RAILROADS, 1902-1908

A decade has passed since Robert H. Wiebe and Samuel P. Hays first suggested that any evaluation of urban progressivism must begin with an analysis of practice rather than ideology.[1] Nonetheless, recent scholarship has failed to move beyond the reform image fashioned by contemporary participants. Historians remain preoccupied in a traditional debate dominated by bosses, reformers, and businessmen. Though winners and losers interchanged roles, the struggle has remained one-dimensional: corrupt corporations subverted direct democracy and thwarted a more equitable distribution of wealth, while reform-minded citizens fought special privilege and economic inequities. This limited approach obscures the fundamental point that progressivism was a give-and-take process in which all sides compromised their positions and occasionally themselves.

In recent years a wide variety of evidence has been marshaled to analyze reform campaigns for home rule, equal taxation, and municipal ownership.[2] Historians have rarely followed the legal battles through the courts as railroads resisted equal taxation, utilities opposed franchise limitation, and legislators impeded self-determination. The judicial process has been widely ignored as a source of assistance in distinguishing the reality from the rhetoric of reform. Though the political arena provided a forum for a multitude of conflicting interest groups, the judicial system was responsible for resolving conflict in an increasingly segmented society. Scholars unhesitatingly have transferred the reform framework from public policy battles to the legal process. Yet, the putative success achieved by progressives in the political arena never was so conclusively matched in the courtroom. The use of litigation as a tactical instrument by competing interests provides the focus for this study. Its major concern is the Jersey City experience, particularly with the equal taxation of railroad property. Litigation should be viewed as an alternative channel of decision making, but one whose reform achievements were less notable than insurgents desired.

In analyzing the impact of the equal tax litigation, several factors pertaining to the development of American law must be considered. By 1900, the physical, demographic and industrial growth that had characterized post-Civil War city-building had not yet subsided. But the exuberant self-confidence with which urban dwellers had once embraced technological advances in transportation and communication was transformed into a recognition of the less admirable consequences of such change—municipal corruption, increasing socioeconomic inequality, and corporate irresponsibility. This shift in public opinion paralleled government's changing relationship with the private sector from a position of unrestrained boosterism to one of more active regulation and stewardship.

Scholars long have noted that American law was molded and shaped by the interplay of government with emerging autonomous segments representing minorities, business, labor, and agriculture. Though serving as an intermediary, the governmental process failed to integrate or provide a central direction for competing groups. Indeed, the law reinforced and preserved existing divisions by negotiating compromises and coordinating an increasingly compartmentalized society.[3] The post-Civil War years reflected the attempted, though largely unsuccessful, use of law to redress inequities concerning race, temperance, and suffrage. At the same time, the law had an equally dramatic impact on another interest group —the nation's cities. One need look no further than the explosion of treatises on municipal corporations after 1880 to realize that the problems of local government were occupying larger amounts of judicial and legislative attention.[4] Local reformers asked the courts to consider the positive utilization of law to redress economic imbalance. In making this request, it appears that progressives may have misconstrued the economic and social interests of most state judges. A majority of the bench and bar were purists, believing that the judiciary ought not to interfere with legislative (or administrative) judgment unless that judgment was clearly unconstitutional or unreasonable. The courts intervened infrequently, and then only as "indispensable referees in a vital and ragged game."[5]

The legal system was itself the product of a society in which the allocation of political and economic power was not always compatible with equality of opportunity. The degree of imbalance varied across the nation, but power over public policy-making rested by the late nineteenth century with autonomous interests who monopolized the politics of opportunity. No state was more proficient in the development of monopoly capitalism than the "home of the trusts"—New Jersey, whose liberal incorporation laws enabled that state's railroads to emerge as an independent political force.[6] Capitalizing upon their political connections and what Robert W. Fogel has described as the "axiom of indispensability," New Jersey's railroads secured preferential tax treatment and immunity from government control.[7] Though recent accounts of the railroad industry during the Progressive Era have differed markedly over the origins and effects of regulation, most scholars have noted the tendency of supervising authority to be located with the national as opposed to state governments.[8] The New Jersey experience similarly reveals that the decision-making power usually rested with the state as opposed to local jurisdictions.

Two issues that underwent intense public scrutiny during the first decade of the twentieth century related directly to the power of the railroads in New Jersey. One was the monopolization of the state's political and economic life by an alliance of political bosses and corporate magnates. The second issue, stemming in large part from the first, was the equal taxation of railroads.

The latter question was integrally connected with the fiscal survival of New Jersey's cities. During the late nineteenth century, soaring municipal costs had forced the local tax rate upward. Urban leaders, seeking new funds, protested that the taxes paid by the railroads failed to keep pace with the lines' growing income.[9] By the 1880s it was estimated that railroad holdings represented 25 percent of New Jersey's property values.[10] Cities and counties, however, received no tax revenue from this real estate, despite the fact that it included some of the richest meadowland and river frontage in the state.[11] Taxpayers soon found themselves in an ambivalent position with respect to railroads. On the one hand, many citizens had come to accept them as indispensable to economic growth; but at the same time, many others questioned the railroads' arrogance toward the problems of cities located along their routes.

In the railroads' behalf it should be noted that although they drastically rearranged urban land use, they did not emerge from their own rapid development without serious problems. Enormous property expenditures resulted in overcapitalization. Shoddy construction, watered stock, obsolete equipment, and overexpansion were other problems that continued to plague the industry into the twentieth century.[12] Moreover, while the railroads contributed to the corruption and segmentation of state politics and the growth of monopolistic practices, their presence also facilitated intrastate communication and provided mass employment through the attraction of new businesses and the creation of new markets.

The matter was further complicated by the divergent political and economic developments emerging within New Jersey. If all property were to be taxed and assessed at true value, there would have to be a considerable increase in the valuations of private property owners, who previously had been assessed at never more than 60–75 percent of full value. But only those property holders residing in cities with significant railroad real estate would enjoy the benefits of a reduced tax rate resulting from the full local taxation of railroad property. In practical terms this usually meant that Republican legislators from predominantly agrarian South Jersey opposed the equal tax proposals of representatives from the northeastern counties, where railroad development was most pronounced and where Democratic majorities generally prevailed.

A persistent theme in late nineteenth-century legal development was the protection of more productive, large-scale economic operations against the limits that more parochial interests sought to impose. Though praised as an integrating force, railroad growth raised a question of priorities by placing community stability in opposition to statewide development. Should the legislature and the courts have championed railroad expansion and preferential treatment without considering the inevitable consequences for competing interests? We need to ask: Which public is it whose interest must be weighed, the public of a single community, or the public of broader market areas served by the railroads, whose own economic growth was often hampered by the tax-raising efforts of localities?[13]

The crux of the dilemma was that railroad property was never listed in the record of municipal ratables. An 1884 Railroad Tax Act had created this imbalance. Responding to the railroad lobby's contention that local taxing authorities established inconsistent valuations of their property, the legislature had practically eliminated municipal taxation of railroad holdings in the state. The State Board of Assessors created by the new law had classified railroad property into three taxable divisions. The first class included the franchise and the "main stem," which represented the 100-foot-wide roadbed on either side of the track, and all personal property including rails, sleepers, and depots. First-class property was taxed by the State Board of Assessors at the rate of $5 per thousand ratables, but the railroads paid nothing to the municipalities through which the main stem passed. All other real property beyond 100 feet in width used for railroad purposes constituted the second class of railroad property and was taxed at a rate not exceeding $15 per thousand ratables. Only third-class railroad property, denoting land not as yet used for railroad purposes, was taxable at full local rates.[14] This arrangement had prevented the effective revenue yields from significant parcels of urban land, constricted the tax base, and forced other property owners to bear the municipal mortgage and rising costs.

The condition bore most heavily upon Jersey City. Since 1875, fourteen railroads had operated there, making the city an industrial center as well as a terminus for the major trunk lines of the Northeast.[15] Over the years railroad expansion along the warehouse and waterfront districts had inevitably encroached upon adjacent commercial and residential areas, resulting in the carriers' emergence as the single largest municipal property owners. By 1901 the railroads held rights to approximately one-third of Jersey City's land. But due to the preferential classification of their property, the railroads paid taxes upon only half of this area (16 percent of the city's land) and contributed only 10 percent of the municipal realty revenues. Local homeowners and corporate property owners paid over 90 percent of the tax burden on the remaining two-thirds of city real estate.[16] It would be misleading to assume, however, that the railroads were unfairly advantaged while the city was unfairly disadvantaged. The railroads' locally taxable property was forced to bear a disproportionate share of the municipal tax burden due to the wide discrepancy between equality of valuation and taxation.[17] Nevertheless, the crisis in Jersey City represented the most flagrant example of the legislature's disregard for the principle that all taxable property should share public burdens equally.

As the railroads absorbed larger areas of municipal property, the struggle for equal taxation emerged as the major priority of the progressive Republican administration of Mark M. Fagan, mayor of Jersey City from 1902 to 1908.[18] Rising out of the impoverished surroundings of downtown Jersey City's Fifth Ward, Fagan adroitly took advantage of internal turmoil in the local Democratic party to become the youngest mayor and only the third Republican chief executive in his city's history. Although apparently "100 percent an organization man" during his first campaign, Fagan had pledged that he would prevent "the encroachment of railroad interests . . . and insist upon the payment of an equitable share of the taxes by all corporations. . . ."[19] The mayor was encouraged along those lines by his corporation counsel, George L. Record, who joined him in seeking to end Jersey City's economic dependence upon the railroads and utilities through a program of regulation, franchise limitation, and taxation.

Though Mayor Fagan was primarily interested in achieving economic democracy, he was instrumental in developing an advanced program of social justice. His administration ultimately supported the establishment of free medical clinics, public baths, playgrounds, free concerts in the parks, and the elimination of unprotected railroad crossings, adulterated milk and impure water. His overriding concern with child welfare led him to support the creation of the city's first juvenile court, movements for tenement and child labor reform, and a seat for every child in the public schools.[20] Once in office, however, Fagan quickly discovered that his administration would be unable to provide even the most basic municipal services unless Jersey City's tax base was significantly broadened.

Consequently, in his first major move, Fagan sought to alert the public to the evils of corporate tax-dodging and the need for the taxation of all local property at the same rates. Through an intensive educational campaign, supported by the local newspapers, city officials exposed many corporations as benefiting from preferential treatment at the expense of other taxpayers. To redress this situation, the local board of assessors increased valuations over $1 million on ten corporations, including members of the beef, sugar, oil, and tobacco trusts.[21] Further revenues were obtained by assessing all corporation trust companies upon the basis of the actual amount of their property rather than on the par value of their stock as in previous years.[22] By 1903 the Fagan administration had successfully increased assessments on delinquent corporations by over $2.5 million.

Progress towards the elimination of corporate tax-dodging inevitably led Jersey City's reformers to consider the fundamental problem—the maldistribution of the municipal tax burden. Mayor Fagan recognized the disadvantage of laboring under a system of taxation that made the city's largest property owners, the railroads, "financially indifferent to the character of city government."[23] On several occasions the mayor advised the legislature that continued railroad tax evasion threatened the city's very existence. Yet equal taxation, the favored goal of reformers, met repeated defeat at the hands of conservative Republican legislators from South Jersey. Following a particularly unproductive legislative session early in 1904, Fagan charged that the tax reform proposals "demanded by practically unanimous sentiment in all North Jersey ... have been buried ... at the command of the railroad corporations while the interests of the people are being betrayed."

This is a condition which ... if unchecked, means the virtual control of our state ... by corporations. ... As a public official I protest against the injustice done to Jersey City. As a member of the Republican Party, I deplore its subserviency to corporate greed and injustice.[24]

The conflict over railroad taxation, though apparently a city-state confrontation, also reflected marked political and economic differences between the two sides. Recognizing that the conservative Republican legislators would remain obstructive, the Fagan administration turned to the courts in the hopes of salvaging its tax reform proposals.[25] But past experience and an examination of earlier decisions should have taught progressives that the judiciary would be reluctant to interfere in an area traditionally left to legislative initiative. As Willard Hurst has noted, "when local interests resorted to municipal licensing, regulation, or taxation, state courts showed more energy than state legislatures in resisting these thrusts of localism."[26]

Much of New Jersey's turn-of-the-century equal tax litigation stemmed from an 1886 case *(State, The Central Railroad Co. of N. J. v. State Board of Assessors, et al.)* questioning the legality of the Railroad Tax Act of 1884. The legal problem concerned the equal protection theory in the state constitution, i.e., that all property be taxed uniformly. Attorneys for the New Jersey Central Railroad and thirty-three other companies had appeared before the state supreme court to request denial of the first assessments set by the State Board of Assessors. The railroads had argued that the constitution required that all property be assessed for taxes under general laws.[27] The act of 1884 had been, in their opinion, unconstitutional; it had discriminated against both railroad and canal companies in terms of taxation and valuation.

In its decision, the supreme court adopted the arguments of the railroads' counsel holding that the legislation was unconstitutional because it segregated railroad property from other corporate franchises.[28] Attorney General John P. Stockton filed an appeal before the state's highest tribunal, the Court of Errors and Appeals.[29] While railroad attorneys reiterated their arguments about the evils of special legislation, Stockton's contention that "courts cannot annul tax laws simply because they operate unjustly" seemed to represent a partial admission of the law's discriminating intent. He reaffirmed, nonetheless, the state's authority to tax through the legislative branch.[30] In an eleven-to-one reversal the high court upheld the constitutionality of the 1884 statute. The court observed that because railroads were peculiar property, the method of taxing them deserved to be the subject of separate legislation.[31]

It was ironic that New Jersey's railroads should have reacted so vehemently against such legislation and its enforcement by the State Board of Assessors. Hindsight revealed that the roads benefited greatly from the 1884 act. The law assured them a far less onerous tax rate than that borne by other corporate and personal property. The real victims of both the legislation and the 1886 litigation were not the railroads but the cities of North Jersey. In approving the need for such special legislation, the courts had noted that there could be no objection that railroad property paid less than its fair share of municipal taxation.

By 1900 New Jersey municipal reformers were grappling with these consequences. From their vantage point the State Board of Assessors had become the railroads' guardian and buffer against competing interests. In addition, the sizable array of former state officials and ex-supreme court justices under retainer by the railroads impressed many reformers as indicative of the community of interest linking business and government. Mayor Fagan denounced the "aggregation of malign forces" operating as a "commercial unit against the public interest."[32] In fact, the relationship was far from conspiratorial. The progressives realized that judges make laws but apparently did not consider that New Jersey's justices would not make the laws reformers desired.[33]

City officials were also hampered by a public seriously divided in its attitudes and enthusiasm for equal taxation. By the turn of the century, the business community that once had welcomed railroad development as a sign of industrial growth had come to view each new track and terminal as a streak of blight that despoiled neighborhoods, reduced property values, and contributed to a rising tax rate. On the other hand, urban leaders were hard pressed to convince non-property owners that the railroads' presence was entirely detrimental. This was especially true in Jersey City, where the trade and transportation sector employed over 25,000 workers.[34] The problem was particularly acute for Mark Fagan, a Republican mayor in an overwhelmingly Democratic city. His reelection depended upon satisfying two diverse interest groups—taxpayers seeking a reduced tax rate and a working class eager for expanded social services. Since tax reform seemed to be a concern only of the middle-class, taxpaying minority, the mayor was forced to argue that basic municipal services as well as proposals for free medical care and better schools depended upon the attainment of equal taxation.

Mark Fagan's decision to seek equal taxation through legal action was neither novel nor original. Indeed, much of the litigation involving Jersey City and the railroads between 1902 and 1908 consisted of cases inherited from prior administrations. Conservative opposition in the legislature, however, forced reformers to be more active and dependent upon judicial action to redress perceived railroad transgressions. The Fagan administration was consequently much more at ease and familiar with court tactics than its predecessors and more willing to use litigation to create favorable public opinion at home. The contrast between reformer rhetoric and the harsh reality of their limited accomplishments in court is suggestive of the failure of litigation as a progressive tactic.

Jersey City and other railroad cities could ill have afforded to absorb repeated financial reversals without contesting practically every revenue question in the courts. On one occasion attorneys for the city, the Erie Railroad, and the State Board of Assessors appeared before the Court of Errors and Appeals as parties to a twenty-year-old jurisdictional dispute.

Unpaid taxes amounting to over $345,000 by 1900 had been assessed by city officials against a pier and elevator building leased but not owned by the railroad. This same property had also been assessed by the State Board of Assessors for the period 1884 to 1897. Both the city and the state asserted their right as the proper taxing authority.

Speaking for the court, Justice Charles Garrison warned that if all property used for railroad purposes but not owned by them were to be eliminated from state taxation and subjected to local assessment, the consequences would be disastrous for New Jersey's economy. In this instance, as on many occasions, critics of the railroads disputed the proper basis of taxation but never once contested the indispensability of the railroads' contributions to economic growth.[35] Overruling a lower court's decision, Justice Garrison held that all property in possession of a railroad company and used for its purposes was taxable by the state alone.[36] This interpretation was later broadened to include all property held for "fairly anticipated" railroad purposes.[37] The court's decision, which appeared contrary to the 1884 statute's description of second-class property, further narrowed local taxing authority.

Though clarifying the larger jurisdictional question, the court's opinion left unpaid the sum of $345,000 in back taxes ordered due to Jersey City in 1898 by order of a special legislative committee. The Erie Railroad's threat to continue litigation over this point prompted the Fagan administration to settle out of court. The railroad agreed to pay all claims owed the city between 1884 and 1897 plus an additional 2 percent in interest. As a result of the settlement, local authorities received over $265,000 in back taxes.

The Erie tax compromise proved to be a major campaign issue during Mayor Fagan's bid for reelection in 1903. The Democrats denounced the settlement as a "wholly unjustifiable and illegal action" that deprived the city of over $100,000 in interest and penalties for the years 1897 to 1902. In an interesting juxtaposition of fact and fiction, critics charged that the Fagan administration had demonstrated "outrageous favoritism" toward the railroad corporation while exacting every cent of penalty from delinquent homeowners.[38] In fact, city assessors had been instructed to undervalue private property in order to force a greater burden upon the railroads. Despite such unfounded accusations, Mark Fagan was reelected by a comfortable margin. His victory was due largely to the sweeping majorities he received from voters in the city's residential wards, whose support reflected the effect of a half-dollar reduction in the 1903 tax rate.[39]

The Fagan administration's much publicized commitment to equal taxation should more accurately be portrayed as part of a struggle to shift the tax burden from homeowners onto railroad corporations. City officials were fond of maintaining that the full local taxation of railroad-owned property (valued at over $50 million in 1904) would triple municipal revenue and reduce the tax rate by $10 per thousand ratables. The railroads alleged that the city's professed interest in equal taxation was farcical since some private property escaped taxation entirely and non-railroad real estate was never assessed beyond 60-70 percent of actual value. They noted that local property was assessed at a value of $9,796 per acre in 1903, while second-class railroad property was assessed at $27,505 per acre. Thus, although the railroads were assessed at a lower rate of taxation ($15 per thousand ratables on second-class property in 1904, as opposed to $27.50 for homeowners), their locally taxable property was often forced to bear a disproportionate share of the tax burden.[40] This situation contributed to a circle of inequities with neither side willing to concede.

The progressives' pursuit of tax equalization through legal action stemmed in part from the almost complete absence of cooperation accorded reformers by the state legislature. The loose aggregation of Republican reformers collectively known as the "New Idea" movement lacked the political influence, voter support, and financial backing to sustain legislative majorities. Their periodic campaigns for tax reform depended upon transient, politically diverse coalitions that quickly dissolved once legislative compromises were enacted.

Two such measures were passed during the 1905 and 1906 legislative sessions. The Duffield Act, introduced by the Republican Assembly caucus with railroad approval, provided for the taxation of second-class property at full local rates. In practical terms, this meant that the railroads would be taxed at the rate of $27.50 per thousand ratables (instead of at the previous rate of $15) on approximately $22 million worth of property in Jersey City.[41] The Republican-controlled State Senate managed to negate much of the gains of this bill by coupling its passage with a maximum tax act that would limit the Jersey City tax rate to $17 per thousand ratables unless the voters approved a tax increase.[42] In criticizing the Duffield Act as a "halfway measure," Mayor Fagan called for a "continued and persistent fight" to obtain the full local taxation of main stem property. "Nothing short," he declared, "will satisfy the demands of justice."[43]

Those demands appeared to reach fruition in 1906 with passage of the Perkins Act.[44] This measure taxed all railroad-owned main stem, franchises, and personal property at the average tax rate of the state ($18 per thousand ratables) rather than at the previous $5. The revenue obtained from such taxation could only be distributed among the various

counties for school purposes. Equal-tax advocates had supported a measure that would have divided the revenue among participating municipalities for general purposes. In an effort to offset even this minimal
triumph, the Republican organization pushed through the Avis Tax Act,
which authorized county tax boards to assess all property at true value.[45]
The increased assessments of personal property did not adversely affect
the railroads, since their valuations remained in the hands of the State
Board of Assessors. Consequently, the railroads benefited from the reduced tax rate created by the true valuation of nonrailroad property.

Two aspects of the 1905/1906 legislative sessions deserve comment.
Though the legislation was the result of political and economic bargaining, it was the railroads who established the parameters of discussion
and then set the limits of compromise. Secondly, the minimal success
achieved by reformers can be attributed to the issue-oriented campaign
conducted by progressives. The movement's catalyst remained Mark
Fagan, whose reelection in 1905 was recognized as an acknowledgment
of his leadership in the struggle. Commending the mayor as "the first
man with courage enough to make the people's cause his own," the
Newark News concluded that he was the statewide leader in the fight
against "corporate arrogance."[46] Unfortunately, reformers found it
exceedingly difficult to sustain public interest in tax reform. As one
scholar has observed, "all the passion went toward the passage of these
laws. After enactment, passion died down."[47]

Although the legislators were the real culprits in obstructing equal
taxation, progressives considered the courts a more immediate vehicle
for social change. City officials often utilized time-consuming litigation
to cripple legislation when they were unable to alter the composition
of the legislature or effect a change in the overly protective policy of the
State Board of Assessors. The single most important source of litigation
involving both Jersey City and the railroads continued to be the determination of the proper taxing authority. The Fagan administration considered
the token assessments of the State Board of Assessors to be an unrealistic
appraisal of railroad valuation. In *Jersey City* v. *State Board of Assessors
and United New Jersey Railroad and Canal Co.* (1906), Corporation
Counsel George Record contended that a recent decision by the state
board had improperly classified as main stem three pieces of railroad
property that deserved to be taxed by local authorities. The court held
that the determination of a railroad line as main stem depended upon its
use at the time of assessment. After examining the three disputed lines,
the justices decided that each was used for freight purposes and did not
fall within the main stem category. The State Board of Assessors was ordered to reclassify the disputed property.[48] This meant increased tax

revenue for Jersey City, although the state continued to administer the assessment, collect the taxes, and distribute the city's local share. Though representing a revenue gain, the decision was simply a holding action against the absorption of municipal property into the main stem category, which, despite the Perkins Act, still remained exempt from full local taxation.[49]

The city's triumph proved to be short-lived. Thirteen months after the supreme court's decisions in the United New Jersey and Lehigh Valley cases, Attorney General Robert H. McCarter appealed the lower court's judgment to the Court of Errors and Appeals.[50] Speaking for the court, Justice John F. Fort held that the classification of railroad property was the sole responsibility of the State Board of Assessors and concluded that the original main stem assessment applied, regardless of whether the company operated a passenger or freight business.[51]

Although the courts persisted in broadly construing the class of state-protected railroad property, it would be incorrect to characterize the bench's actions as constituting judicial interference or obstruction. Beginning with the 1886 litigation over the Railroad Tax Act, the courts had demonstrated a willingness to follow legislative initiative in the area of railroad taxation. It was gradually becoming apparent to contemporaries that the courts were unwilling to develop, perhaps incapable of developing, rules for the complex relationships created by industrial capitalism. The only real consistency in the courts' decisions was in meeting the immediate needs of the broadest possible market areas. An increasing number of jurists recognized that the legislature represented "the more direct and accurate expression of the general will."[52] Unlike national reformers, who were occasionally able to secure desired legislation (though the United States Supreme Court might declare such laws unconstitutional), New Jersey's progressives lost out in both the courts and legislature.

The state judiciary's willingness to follow legislative initiative did not reflect an abandonment of judicial prerogative, but simply represented a recognition of the regulatory powers of the newly created (1905) State Board of Equalization of Taxes.[53] The courts' ability to work within this new framework was evident in a 1907 case involving Jersey City with the New York and Jersey Railroad Company. The focus of the dispute was a 1905 decision by the local tax board assessing the railroad's property at $815,000. The carrier appealed the city's action to the Board of Equalization, contending that the property was being used for railroad purposes. In reducing the assessment to $43,000 the board held the city's estimate erroneous because it was based upon a third-class evaluation of the disputed property. The Fagan administration appealed the ruling to the state supreme court.

The court held that since the property was part of the route of the Hudson Tunnel Railroad, it fulfilled the requirements of property being used for railroad purposes. The order of the Board of Equalization of Taxes was upheld.[54] In accepting the new regulatory apparatus the state courts again demonstrated deference to legislative and administrative authority, as well as a noticeable pro-railroad attitude.[55]

Mark Fagan's electoral defeat in 1907 brought a premature conclusion to the pursuit of equal taxation. His attacks on the Republican establishment, participation in the equal tax crusade, and creation of a separate reform machine had contributed to his estrangement from the regular party organization. The mayor was also attacked by the city's religious community for failing to enforce saloon closing laws and by disillusioned homeowners over the failure of tax reform to create a more equitable distribution of wealth. Although the Perkins and Duffield acts had enabled the Fagan administration to lower the tax rate from $24.90 per thousand ratables in 1906 to $16.08 in 1907, homeowners did not actually benefit from this apparent decrease. For, as the Hudson County Tax Board proceeded to assess all property at full value, ratables in Jersey City rose from $168 million in 1906 to $267 million in 1907, an increase of 58.3 percent. As a result of the rise in individual valuations, the actual tax rate rose 71¢ to $25.61.[56]

The tax reform litigation was not, of course, an isolated occurrence and must be viewed as but one aspect of the Fagan administration's primary concern for economic change. The struggle for equal taxation in the courts paralleled the progressives' campaign in the legislature for the assessment of all property at full local rates. At the height of their mass-based campaign for tax reform, Jersey City's reformers initiated litigation designed to achieve the same purpose. One must not assume, however, that all of the municipally initiated lawsuits were introduced for the purpose of protecting the public interest; some were aimed primarily at defending the city's interest, by undermining legislation favorable to market areas served by the railroads. Moreover, although railroad property was assessed at true value, the local tax board tended to undervalue the property of homeowners by as much as 40 percent. The inability of insurgents to translate local-level support into judicial approval suggests that "progressive" may have been a term used to conceal less than admirable objectives.[57] Urban reformers did not emerge from the equal tax litigation entirely blameless. As Lawrence M. Friedman has observed, "railroad tracks once laid could not run away, and the temptation was to get all one could from a captive giant."[58]

Reformers' success in shaping contemporary public opinion and the subsequent historical debate was rarely matched by equal effectiveness in the courts. The ultimate failure of litigation as a reform tactic is suggestive of how the anti-railroad sentiment avowed by progressives assumed far more meager form in action. Inconsistent judicial decisions reflected the blurring of authority and confusion characteristic of early twentieth-century policy formation. The segmentation of political and economic power among many hostile, competing groups rendered it impossible for the courts to do more than preserve existing divisions. Historians have yét to explain adequately the degree of ambivalence that pervaded public attitudes toward the railroad industry. In part, this deficiency has stemmed from the failure to perceive the many different "publics" whose interests were involved. Evidence portraying the railroads in sharply dichotomous stereotypes as either "engines of salvation" or "smoking black devils" has further obscured the issues. The classic conception of reform, which sees popular government confronting the power of corrupt corporations and special interests, seems to be at variance with the Jersey City experience. If urban reform was indeed a give-and-take process, then neither the city nor the railroads were as angelic or as villainous as they were portrayed to be.

MICHAEL H. EBNER and EUGENE M. TOBIN

A BIBLIOGRAPHIC GUIDE TO SELECTED
RECENT LITERATURE

What follows is not a full-scale comprehensive bibliography but a guide to the most recent pertinent historical literature on urban progressive reform. Every serious student of the period will want to consult the exemplary documentation provided in Ernest S. Griffith, *A History of American City Government: The Progressive Years and Their Aftermath, 1900-1920* (New York: Praeger for the National Municipal League, 1974). A volume in a distinguished series dating back to 1937 and still to be completed, it is superbly grounded in primary and secondary literature, published as well as unpublished.

ANTECEDENTS OF URBAN PROGRESSIVISM

Instrumental to understanding urban affairs in the early twentieth century are several recent studies on the origins of municipal government and the issues that public officials confronted as it evolved. Foremost among these, because it delves into the English roots of local government and offers a convincing interpretation of the changing nature of political authority in the cities, is Jon C. Teaford, *The Municipal Revolution in America: Origins of Modern Urban Government, 1650-1825* (Chicago: University of Chicago Press, 1975). Judith Diamondstone, "Philadelphia's Municipal Corporation, 1701-1776," *Pennsylvania Magazine of History and Biography,* 90:2 (April, 1966), 183-201, is a model case study. The centralization of local governmental authority in Boston resulting from the charter of 1821 is the focus of Milton Kotler, "The Disappearance of Municipal Liberty," *Politics and Society,* 3:1 (Fall, 1972), 83-116, and

Robert McCaughey, "From Town into City: Boston in the 1820s," *Political Science Quarterly,* 88:2 (June, 1973), 191-213. Edward Pessen, "Who Governed the Nation's Cities in the 'Era of the Common Man'?" *Political Science Quarterly,* 87:4 (December, 1972), 591-614, and M. J. Heale, "From City Fathers to Social Critics: Humanitarianism and Government in New York, 1790-1860," *Journal of American History,* 63:1 (June, 1976), 21-41, although narrowly focused on leadership elites, add critical chapters—of which many more are needed—to the early history of municipalism.

The post-Civil War situation is best reviewed in Ernest S. Griffith, *A History of American City Government: The Conspicuous Failure, 1870-1900* (New York: Praeger for the National Municipal League, 1974), although it lacks some of the sharp insights of the 1900-1920 sequel. Highly suggestive and conceptually innovative is Seymour J. Mandelbaum, *Boss Tweed's New York* (New York: John Wiley and Sons, Inc., 1965); also informative is Alexander B. Callow, Jr., *The Tweed Ring* (New York: Oxford University Press, 1966). That many of the reforms generally associated with the Progressive Era actually originated in the "Gilded Age" is the thesis of Herbert G. Gutman, "Class, Status, and the Gilded Age Radical: A Reconsideration, The Case of a New Jersey Socialist," in *Many Pasts: Readings in American Social History,* eds. Herbert G. Gutman and Gregory S. Kealey, vol. 2 (Englewood Cliffs: Prentice-Hall, 1973), 125-151. A significant case study by a former student of Gutman is Douglas V. Shaw, "The Politics of Nativism: Jersey City's 1871 Charter Commission," in *Urban New Jersey Since 1870,* ed. William C. Wright (Trenton: New Jersey Historical Commission, 1975), 84-95. Vincent J. Falzone, "Terence V. Powderly: Politician and Progressive Mayor of Scranton, 1878-1884," *Pennsylvania History,* 41:3 (July 1974), 289-310, should also be consulted. Finally, a full-scale analysis of the late nineteenth-century origins of reform that must be studied by every careful student is David P. Thelen, *The New Citizenship: Origins of Progressivism in Wisconsin, 1885-1900* (Columbia, Mo.: University of Missouri Press, 1972).

PROGRESSIVE HISTORIOGRAPHY

Richard Hofstadter's *The Age of Reform: From Bryan to F. D. R.* (New York: Alfred A. Knopf, 1955), remains the essential beginning for understanding progressivism. The most recent historiographical essays are Robert H. Wiebe, "The Progressive Years, 1900-1917," in *The Reinterpretation of American History and Culture,* eds. William H. Cartwright and Richard L. Watson, Jr. (Washington, D. C.: National Council for the Social Studies, 1973), 425–442; William G. Anderson, "Progressivism: An Historiographical Essay," *History Teacher*, 6:3 (May, 1973), 427–452; and David M. Kennedy, "Overview: The Progressive Era," *The Historian*, 37:3 (May, 1975), 453–468. A valuable collection of original essays is Lewis L. Gould, ed., *The Progressive Era* (Syracuse: Syracuse University Press, 1974), which includes an illuminating contribution by Melvin G. Holli entitled "Urban Reform in the Progressive Era," (pp. 133–152). Re-surveying the period with an eye toward reinterpretation and synthesis are Otis L. Graham, Jr., *The Great Campaigns: Reform and War in America, 1900-1928* (Englewood Cliffs: Prentice-Hall, 1971); Arthur A. Ekirch, Jr., *Progressivism in America: A Study of the Era from Theodore Roosevelt to Woodrow Wilson* (New York: New Viewpoints, 1974); and William L. O'Neill, *The Progressive Years: America Comes of Age* (New York: Dodd, Mead and Company, 1975). An up-to-date compendium providing the historiographic context in a "problems and issues" format is Arthur Mann, ed., *The Progressive Era: Major Issues of Interpretation*, 2d ed. (Hinsdale: The Dryden Press, 1975). Somewhat older but nevertheless useful is the bibliographic compilation by Arthur S. Link and William M. Leary, Jr., *The Progressive Era and the Great War, 1896-1920* (New York: Appleton-Century-Crofts, 1969).

CLASS, POLITICS, AND REFORM

A widely anthologized article correcting Hofstadter's contention that working-class ethnics were dominated by political "bosses" and hence opposed to reform is J. Joseph Huthmacher, "Urban Liberalism and the Age of Reform," *Mississippi Valley Historical Review*, 49:2 (September, 1962), 231-241. A full-scale analysis of the working-class liberal as reformer is Huthmacher's *Senator Robert F. Wagner and the Rise of Urban Liberalism* (New York: Atheneum, 1968). Further elaborating on this thesis is a study of seven northeastern and middle-western states by John D. Buenker, *Urban Liberalism and Progressive Reform* (New York: Charles Scribner's Sons, 1973), originally a doctoral dissertation directed by Huthmacher; in addition, Buenker has contributed almost twenty articles to scholarly journals since 1968 documenting the role of urban ethnic-stock politicians. Nancy J. Weiss, *Charles Francis Murphy, 1858-1924: Respectability and Responsibility in Tammany Politics* (Northampton: Smith College, 1968), is a good case study. Assaying emergent historiographic trends is David R. Colburn and George E. Pozzetta, "Bosses and Machines: Changing Interpretations in American History," *History Teacher*, 9:3 (May, 1976), 445–464.

Ethnic-stock voters, of course, represented only one segment of continually shifting reform coalitions. In a highly influential article, "The Politics of Reform in Municipal Government in the Progressive Era," *Pacific Northwest Quarterly* 55:4 (October, 1964), 157-169, Samuel P. Hays contends that the motives of municipal charter reformers included centralization of political authority to curb the ascendant electoral power of ethnic groups. Lloyd Sponholtz, "The Initiative and Referendum: Direct Democracy in Perspective, 1898-1920," *American Studies,* 14:2 (Fall, 1973), 43-64, raises specific questions about the rhetoric espoused by reformers; however, Otis A. Pease, "Urban Reformers in the Progressive Era: A Reassessment," *Pacific Northwest Quarterly,* 62:2 (April, 1971), 49-58, questions aspects of this social-control thesis.

Richard M. Bernard and Bradley R. Rice, "Political Environment and the Adoption of Progressive Municipal Reform," *Journal of Urban History,* 1:2 (February, 1975), 149-174, is a quantitative analysis measuring the predictability of electoral support based on such variables as population composition, date of incorporation, home ownership, region, etc. Case studies include Michael H. Ebner, "Socialism and Progressive Political Reform: The 1911 Change of Government in Passaic," in *Socialism and the Cities,* ed. Bruce M. Stave (Port Washington, N. Y.: Kennikat Press, 1975), 116-140; Geoffrey W. Clark, "The Progressives v. the Political Machine in Hoboken, 1911-1915," in *Hoboken: A Collection of Essays,* eds. Edward Halsey Foster and Geoffrey W. Clark (New York: Irvington Publishers, Inc., 1976), 63-79; Carl V. Harris, "Reforms in Governmental Control of Negroes in Birmingham, Alabama, 1890-1920," *Journal of Southern History,* 38:4 (November, 1972), 567-600; Paul E. Isaac, "Municipal Reform in Beaumont, Texas, 1902-1909," *Southwestern Historical Quarterly,* 78:4 (April, 1975), 409-430; Anthony R. Travis, "Mayor George Ellis: Grand Rapids Political Boss and Progressive Reformer," *Michigan History,* 58:2 (Summer, 1974), 101-130; and Mark S. Foster, "Frank Hague of Jersey City: 'The Boss' as Reformer," *New Jersey History,* 86:2 (Summer, 1968), 106-117.

ELECTORAL STUDIES

While studies of voting behavior in the nineteenth century have flourished, a great deal of research still is needed on cities and metropolitan regions during the early twentieth century. Carl N. Degler, "American Political Parties and the Rise of the City: An Interpretation," *Journal of American History,* 51:1 (June, 1964), 41-59, remains a touchstone. Critical conceptual issues are developed by Samuel P. Hays in two articles ("The Social Analysis of American Political History, 1880-1920," *Political*

Science Quarterly, 80:3 [September, 1965], 373-394, and "The Changing Political Structure of the City in Industrial America," *Journal of Urban History*, 1:1 [November, 1974], 6-38) that surely are influencing current research. John M. Allswang, *A House for All Peoples: Ethnic Politics in Chicago, 1890-1936* (Lexington: University Press of Kentucky, 1971), originally a Hays dissertation based largely on electoral data, has important implications for studying progressivism. Far less successful conceptually and methodologically, but also relying on voting statistics, is Edward R. Kantowicz, *Polish-American Politics in Chicago, 1888-1940* (Chicago: University of Chicago Press, 1975).

Full-length studies on aspects of urban politics that devote varying degrees of attention to electoral behavior include Irwin Yellowitz, *Labor and the Progressive Movement in New York State, 1897-1916* (Ithaca: Cornell University Press, 1965); James B. Crooks, *Politics and Progress: The Rise of Urban Progressivism in Baltimore, 1895-1911* (Baton Rouge: Louisiana State University Press, 1968); Zane L. Miller, *Boss Cox's Cincinnati: Urbanization in the Progressive Era* (New York: Oxford University Press, 1968); and Joel A. Tarr, *A Study in Boss Politics: William Lorimer of Chicago* (Urbana: University of Illinois Press, 1971).

Roger E. Wyman, "Middle-Class Voters and Progressive Reform: The Conflict of Class and Culture," *American Political Science Review*, 68:2 (June, 1974), 488-504, commands scrutiny because of its methodological rigor, its multicity treatment of Wisconsin, and its startling conclusion. Narrower in focus but also examining several urban communities within single states are Joseph F. Mahoney, "Woman Suffrage and the Urban Masses," *New Jersey History*, 87:3 (Autumn, 1969), 151-172; Warren E. Stickle III, "Edward I. Edwards and the Urban Coalition of 1919," *New Jersey History*, 90:2 (Summer, 1972), 83-96; and Melvin G. Holli, "Mayor Pingree Campaigns for the Governorship," *Michigan History*, 57:2 (Summer, 1973), 151-173. Two excellent case studies of voting in specific cities are Louise Rickard, "The Politics of Reform in Omaha, 1918-1921," *Nebraska History*, 53:4 (Winter, 1972), 419-445, and Anthony R. Travis, "Mayor George Ellis: Grand Rapids Political Boss and Progressive Reformer," *Michigan History*, 58:2 (Summer, 1974), 101-130.

Four studies examine the nexus of labor and progressivism in California: Alexander Saxton, "San Francisco Labor and the Populist-Progressive Insurgencies," *Pacific Historical Review*, 34:4 (November, 1965), 421-438; Michael P. Rogin, "Progressives and the California Electorate," *Journal of American History*, 55:2 (September, 1968), 297-314; John L. Shover, "The Progressives and the Working Class Vote in California," *Labor History*, 10:4 (Fall, 1969), 584-601; and Mary Ann Mason Burki, "The California Progressives: Labor's Point of View,"

Labor History, 17:1 (Winter, 1976), 24-37; the latter is especially important in reexamining the actual dynamics of political reform and organized labor.

POLITICS AND CITY-BUILDING

Many urban historians ignore systematic analysis of political forces, concentrating instead on questions of structure and growth. Eric E. Lampard, "The Dimensions of Urban History: A Footnote to the 'Urban Crisis,'" *Pacific Historical Review,* 39:3 (August, 1970), 261-278 (esp. 273), has clearly acknowledged this deficiency and subsequently called for its rectification.* Important issues laden with implications for the Progressive Era's political analysts are raised in Kenneth T. Jackson, "Metropolitan Government Versus Political Autonomy: Politics on the Crabgrass Frontier," in *Cities in American History,* eds. Kenneth T. Jackson and Stanley K. Schultz (New York: Alfred A. Knopf, 1972), 442-462. Case studies anchored in the period that pursue themes relevant to those suggested by Jackson include two articles by Michael P. McCarthy: "'Suburban Power': A Footnote on Cleveland in the Tom Johnson Years," *Northwest Ohio Quarterly,* 45:1 (Winter, 1972-1973), 21-27, and "Prelude to Armageddon: Charles E. Merriam and the Chicago Mayoral Campaign of 1911," *Journal of the Illinois State Historical Society,* 67:5 (November, 1974), 505-518; and Carl V. Harris, "Annexation Struggles and Political Power in Birmingham, Alabama, 1890-1910," *Alabama Review,* 27:3 (July, 1974), 163-184. Portions of book-length studies focusing on this issue include chapter 10 of Robert M. Fogelson, *The Fragmented Metropolis: Los Angeles, 1850-1930* (Cambridge: MIT Press, 1967), and chapter 8 of Howard P. Chudacoff, *Mobile Americans: Residential and Social Mobility in Omaha, 1880-1920* (New York: Oxford University Press, 1972).

The corollary issue of urban growth spawning organizational problems with political ramifications yields a rich literature. Part 3 of Sam Bass Warner, Jr., *The Private City: Philadelphia in Three Periods of Its Growth* (Philadelphia: University of Pennsylvania Press, 1968), and Samuel P. Hays, "The Development of Pittsburgh as a Social Order," *Western Pennsylvania Historical Magazine,* 57:4 (October, 1974), 431-448, are broad-gauged overviews of single cities, of which more are needed. Studies of particular municipal "problems" are legion:

---

*Bruce M. Stave, "A Conversation with Eric E. Lampard," *Journal of Urban History,* 1:4 (August, 1975), 462f.

Finance: J. Rogers Hollingsworth and Ellen Jane Hollingsworth, "Expenditures in American Cities," in *The Dimensions of Quantitative Research in History,* ed. William O. Aydelotte et al. (Princeton: Princeton University Press, 1972), 347-389; and C. K. Yearley, *The Money Machines: The Breakdown and Reform of Governmental and Party Finance in the North, 1860-1920* (Albany: State University of New York Press, 1970), esp. 193-250.

Health: C. Kevin McShane, "The 1918 Kansas City Influenza Epidemic," *Missouri Historical Review,* 63:1 (October, 1968), 55-70; Philip A. Kalisch, "The Black Death in Chinatown: Plague and Politics in San Francisco, 1900-1904," *Arizona and the West,* 14:2 (Summer, 1972), 113-136; John Duffy, *A History of Public Health in New York City, 1866-1966* (New York: Russell Sage Foundation, 1974), esp. 238-280; and Stuart Galishoff, *Safeguarding the Public Health: Newark, 1895-1918* (Westport, Conn: Greenwood Press, 1975).

Environment: Mel Scott, *American City Planning since 1890* (Berkeley: University of California Press, 1971), 1-182; Thomas S. Hines, *Burnham of Chicago, Architect and Planner,* (New York: Oxford University Press, 1974); Raymond A. Mohl and Neil Betten, "The Failure of Industrial City Planning: Gary, Indiana, 1906-1910," *Journal of the American Institute of Planners,* 38:4 (July, 1972), 621-640; Martin V. Melosi, " 'Out of Sight, Out of Mind:' The Environment and Municipal Refuse, 1860-1920," *The Historian,* 35:4 (August, 1973), 621-640; Thomas S. Hines, "The Paradox of Progressive Architecture: Urban Planning and Public Building in Tom Johnson's Cleveland," *American Quarterly,* 35:4 (October, 1973), 426-448; Robert Dale Grinder, "The War Against St. Louis's Smoke: 1891-1924," *Missouri Historical Review,* 69:2 (January, 1975), 191-205; Roland M. Smith, "The Politics of Pittsburgh Flood Control: 1908-1936," *Pennsylvania History,* 42:1 (January, 1975), 5-24; and Joel A. Tarr, "From City to Farm: Urban Wastes and the American Farmer," *Agricultural History,* 49:4 (October, 1975), 598-612; and Jon A. Peterson, "The City Beautiful Movement: Forgotten Origins and Lost Meanings," *Journal of Urban History,* 2:4 (August, 1976), 415-434.

Public Safety: James F. Richardson, *Urban Police in the United States* (Port Washington, N. Y.: Kennikat Press, 1974), esp. 62-85; Eugene J. Watts, "The Police in Atlanta, 1890-1905," *Journal of Southern History,* 39:2 (May, 1973), 165-182; Ronald M. Zarychta, "Municipal Reorganization: The Pittsburgh Fire Department as a Case Study," *Western Pennsylvania Historical Magazine,* 58:4 (October, 1975), 471-486; and two articles by Mark H. Haller, "Police Reform in Chicago," *American*

Behavioral Scientist, 13:5-6 (May-June and July-August, 1970), 649-666, and "Historical Roots of Police Behavior: Chicago, 1890-1925," *Law and Society Review,* 10:2 (Winter, 1976), 303-324.

Transportation: Two essays by Glen E. Holt must be read by all students of this subject: "The Changing Perception of Urban Pathology: An Essay on the Development of Mass Transit in the United States," in *Cities in American History,* eds. Kenneth T. Jackson and Stanley K. Schultz (New York: Alfred A. Knopf, 1972), 324-343, and "Urban Mass Transit History: Where We Have Gone and Where We Are Going," in *The National Archives and Urban Research,* National Archives Conferences, vol. 6, ed. Jerome Finster (Athens: Ohio Univeristy Press, 1974), 81-105. Important full-length studies are Sam Bass Warner, Jr., *Streetcar Suburbs: The Process of Growth in Boston, 1870-1900* (Cambridge: Harvard University Press, 1962), and Clay McShane, *Technology and Reform: Street Railways and the Growth of Milwaukee, 1887-1900* (Madison: State Historical Society of Wisconsin, 1974), which can be supplemented with Oliver Zunz, "Technology and Society in an Urban Environment: The Case of the Third Avenue Elevated Railway," *Journal of Interdisciplinary History,* 3:1 (Summer, 1972), 87-102. An intriguing study (especially for onetime collectors of baseball cards) is Steven A. Reiss, "The Baseball Magnates and Urban Politics in the Progressive Era: 1895-1920," *Journal of Sport History,* 1:1 (Spring, 1974), 41-61, which deals in part with the relationship between stadium construction and mass transit. The incipient automotive aspect of the subject is examined in James J. Flink, *America Adopts the Automobile, 1895-1910* (Cambridge: MIT Press, 1970), 124-128; John B. Rae, *The Road and the Car in American Life* (Cambridge: MIT Press, 1971), 197-214; and Howard L. Preston, "The Automobile Business in Atlanta, 1909-1920: A Symbol of 'New South' Prosperity," *Georgia Historical Quarterly,* 58:2 (Summer, 1974), 262-277.

Naturally, the social dimension of the politics of city-building also must be scrutinized. Especially important, despite their nonurban orientations, in raising critical questions about the delicate issue of reform "motivation" are Don S. Kirschner, "The Ambiguous Legacy: Social Justice and Social Control in the Progressive Era," *Historical Reflections,* 2:1 (Summer, 1975), 69-88; Marvin E. Gettleman, "Philanthropy as social control in late nineteenth-century America: Some Hypotheses and Data on the Rise of Social Work," *Societas,* 5:1 (Winter, 1975), 49-60; and William A. Muraskin, "The Social-Control Theory in American History: A Critique," *Journal of Social History,* 9:4 (Summer, 1976),

559-569. Otis A. Pease, "Urban Reformers in the Progressive Era: A Reassessment," *Pacific Northwest Quarterly*, 62:2 (April, 1971), 49-58, asks some interesting questions on the subject, while a model case study is presented in Eugene M. Tobin, "The Progressive as Humanitarian: Jersey City's Search for Social Justice, 1890-1917," *New Jersey History*, 93:3-4 (Autumn-Winter, 1975), 77-98. Again, studies on specific social problems are abundant.

Race: Full-scale organizational studies that focus, at least in part, on the plight of urban blacks are Charles Flint Kellogg, *N. A. A. C. P.: A History of the National Association for the Advancement of Colored People*, vol. 1, *1909-1920* (Baltimore: Johns Hopkins Press, 1967); Arvarh E. Strickland, *History of the Chicago Urban League* (Urbana: University of Illinois Press, 1966); and Nancy J. Weiss, *The National Urban League, 1910-1940* (New York: Oxford University Press, 1974). Book-length case studies of cities, none of them specifically dwelling on progressivism but all necessarily touching upon the issue, should also be referred to—Seth M. Scheiner, *Negro Mecca: A History of the Negro in New York City, 1865-1920* (New York: New York University Press, 1965); Allan H. Spear, *Black Chicago: The Making of a Negro Ghetto, 1890-1920* (Chicago: University of Chicago Press, 1967); Gilbert Osofsky, *Harlem: The Making of a Ghetto: Negro New York, 1890-1930* (New York: Harper and Row, 1966); Constance McLaughlin Green, *The Secret City: A History of Race Relations in the Nation's Capital* (Princeton: Princeton University Press, 1967); and Kenneth L. Kusmer, *A Ghetto Takes Shape: Black Cleveland, 1870-1930* (Urbana: University of Illinois Press, 1975). Another dimension of the issue is the subject of Jack Temple Kirby's *Darkness at the Dawning: Race and Reform in the Progressive South* (Philadelphia: J. B. Lippincott Company, 1972).

Article-length case studies on race include two by August Meier and Elliot Rudwick, "Early Boycotts of Segregated Schools: The East Orange, New Jersey, Experience, 1899-1906," *History of Education Quarterly*, 7:1 (Spring, 1967), 22-36, and "The Boycott Movement Against Jim Crow Streetcars in the South, 1900-1906," *Journal of American History*, 55:4 (March, 1969), 756-775; Michael H. Ebner, "Mrs. Miller and 'The Paterson Show': A 1911 Defeat for Racial Discrimination," *New Jersey History*, 86:2 (Summer, 1968), 88-92; Charles Crowe, "Racial Violence and Social Reform—Origins of the Atlanta Riot of 1906," *Journal of Negro History*, 53:3 (July, 1968), 234-256; Donald H. Bragaw, "Status of Negroes in the Progressive Era: Pensacola, 1896-1920," *Florida Historical Quarterly*, 51:3 (January, 1973), 281-302; Neil Betten and Raymond A. Mohl, "The Evolution of Racism in an Industrial City,

1906-1940: A Case Study of Gary, Indiana," *Journal of Negro History*, 59:1 (January, 1974), 51-65; Carol E. Hoffecker, "The Politics of Exclusion: Blacks in Late Nineteenth-Century Wilmington, Delaware," *Delaware History*, 16:1 (April, 1974), 60-72; and Edward N. Akin, "When a Minority Becomes the Majority: Blacks in Jacksonville Politics, 1887-1907," *Florida Historical Quarterly*, 53:2 (October, 1974), 123-145.

Education: Preeminent book-length studies are David B. Tyack, *The One Best System: A History of American Urban Education* (Cambridge: Harvard University Press, 1974), and Lawrence A. Cremin, *The Transformation of the School: Progressivism in American Education, 1876-1957* (New York: Alfred A. Knopf, 1961), both of which devote ample attention to "urbanism" and "progressivism." Joel H. Spring, *Education and the Rise of the Corporate State* (Boston: Beacon Press, 1972), and Colin Greer, *The Great School Legend: A Revisionist Interpretation of American Public Education* (New York: Basic Books, 1972) are interpretive analyses focusing largely on the motives of pedagogues in the Progressive Era; an antidote is Marvin Lazerson, "Revisionism and American Educational History," *Harvard Educational Review*, 43:2 (May, 1973), 269-283. Three valuable topical studies are Sol Cohen, *Progressives and Urban School Reform: The Public Education Association of New York City, 1895-1954* (New York: Bureau of Publications, Teacher's College of Columbia University, 1964); Marvin Lazerson, *Origins of the Urban School: Public Education in Massachusetts, 1870-1915* (Cambridge: Harvard University Press, 1971); Diane Ravitch, *The Great School Wars, New York City, 1805-1973* (New York: Basic Books, 1974), esp. 107-230: and Selwyn K. Troen, *The Public and the Schools: Shaping the St. Louis System, 1838-1920* (Columbia: University of Missouri Press, 1975).

Article-length case studies on aspects of urban progressivism include Raymond S. Sweeney, "Public Education in Maryland During the Progressive Era," *Maryland Historical Magazine*, 62:1 (March, 1967), 28-46; two articles by William H. Issel: "Teachers and Educational Reform During the Progressive Era: A Case Study of the Pittsburgh Teachers Association," *History of Education Quarterly*, 7:2 (Summer, 1967), 220-233, and "Modernization in Philadelphia School Reform, 1882-1905," *Pennsylvania Magazine of History and Biography*, 94:3 (July, 1970), 358-383; Sol Cohen, "The Industrial Education Movement, 1906-1917," *American Quarterly*, 20:1 (Spring, 1968), 95-110; Robert H. Wiebe, "The Social Functions of Public Education," *American Quarterly*, 21:2, part 1 (Summer, 1969), 147-164; two articles by Timothy L. Smith:

"Immigrant Social Aspirations and American Education, 1880-1930," *American Quarterly*, 21:3 (Fall, 1969), 523-543, and "Native Blacks and Foreign Whites: Varying Responses to Educational Opportunity in America, 1880-1950," *Perspectives in American History*, 6 (1972), 309-335; Elinor M. Gersman, "Progressive Reform of the St. Louis School Board, 1897," *History of Education Quarterly*, 10:1 (Spring, 1970), 3-21; Diana M. Wood, "A Case Study in Local Control of Schools: Pittsburgh, 1900-1906," *Urban Education*, 10:1 (April, 1975), 7-26; Raymond A. Mohl, "Schools, Politics, and Riots: The Gary Plan in New York City, 1914-1917," *Pedagogica Historica*, 15:1 (June, 1975), 39-72; William J. Reese, "Progressive School Reform in Toledo: 1898-1921," *Northwest Ohio Quarterly*, 47:2 (Spring, 1975), 44-59; Wayne J. Urban, "Organized Teachers and Educational Reform during the Progressive Era: 1890-1920," *History of Education Quarterly*, 16:1 (Spring, 1976), 35-52; and Maxine Seller, "The Education of Immigrant Children in Buffalo, New York, 1890-1916," *New York History*, 57:2 (April, 1976), 183-200.

Housing: The outstanding monograph is Roy Lubove, *The Progressives and the Slums: Tenement House Reform in New York City, 1900-1917* (Pittsburgh: University of Pittsburgh Press, 1962). Instructive on urban housing, writ broadly, is Richard O. Davies, "One-third of a Nation: The Dilemmas of America's Housing, 1607-1970," in *The National Archives and Urban Research*, National Archives Conferences, vol. 6, ed. Jerome Finster (Athens: Ohio University Press, 1974), 41-55. Case studies include two articles by John F. Sutherland: "Housing the Poor in the City of Homes: Philadelphia at the Turn of the Century," in *The Peoples of Philadelphia: A History of Ethnic Groups and Lower Class Life, 1790-1940*, eds. Allen F. Davis and Mark H. Haller (Philadelphia: Temple University Press, 1973), 175-202, and "The Origins of Philadelphia's Octavia Hill Association: Social Reform in the 'Contented City,' " *Pennsylvania Magazine of History and Biography*, 99:1 (January, 1975), 20-44; John Modell and Tamara K. Hareven, "Urbanization and the Malleable Household: An Examination of Boarding and Lodging in American Families," *Journal of Marriage and The Family*, 35:3 (August, 1973), 467-479; Paul Dubovik, "Housing in Holyoke and Its Effects on Family Life, 1860-1910," *Historical Journal of Western Massachusetts*, 4:1 (Spring, 1975), 40-50; and Roger D. Simon "Housing and Services in an Immigrant Neighborhood: Milwaukee's Ward 14," *Journal of Urban History*, 2:4 (August, 1976), 435-458.

Labor: A well-done case study (more are needed) is Melvyn Dubofsky, *When Workers Organize: New York City in the Progressive Era* (Amherst: University of Massachusetts Press, 1968). An important companion volume is Irwin Yellowitz, *Labor and the Progressive Movement in New York State, 1897-1916* (Ithaca: Cornell University Press, 1965). Other full-length studies include Gerd Korman, *Industrialization, Immigrants, and Americanizers: The View from Milwaukee, 1866-1921* (Madison: State Historical Society of Wisconsin, 1967); Henry F. Bedford, *Socialism and Workers in Massachusetts, 1886-1912* (Amherst: University of Massachusetts Press, 1967); Donald B. Cole, *Immigrant City: Lawrence, Massachusetts, 1845-1921* (Chapel Hill: University of North Carolina Press, 1963); and Norman H. Clark, *Mill Town: A Social History of Everett, Washington* (Seattle: University of Washington Press, 1970).

Topical monographs with implications for urban labor include Graham Adams, Jr., *Age of Industrial Violence, 1910-1915: The Activities and Findings of the United States Commission on Industrial Relations* (New York: Columbia University Press, 1966); James Weinstein, *The Corporate Ideal in the Liberal State, 1900-1918* (Boston: Beacon Press, 1968); Melvyn Dubofsky, *We Shall Be All: A History of the Industrial Workers of the World* (Chicago: Quadrangle Books, 1969); Walter I. Trattner, *Crusade for the Children: A History of the National Child Labor Committee and Child Labor Reform in America* (Chicago: Quadrangle Books, 1970); Paul T. Ringenbach, *Tramps and Reformers, 1873-1916: The Discovery of Unemployment in New York* (Westport, Conn.: Greenwood Press, 1973); Daniel Nelson, *Managers and Workers: Origins of the New Factory System in the United States, 1880-1920* (Madison: University of Wisconsin Press, 1975); and Stuart D. Brandes, *American Welfare Capitalism, 1880-1940* (University of Chicago Press, 1976). Outstanding because it integrates the milieus of progressive politics and working-class protest is John N. Ingham, "A Strike in the Progressive Era: McKees Rock, 1909," *Pennsylvania Magazine of History and Biography*, 90:3 (July, 1966), 353-377.

Articles not directly examining progressive politics but nonetheless significant include Moses Stambler, "The Effect of Compulsory Education and Child Labor Laws on High School Attendance in New York City, 1898-1917," *History of Education Quarterly*, 8:2 (Summer, 1968), 189-214; three studies by Robert Asher: "Business and Workers' Welfare in the Progressive Era: Workmen's Compensation Reform in Massachusetts, 1880-1910," *Business History Review*, 43:3 (Winter, 1969), 452-475, "Radicalism and Reform: State Insurance of Workmen's Compensation in Minnesota, 1910-1933," *Labor History*, 14:1 (Winter, 1973), 19-41 and "The Origins of Workers' Compensation in Minnesota," *Minnesota History*, 44:4 (Winter, 1974), 142-154; Frederick M. Heath, "Labor and the Progressive Movement in Connecticut," *Labor History*, 12:1 (Winter, 1971), 52-67; Robert F. Wesser, "Conflict and Compromise: The Workmen's Compensation Movement in New York, 1890s-1913," *Labor History*, 12:3 (Summer, 1971), 345-372; Robert Asher, "Communications," *Labor History*, 13:2 (Spring, 1972), 312-316; Thomas J. Kerr IV, "The New York Factory Investigating Commission and the Minimum Wage Movement," *Labor History*, 12:3 (Summer, 1971), 373-391; Robert J. Goldstein, "The Anarchist Scare of 1908: A Sign of Tensions in the Progressive Era," *American Studies*, 15:2 (Fall, 1974), 55-78; Rhodri Jeffreys-Jones "Violence in American History: Plug Uglies in the Progressive Era," *Perspectives in American History*, 8 (1974), 465-579; and Allis Rosenberg Wolfe, "Women, Consumerism, and the National Consumers' League in the Progressive Era, 1900-1923," *Labor History*, 16:3 (Summer, 1975), 387-392. Finally, on the California situation consult the articles by Saxton, Rogin, Shover, Burki cited under "Electoral Studies."

Social Welfare: While no full-length volume on the urban dimension of this subject is available, several excellent case studies and biographies can be consulted. Two books, neither of them specifically urban in focus, should be examined for chronological perspective: Hace Sorel Tishler, *Self-Reliance and Social Security, 1870-1917* (Port Washington, N. Y.: Kennikat Press, 1971), and Roy Lubove, *The Struggle for Social Security, 1900-1935* (Cambridge: Harvard University Press, 1965). Good topical studies include Robert H. Bremner, *From the Depths: The Discovery of Poverty in the United States* (New York: New York University Press, 1956); two books by Roy Lubove: *The Progressives and the Slums: Tenement House Reform in New York City, 1900-1917* (Pittsburgh: University of Pittsburgh Press, 1962), and *The Professional Altruist: The Emergence of Social Work as a Career, 1880-1930* (Cambridge: Harvard University Press, 1965); Allen F. Davis, *Spearheads For Reform: The Social Settlements and the Progressive Movement, 1890-1914* (New York: Oxford University Press, 1967); Anthony M. Platt, *The Child Savers: The Invention of Delinquency* (Chicago: University of Chicago Press, 1969); Walter I. Trattner, *Crusade for the Children: A History of the National Child Labor Committee and Child Labor Reform in America* (Chicago: Quadrangle Books, 1970); and Jack M. Holl, *Juvenile Reform in the Progressive Era: William R. George and the Junior Re-*

public Movement (Ithaca: Cornell University Press, 1971). Studies examining important leaders are Louise C. Wade, *Graham Taylor: Pioneer for Social Justice* (Chicago: University of Chicago Press, 1964); Walter I. Trattner, *Homer Folks: Pioneer in Social Welfare* (New York: Columbia University Press, 1968); Clarke A. Chambers, *Paul U. Kellogg and the Survey: Voices for Social Welfare and Social Justice* (Minneapolis: University of Minnesota Press, 1971); Charles Larsen, *The Good Fight: The Life and Times of Ben B. Lindsey* (Chicago: Quadrangle Books, 1972); and James B. Lane, *Jacob A. Riis and the American City* (Port Washington, N. Y.: Kennikat Press, 1974). Interpretations of Jane Addams include John C. Farrell, *Beloved Lady: A History of Jane Addams' Ideas on Reform and Peace* (Baltimore: Johns Hopkins Press, 1967); Daniel Levine, *Jane Addams and the Liberal Tradition* (Madison: State Historical Society of Wisconsin, 1971); and Allen F. Davis, *American Heroine: The Life and Legend of Jane Addams* (New York: Oxford University Press, 1973).

Article-length case studies on social welfare include Philip Gleason, "An Immigrant Group's Interest in Progressive Reform: The Case of German-American Catholics," *American Historical Review,* 88:2 (December, 1967), 367-379; Robert L. Buroker, "From Voluntary Association to Welfare State: The Illinois Immigrants' Protective League, 1908-1926," *Journal of American History,* 53:3 (December, 1971), 643-660; Jill Conway, "American Reformers and American Culture, 1870-1930," *Journal of Social History,* 5:2 (Winter, 1971-72), 164-177; Arnold Rosenberg, "The Rise of John Adams Kingsbury," *Pacific Northwest Quarterly,* 63:2 (April, 1972), 55-62; Jeremy P. Felt, "Vice Reform as a Political Technique: The Committee of Fifteen in New York, 1900-1901," *New York History,* 54:1 (January, 1973), 24-51; Kenneth L. Kusmer, "The Functions of Organized Charity in the Progressive Era: Chicago as a Case Study," *Journal of American History,* 60:3 (December, 1973), 657-678; Raymond A. Mohl and Neil Betten, "Paternalism and Pluralism: Immigrants and Social Welfare in Gary, Indiana, 1906-1940," *American Studies,* 15:1 (Spring, 1974), 5-30; John F. McClymer, "The Pittsburgh Survey, 1907-1914: Forging an Ideology in the Steel District," *Pennsylvania History,* 41:2 (April, 1974), 169-188; Peter Romanofsky," 'To Save their Souls': The Case of Dependent Jewish Children in New York City, 1905-1906," *Jewish Social Studies,* 36:3-4 (July-October, 1974), 253-261; and Eugene M. Tobin, "The Progressive as Humanitarian: Jersey City's Search for Social Justice, 1890-1917," *New Jersey History,* 93:3-4 (Autumn-Winter, 1975), 77-98.

POLITICAL LEADERSHIP

Case studies of progressive mayors provide superb opportunities for undertaking analyses of urban political leadership. The outstanding book is Melvin G. Holli, *Reform in Detroit: Hazen S. Pingree and Urban Politics* (New York: Oxford University Press, 1969). Its widely anthologized eighth chapter, entitled "Social and Structural Reform," has become a frame of reference for subsequent scholarship. Other full-length analyses include Edwin R. Lewinson, *John Purroy Mitchel: The Boy Mayor of New York* (New York: Astra Books, 1965); Jack Tager, *The Intellectual As a Reformer: Brand Whitlock of Toledo* (Cleveland: Case Western Reserve University Press, 1968); Robert M. Crunden, *A Hero In Spite of Himself: Brand Whitlock in Art, Politics, and War* (New York: Alfred A. Knopf, 1969); and Gerald Kurland, *Seth Low: The Reformer in an Urban Industrial Age* (New York: Twayne Publishers, Inc., 1971). Article-length studies are Donald W. Disbrow, "Reform in Philadelphia under Mayor Blankenburg, 1912-1916," *Pennsylvania History*, 27:4 (October, 1960), 379-396; John D. Buenker, "Edward F. Dunne: The Urban New Stock Democrat as Progressive," *Mid-America*, 50:1 (January, 1968), 3-21; two articles on Mark Fagan by Eugene M. Tobin: "The Progressive as Politician: Jersey City, 1896-1907," *New Jersey History*, 91:1 (Spring, 1973), 5-23, and "The Progressive as Single Taxer: Mark Fagan and the Jersey City Experience, 1900-1917," *American Journal of Economics and Sociology*, 33:3 (July, 1974), 287-298; Anthony R. Travis, "Mayor George Ellis: Grand Rapids Political Boss and Progressive Reformer," *Michigan History*, 58:2 (Summer, 1974), 101-130; and Martin J. Schiesl, "Progressive Reform in Los Angeles under Mayor Alexander, 1909-1913," *California Historical Quarterly*, 54:1 (Spring, 1975), 37-56.

Full-length case studies of urban reform are James B. Crooks, *Politics and Progress: The Rise of Urban Progressivism in Baltimore, 1895-1911* (Baton Rouge: Louisiana State University Press, 1968), and Philip S. Benjamin, *The Philadelphia Quakers in the Industrial Age, 1865-1920* (Philadelphia, Temple University Press, 1976). Jack Tager, "Progressives, Conservatives and the Theory of Status Revolution," *Mid-America*, 48:3 (July, 1966), 162-175, and Bonnie R. Fox [Schwartz], "The Philadelphia Progressives: A Test of the Hofstadter-Hays Thesis," *Pennsylvania History*, 34:4 (October, 1967), 372-394, offer variants on the often debated issue of "motivation." Examination of specific settings include Joel A. Tarr, "William Kent to Lincoln Steffens: Origins of Progressive Reform in Chicago," *Mid-America*, 47:1 (January, 1965), 48-57; Mansel G. Blackford, "Reform Politics in Seattle During the Progressive Era, 1902-

1916," *Pacific Northwest Quarterly,* 59:4 (October, 1968), 177-185; Richard Skolnik, "Civic Group Progressivism in New York City," *New York History,* 51:4 (July, 1970), 411-439; Elliot West, "Cleansing the Queen City: Prohibition and Urban Reform in Denver," *Arizona and the West,* 14:4 (Winter, 1972), 331-346; Michael P. McCarthy, "Politics and the Parks: Chicago Businessmen and the Recreation Movement," *Journal of the Illinois State Historical Society,* 65:2 (Summer, 1972), 158-172; J. Paul Mitchell, "Boss Speer and the City Functional: Boosters and Businessmen versus Commission Government in Denver," *Pacific Northwest Quarterly,* 63:4 (October, 1972), 155-164; Augustus Cerillo, Jr., "The Reform of Municipal Government in New York City: From Seth Low to John Purroy Mitchel," *New-York Historical Society Quarterly,* 57:1 (January, 1973), 51-71; Donald A. Ritchie, "The Gary Committee: Businessmen, Progressives, and Unemployment in New York City, 1914-1915," *New-York Historical Society Quarterly,* 57:4 (October, 1973), 327-347; Jack D. Elenbass, "The Boss of the Better Class: Henry Leland and the Detroit Citizens League, 1912-1924," *Michigan History,* 58:2 (Summer, 1974), 131-150; Lee F. Pendergrass, "The Formation of a Municipal Reform Movement: The Municipal League of Seattle," *Pacific Northwest Quarterly,* 66:1 (January, 1975), 13-25; Bradley R. Rice, "The Galveston Plan of City Government by Commission: The Birth of a Progressive Idea," *Southwestern Historical Quarterly,* 78:4 (April, 1975), 365-408; and Richard G. Miller, "Fort Worth and the Progressive Era: The Movement for Charter Revision, 1899-1907," in *Essays on Urban America,* eds. Margaret Francine Morris and Elliot West (Austin: University of Texas Press, 1975), 89-126. The important article, already cited, by Samuel P. Hays, "The Politics of Reform in Municipal Government in the Progressive Era," *Pacific Northwest Quarterly,* 55:4 (October, 1964), 157-169, deserves consultation by every serious student of urban political reform.

A full-length study on the intellectual currents of urban progressivism remains unwritten. Excellent on the origins of this ideology is John G. Sproat, *'The Best Men': Liberal Reformers in the Gilded Age* (New York: Oxford University Press, 1968). It should be followed by Jean B. Quandt, *From Small Town to the Great Community: The Social Thought of Progressive Intellectuals* (New Brunswick, N. J.: Rutgers University Press, 1970); Stanley K. Schultz, "The Morality of Politics: The Muckrakers' Vision of Democracy," *Journal of American History* 52:3 (December, 1965), 527-547; Kenneth McNaught, "American Progressives and the Great Society," *Journal of American History,* 53:3 (December, 1966), 504-520; and G. Edward White, "The Social Values of the Progressives:

Some New Perspectives," *South Atlantic Quarterly*, 70:1 (Winter, 1971), 62-76. A convincing analysis with a distinctively urban focus is Roy Lubove, "The Twentieth-Century City: The Progressive as Municipal Reformer," *Mid-America*, 41:4 (October, 1959), 195-209. The respective biographies by Jack Tager and Robert Crunden of Toledo's Brand Whitlock, cited elsewhere in this section, offer important insights regarding a progressive politician. An interesting study of a major thinker on municipal problems is Lurton W. Blassingame, "Frank J. Goodnow: Progressive Urban Reformer," *North Dakota Quarterly*, 40:2 (Summer, 1972), 22-30.

August, 1976

NOTES

INTRODUCTION

1.   Richard Hofstadter, *The Age of Reform: From Bryan to F. D. R.* (New York, 1955), has been described as "perhaps the most widely read work on modern history published in the last generation" (see J. A. Thompson, "The 'Age of Reform' in America," *The Historical Journal*, 19:1 [March, 1976], 257). Although Hofstadter's work acted as a catalyst for renewed interest in progressivism, his thesis built upon earlier works by George E. Mowry (*The California Progressives* [Berkeley, 1951]) and Alfred D. Chandler, Jr. ("The Origins of Progressive Leadership," in Elting Morrison, ed., *The Letters of Theodore Roosevelt*, vol. 8 [Cambridge, 1954], 1462-1465). Students should also consult such recent historiographical essays as David M. Kennedy, "Overview: The Progressive Era," *The Historian*, 37:3 (May, 1975), 453-468; Robert H. Wiebe, "The Progressive Years, 1900-1917," in *The Reinterpretation of American History and Culture*, ed. William H. Cartwright and Richard L. Watson, Jr. (Washington, D. C., 1973), 425-441; and Otis A. Pease, "Urban Reformers in the Progressive Era: A Reassessment," *Pacific Northwest Quarterly*, 62:2 (April, 1971), 49-58.

2.   Robert H. Wiebe, *The Search for Order, 1877-1920* (New York, 1967); and Samuel P. Hays, *The Response to Industrialism, 1885-1914* (Chicago, 1957).

3.   Jack Tager, "Progressives, Conservatives and the Theory of the Status Revolution," *Mid-America*, 48:3 (July, 1966), 162-175; and Robert W. Doherty, "Status Anxiety and Reform: Some Alternatives," *American Quarterly*, 19:2. Pt.2 (Summer 1967), 329-337. For a trenchant critique of "status revolution" as a social scientific concept applicable to history, consult David P. Thelen, "Social Tensions and the Origins of Progressivism," *Journal of American History*, 56:2 (September, 1969), 323-341.

4.   Wiebe, *The Search for Order*, 111-132.

5.   James Weinstein, *The Corporate Ideal in the Liberal State, 1900-1918* (Boston, 1968), 3-39; and Samuel P. Hays, "The Politics of Reform in Municipal Government in the Progressive Era," *Pacific Northwest Quarterly*, 55:4 (October, 1964), 157-169.

6.   J. Joseph Huthmacher, "Urban Liberalism and the Age of Reform," *Mississippi Valley Historical Review*, 49:2 (September, 1962), 231-241; and John D. Buenker, *Urban Liberalism and Progressive Reform* (New York, 1973).

7.   David P. Thelen, "Progressivism as a Radical Movement," in *Main Problems in American History*, ed. Howard H. Quint et al., vol. 2 (Homewood, Ill. 1972), 149-158; Thelen, *The New Citizenship: Origins of Progressivism in Wisconsin, 1885-1900* (Columbia, Mo., 1972), 308; and Thelen, *Robert M. LaFollette and the Insurgent Spirit* (Boston, 1976), 23-51.

8.   Stanley P. Caine, "The Origins of Progressivism," in *The Progressive Era*, ed. Lewis L. Gould (Syracuse, 1974), 34.

9.   Hays, *The Response to Industrialism;* Gabriel Kolko, *The Triumph of Conservatism: A Reinterpretation of American History, 1900-1916* (Princeton, 1963); and Melvin G. Holli, *Reform in Detroit: Hazen S. Pingree and Urban Politics* (New York, 1969).

10.   Thelen, "Social Tensions and the Origins of Progressivism," 323-341.

11.   Charles Forcey, *The Crossroads of Liberalism: Croly, Weyl, Lippmann and the Progressive Era, 1900-1925* (New York, 1961).

12.   Eric E. Lampard, "The Dimensions of Urban History: A Footnote to the 'Urban Crisis,'" *Pacific Historical Review*, 39:3 (August, 1970), 261-278; Roy Lubove, "The Urbanization Process: A Historical Approach," *Journal of the Institute of American Planners*, 33:1 (January, 1967), 33-39; and Samuel P. Hays, "The Social Analysis of American Political History, 1880-1920," *Political Science Quarterly*, 80:3 (September, 1965), 373-394.

13.   Carl Abbott, "Building Urban-Industrial America," *Journal of Urban History*, 2:3 (May, 1976), 369-372; and Samuel P. Hays, "The Changing Political Structure of the City in Industrial America," *Journal of Urban History*, 1:1 (November, 1974), 6-38.

14.   Bruce M. Stave, "A Conversation with Eric E. Lampard," *Journal of Urban History*, 1:4 (August, 1975), 462f.

15.   Hays, "The Politics of Reform in Municipal Government," 157-169.

16.   Students interested in the literature of this rapidly growing field should consult David B. Tyack, *The One Best System: A History of American Urban Education* (Cambridge, 1974); Selwyn K. Troen, *The Public and the Schools: Shaping the St. Louis System, 1838-1920* (Columbia, Mo., 1975); Joel H. Spring, *Education and the Rise of the Corporate State* (Boston, 1972); Sol Cohen, *Progressives and Urban School Reform: The Public Education Association of New York City, 1895-1954* (New York, 1964); Raymond E. Callahan, *Education and the Cult of Efficiency* (Chicago, 1962); and Lawrence A. Cremin, *The Transformation of the School: Progressivism in American Education, 1876-1957* (New York, 1961).

17.   Benjamin Parke DeWitt, *The Progressive Movement* (New York, 1915), viii-ix.

1. THE ENVIRONMENTS OF REFORM

The author wishes to acknowledge the valuable suggestions of Morton Keller in the preparation of this chapter.

1.   Richard Hofstadter, *The Age of Reform: From Bryan to F. D. R.* (New York, 1955); James Weinstein, *The Corporate Ideal in the Liberal State: 1900-1918* (Boston, 1968); and John D. Buenker, *Urban Liberalism and Progressive Reform* (New York, 1973), are illustrative of the many works that form part of this appraisal.

2.   Samuel P. Hays, "The Social Analysis of American Political History, 1880-1920," *Political Science Quarterly*, 80:3 (September, 1965), 374.

3.   Walter M. Pratt, *Seven Generations: A Story of Prattville and Chelsea* (n.p., 1930), 106. Pratt's *The Burning of Chelsea* (Boston, 1908) gives an extended personal view of the conflagration.

4. Pratt, *Seven Generations*, and *Chelsea Gazette*, April 17, 1909. The displacement of population in the Chelsea fire was almost 70 percent greater proportionally than in even the Great Chicago Fire of 1871; cf. Elias Colbert and Everett Chamberlin, *Chicago and the Great Conflagration* (Chicago, 1872). All Chelsea newspapers cited are available in the Chelsea Public Library.

5. Chelsea *Gazette*, April 18, 1908.

6. Chelsea *Gazette*, December 5, 1908, and August 27, 1910; J. P. Heaton, "A Study in Industrial Evolution, 6: Chelsea," *Current Affairs* (February 27 and March 6, 1922), passim.

7. Heaton, "A Study in Industrial Evolution," passim.

8. "History of the City of Chelsea from the Time of Pawtucket Indians to the Present Industrial Community," typescript, n.a., n.d., in the Chelsea Public Library, 18, 19, 25.

9. *The Census of Massachusetts, 1885* (Boston, 1888), vol. 2, 1335-1340.

10. Edward J. Kopf, "The Intimate City: A Study of Urban Social Order: Chelsea, Massachusetts, 1906-1915" (Ph.D. diss., Brandeis University, 1974), Table 1, 35; Massachusetts Bureau of Statistics, *Report of the Statistics of Manufactures . . . 1915* (Boston), v.

11. *Massachusetts State Census, 1915* (Boston), p. 503; Kopf, "The Intimate City," 35.

12. Kopf, "The Intimate City," 44.

13. Ibid.

14. Ibid., chapter 4.

15. Kopf, "The Intimate City," 108, Table 5. Pages 101-114 explain the Index and the basis of the comparisons. All available evidence suggests no significant reordering of the city occurred between 1908 and 1915.

16. Kopf, "The Intimate City," 122.

17. Ibid., 49.

18. A comparison of Maps 1-2 and 1-3 should make this evident. Tables 1-1 and 1-2 give fuller data on these divisions.

19. E.g., Chelsea *Gazette*, April 25 and May 2, 1908.

20. Chelsea *Gazette*, April 25, May 2, June 6, 1908.

21. Quoted from the Citizens' Committee's petition to the General Court as printed in Chelsea *Gazette*, April 25, 1908.

22. See *Chelsea City Documents, 1907*, and *Chelsea City Directory, 1908*, for identity and occupation of aldermen. Both are available in the Chelsea Public Library.

23. Alderman Melvin Breath in Chelsea *Gazette*, May 30, 1908.

24. See Robert H. Wiebe, *The Search for Order* (New York, 1967), chapter 5.

25. Henry F. May's *Protestant Churches and Industrial America* (New York, 1949) is one of many works describing this apprehension.

26. John Higham traces these shifts in *Strangers in the Land* (New Brunswick, N. J., 1955).

27. Pratt, *The Burning of Chelsea*, 28-30.

28. Chelsea *Gazette*, December 10, 1910. Samuel P. Hays, in "The Politics of Reform in Municipal Government in the Progressive Era," *Pacific Northwest Quarterly*, 55:4 (October, 1964), 157-169, presents this line of argument.

29. Chelsea *Evening Record*, November 10 to December 10, 1910, passim.

30. Chelsea *Evening Record*, December 30, 1910.

31. See Table 1-3.

32. Chelsea *Evening Record*, December 3, 1910.

33. The printer was Alexander Cook and the roofer was William A. O'Brien (*Chelsea City Documents, 1912: Chelsea City Directory, 1910, 1912*).

34. These members were McClintock, Dunham and Briggs.

35.   Chelsea *Catholic Citizen*, February 20, 1915; *Chelsea City Documents, 1907;* and *Chelsea City Directory, 1908.*
36.   Chelsea *Catholic Citizen*, February 20, 1915; *Chelsea City Documents, 1912;* and *Chelsea City Directory, 1910, 1912.*
37.   Chelsea *Evening Record*, October 23, 30, November 6, 1911.
38.   See Table 1-2.
39.   See Table 1-1.
40.   See Table 1-3.
41.   See Table 1-3; also see Kopf, "The Intimate City," 131–132, on Irish population in Chelsea.
42.   Table 1-3.
43.   Table 1-3.
44.   *Chelsea City Documents, 1907, 1912;* Chelsea *Gazette*, June 6, 1908.
45.   Mayor John Beck in the Chelsea *Gazette*, January 11, 1908.
46.   Chelsea *Gazette*, December 6, 1910.
47.   Quoted from *The Dethronement of the City Boss* (1910) in Chelsea *Gazette*, December 7, 1910.
48.   For example, it gave a Republican mayoral candidate 456 votes in 1914 to his opponent's 147 (Chelsea *Gazette*, December 19, 1914).
49.   Chelsea *Gazette*, May 9, 1908.
50.   *Chelsea City Documents, 1907, 1912; Chelsea City Directory, 1908, 1910, 1912.*
51.   Hofstadter, *Age of Reform*, and Weinstein, *Corporate Ideal*, lean toward monism.
52.   Quoted from the *Christian Science Monitor* in the Chelsea *Record*, December 6, 1910.
53.   Higham, *Strangers*, passim.
54.   Kopf, "The Intimate City," 95.
55.   David P. Thelen's *The New Citizenship: The Origins of Progressivism in Wisconsin, 1885-1900* (Columbia, Mo., 1972) provides such an example.
56.   Buenker, *Urban Liberalism.*

2. CITY-BUILDING AND PROGRESSIVE REFORM

1.   For an introduction to urban historiography, see Roy Lubove, "The Urbanization Process: An Approach to Historical Research," *Journal of the American Institute of Planners,* 33:1 (January, 1967), 660–671; and Raymond A. Mohl, "The History of the American City," in William H. Cartwright and Richard L. Watson, Jr., eds., *The Reinterpretation of American History and Culture* (Washington, D. C., 1973), 173–189. For the current status of Progressive Era studies, consider Robert H. Wiebe, "The Progressive Years, 1900-1917," in Cartwright and Watson, 425–442.
2.   Wiebe's definition of "modernization" is appropriate for the purposes of this paper. See "The Progressive Years," 425–426. Also consider two of his important works, *The Search for Order, 1877-1920* (New York, 1967), chaps. 5-8; and *The Segmented Society: An Introduction to the Meaning of America* (New York, 1975), 24-27, 103-110.
3.   Cf. Samuel P. Hays, "The Politics of Reform in Municipal Government in the Progressive Era," *Pacific Northwest Quarterly,* 55:4 (October, 1964), 157-169; Melvin G. Holli, *Reform in Detroit: Hazen S. Pingree and Urban Politics* (New York, 1972), 157-181; and Michael H. Frisch, *Town into City: Springfield, Massachusetts, and the Meaning of Community, 1840-1880* (Cambridge, 1972), 238-250.
4.   Alwyn Barr, *Reconstruction to Reform: Texas Politics 1876-1906* (Austin, 1971); S. G. Reed, *A History of the Railroads of Texas* (Houston, 1941); and *History of Houston and Galveston* (Chicago, 1895).

5. The best history of the city in the antebellum period places Houston in a comparative context. Kenneth W. Wheeler, *To Wear a City's Crown: The Beginning of Urban Growth in Texas, 1836-1865* (Cambridge, 1965), 3-19, 45-132, 151-163. For perspectives on the Houston-Galveston commercial rivalry, consider Marilyn McAdams Sibley, *The Port of Houston: A History* (Austin, 1968), 62-129; and James P. Baughman, "The Evolution of Rail-Water Systems of Transportation in the Gulf Southwest, 1836-1890," *Journal of Southern History*, 34:3 (Autumn, 1968), 357-381. Biographical approaches include David G. McComb, *Houston: The Bayou City* (Austin, 1969), and Benajah Harvey Carroll, *Standard History of Houston, Texas* (Knoxville, 1912).

6. Morrison and Fourmy, comps., *Directory of the City of Houston* (Houston and Galveston, 1890-1902), passim (hereafter cited as *City Directory*); Andrew Morrison, *The City of Houston* (n.p., 1891); I. J. Isaacs, ed., *The Industrial Advantages of Houston . . .* (Houston, 1894); U. S., Census Office, *Eleventh Census of the United States: 1890, Compendium*, 738-739; U. S., Bureau of the Census, *Special Report: Statistics of Cities Having a Population of over 30,000: 1906*, 87-89; Harold L. Platt, "Urban Public Services and Private Enterprise: Aspects of the Legal and Economic History of Houston, Texas, 1865-1905" (Ph.D. diss., Rice University, 1974), chap. 2.

7. Platt, "Urban Public Services," chaps. 1, 3. For a sketch of Browne's Horatio Alger rise to wealth, see *The Industries of Houston . . .* (Houston, 1887), 50-51. The central importance of private decision makers in nineteenth-century cities is analyzed in Sam Bass Warner, Jr., *The Private City: Philadelphia in Three Periods of Its Growth* (Philadelphia, 1968); Robert M. Fogelson, *The Fragmented Metropolis: Los Angeles, 1850-1930* (Cambridge, 1967), 24-42, 85-107; and Frisch, *Town into City*, 92-113.

8. *City Directory, 1890*, 54-70, and *1905*, 36-53. The development of organizational life is explored by Louis Galambos, "The Emerging Organizational Synthesis in Modern American History," *Business History Review*, 44:3 (Autumn, 1970), 279-290; and Samuel P. Hays, "Introduction: The New Organizational Society," in *Building the Organizational Society: Essays on Associational Activity in Modern America*, ed. Jerry Israel (New York, 1972), 1-15.

9. *Minutes of the City Council* (Houston: City Secretary's Office, 1892), Book H, 101-102 (hereafter cited as *Minutes*).

10. The complicated tactics of city officials, creditors, and the national judiciary is detailed in Platt, "Urban Public Services," chap. 3. For more general perspectives on the rash of municipal bond defaults after 1860, see Charles Fairman, *Reconstruction and Reunion, 1864-1888*, vol. 6, part 1, of *The Oliver Wendell Holmes Devise: History of the Supreme Court of the United States*, ed. Paul A. Freund (New York, 1971), chaps. 17-18; A. M. Hillhouse, *Municipal Bonds: A Century of Experience* (New York, 1936). A seminal contribution is made by C. K. Yearley, *The Money Machines: The Breakdown and Reform of Governmental and Party Finance in the North, 1860-1920* (Albany, 1970).

11. The tax rate in Houston remained a constant 2 percent ad valorum throughout the period. Contradictory figures of "true," or market, value were reported ranging from 50 to 75 percent. Cf. *Daily Herald, Houston Illustrated . . .* (Houston: Daily Herald, 1893), 19-21; Isaacs, ed., *Industrial Advantages*, 33; and U. S., Bureau of the Census, *Special Reports: 1906*, 282-284. The city's bonded debt limitations were set in special and general state laws. Consult H. P. N. Gammel, comp., *Laws of Texas, 1822-1897*, 10 vols., (Austin, 1898), 9:848-851, and 10: 486-490; and Robert C. Cotner, *James Stephen Hogg: A Biography* (Austin, 1959), 333-338.

12. *Minutes, H* (Dec., 1892-May, 1894), 101-102, 126-129, 149-155, 207; "Water and Light," *Houston Post*, October 23, 1893. Negotiations with the Citizens' Light and Power Company can be followed in *Minutes, H* (April-June, 1894), 200-

223. The first proposals for municipal ownership were voiced by Browne's predecessor in 1891 for similar conservative reasons of budgetary savings. Throughout the period under consideration, public ownership remained a nonideological issue. Yet, every politician paid at least lip service to the ideal of municipally owned utilities. See David P. Thelen, *The New Citizenship: Origins of Progressivism in Wisconsin, 1885-1900* (Columbia, Mo., 1972), 55–60, 130–202. Also see below, n. 22.

13.   Charles O. Green, *Fire Fighter of Houston, 1838-1915* (Houston, 1915), 115–117; *Minutes, H* (October, 1894–June, 1895), 336–338, 367–368, 446, 542; *Houston Post,* November 6, 1894; October 26, 1895; July 8, 1897. Also see below, n. 38.

14.   *Higgins v. Bordages,* 88 Texas 458, 464 (1895). For a similar judicial adventure on a national level, cf. *Village of Norwood v. Baker,* 172 U. S. 269 (1895).

15.   "The Day at Houston," *Galveston Daily News,* April 11, 1895; *Houston Post,* April 11–13, 1895; *City Directory* (1895), 3; *Storrie v. City of Houston,* no. 1779, U. S. Circuit Court, East District of Texas at Galveston (Galveston, 1895).

16.   *Minutes, H* (July–September, 1895), 566–575, 602–604; "Paving and Progress," *Houston Post,* September 15, 1895; "Public Spirit Once More Awake," *Houston Post,* December 1, 1896. Also see John Brinckerhoff Jackson, *American Space: The Centennial Years, 1865-1876* (New York, 1972), 78.

17.   "Houston's Water Supply," *Fire and Water,* 17 (June, 1895), 289; "The Day at Houston," *Galveston Daily News,* July 16, August 1–13, 1895.

18.   Robert E. Zeigler, "The Workingman in Houston, Texas, 1865-1914" (Ph.D. diss., Texas Tech University, 1972), 141–188; "The Bond Issue Defeated," *Houston Post,* September 22, 1895. About 20 percent of the taxpayers participated. For voter registration figures, see *Houston Post,* March 26, 1896, November 30, 1897.

19.   For biographical information, see *History of Texas,* 470–472, and Derman H. Hardy and Ingham S. Roberts, *Historical Review of Southeast Texas,* 2 vols. (Chicago, 1910), 2:491–492. For the campaign, review *Houston Post,* December 12, 1895–March 8, 1896.

20.   An introduction to rapid change in Texas public utility law can be gained in *Galveston and Western Railroad Company v. City of Galveston,* 90 Texas 398 (1897); *San Antonio Street Railway v. Elmendorp,* 90 Texas 520 (1897); and *Palestine Water and Power Company v. City of Palestine,* 91 Texas 540 (1898). For more general insights into the enlarging role of the judiciary, consider Charles W. McCurdy, "Justice Field and the Jurisprudence of Government-Business Relations: Some Parameters of Laissez-Faire Constitutionalism, 1863–1897," *Journal of American History,* 61:4 (March, 1975), 970–1005; James Williard Hurst, *Law and the Conditions of Freedom in the Nineteenth-Century United States* (Madison, 1956), chap. 3; and Harold M. Hyman, *A More Perfect Union: The Impact of Civil War and Reconstruction on the Constitution* (New York, 1973), 307–414.

21.   *Minutes, J* (April–May, 1897), 255–256; *Houston Post,* April 15, May 9, 12, November 18, 30, 1897, and January 8, 1898; see above, n. 12.

22.   *Minutes, J* (August, 1897–January, 1898), 330, 342–351, 374–393. The final vote was 704 to 529. A second referendum on the issue in 1899 also reflected widespread support by property-taxpayers. See also *Minutes, J* (October–November, 1899), 86–87, 106–109.

23.   *Massachusetts Loan and Trust Company v. Citizens' Electric Light and Power Company,* nos. 343 and 369 (Equity), U. S. Circuit Court (Galveston, 1898); *Parlan, et al. v. Houston City Railway Company,* no. 302 (Equity), ibid., (1895); *International Trust Company v. Houston Electric Street Railway Company,* no. 30811, 55th District Court of Texas (Houston, 1901).

24.   For an informed discussion of these ideas, see Paul M. Gaston, *The New South Creed: A Study in Myth Making* (New York, 1970), 92–150. For analysis of politically restrictive, racist patterns in the South, see J. Morgan Kousser, *The Shaping of Southern Politics: Suffrage Restriction and the Establishment of the One-Party*

South, 1880-1910 (New Haven, 1974); and Jack Temple Kirby, *Darkness at the Dawning: Race and Reform in the Progressive South* (Philadelphia, 1972), chaps. 1-5. For the candidates' positions, see *Houston Post*, January 7-March 26, 1898. Of the 9,450 registered voters in 1898, 2,025 were black.

25. Zeigler, "Workingman in Houston," 203-226. General community support, including the police, for labor and against outside corporations was not peculiar to Houston. See Herbert G. Gutman, "The Workers' Search for Power," *The Gilded Age: A Reappraisal*, ed. H. Wayne Morgan (Syracuse, 1963), 38-68.

26. Building a sewer system to eliminate pollution in the bayou was an exceptional concession to regional interests that subsequently secured federal funding for a new ship channel. See Sibley, *Port of Houston*, 90-136, and Martin V. Melosi, " 'Out of Sight, Out of Mind': The Environment and Disposal of Municipal Refuse, 1860-1920," *The Historian*, 35:4 (August, 1973), 621-640.

27. *City of Houston v. Houston City Street Railway Company*, no. 24864, 11th District Court of Texas (Houston, 1900); *Houston Electric Street Railway Company v. City of Houston*, no. 28686, 11th District Court (1900), ibid., no. 30319, 55th District Court (1901).

28. Brashear's surprising resignation led to a special election, in which one of his aldermanic supporters, J. D. Woolford, won a plurality (1,510 votes) over another regular (289 votes) and two antiadministration men (2,140 votes) (see *Houston Post*, January 26-27, February 17-19, 1901). Woolford maintained a precarious position as mayor against continued council pressures that included an impeachment threat (*Houston Post*, November 26-27, 1901). The abolition of the Light Board was one of the council's first acts after the resignation. See *Minutes, L* (March, 1901), 36-47.

29. The sources of Brashear's opposition outside the council are difficult to identify. Because Browne bolted the Democratic primary in 1900, most community leaders and the *Houston Post* supported the regular party candidate (see *Houston Post*, February 27-April 4, 1900).

30. On the Galveston disaster, see Herbert Molloy Mason, Jr., *Death from the Sea* (New York, 1972), and Bradley R. Rice, "The Galveston Plan of City Government by Commission: The Birth of a Progressive Idea," *Southwestern Historical Quarterly*, 78:4 (April, 1975), 365-408. On the discovery of oil, see Harold F. Williamson, et al., *The American Petroleum Industry*, vol. 2, *The Age of Energy, 1899-1959* (Evanston, 1963), 3-65. The impacts of the discovery on Houston's wealth and energy use can be followed in McComb, *Houston*, 113-120, and *Houston Post*, January 29, March 22, May 14, 1901.

31. For biographical data on Holt, see two articles in *Houston Post:* "O. T. Holt," January 21, 1902, and "Holt Aldermanic Ticket," March 31, 1902; see also E. W. Winkler, ed., *Platforms of Political Parties in Texas* (Austin, 1916), passim. The two newspapers gave extensive coverage of the primary campaign; see *Houston Post*, January 21-April 5, 1902, and *Houston Chronicle*, March 3-April 3, 1902.

32. The flow of communications on national urban reform currents began in earnest during the late nineties through *Houston Post* editorials. In addition, private organizations such as the Labor Council, Good Government League, and the Business League began operating municipal research committees, including membership in the National Municipal League for the latter two associations. The city joined and participated in the League of American Municipalities. Limitations of space preclude documentation here, but see Platt, "Urban Public Services," chaps. 5-7.

33. Kirby's personal and economic history is traced in John Ozias King, "The Early History of the Houston Oil Company, 1901-1908," (Master's thesis, University of Houston, 1958), 37-40, passim. The influential work of Haskins and Sells is outlined in "Charles Waldo Haskins," *National Cyclopaedia of American Biography*, 54 vols. (New York, 1937), 9:514-515; and "Elijah Watt Sells," ibid.,

12:594. The central place of fiscal control in municipal reform is carefully examined by Yearley, *The Money Machines.*

34. "The Proposed City Charter," *Houston Post,* October 22, 1902. Cf. the National Municipal League, *A Municipal Program: A Report of a Committee of the National Municipal League* (New York, 1900), and Robert C. Brooks, "Review of A Municipal Program," *Municipal Affairs,* 4 (1900), 235-238.

35. Houston, *Charter and Revised Code of Ordinances* (1904), 3-63. Residents of the proposed annexed areas strongly objected against being brought under municipal authority. The suburbanites believed their taxes would benefit only the central areas (see *Houston Post,* February 7, 16, 22, 27, 1903). For a comparative context that includes Houston in the twentieth century, see Kenneth T. Jackson, "Metropolitan Government Versus Political Autonomy: Politics on the Crabgrass Frontier," *Cities in American History,* ed. Jackson and Stanley K. Schultz (New York, 1972). 442-462.

36. *City Directory,* (1903), 5-7; *Massachusetts Loan v. Citizens' Electric,* nos. 343 and 369 (Equity), U. S. Circuit Court; *Moody's Manual of Railroad and Corporation Securities* (New York, 1903), 1047; Russel Robb, "Early History of the Firm," *Stone and Webster Public Service Journal,* 1 (1907), 4-5, 48, 233-235; E. C. Brown, comp., *Brown's Directory of American Gas Companies* (New York, 1899), 119; and Arthur L. Hunt, "Manufactured Gas," in U. S., Bureau of the Census, *Twelfth Census of the United States: 1900, Manufacturing: Special Reports on Selected Industries,* 10, part 4, 705-722.

37. A copy of the settlement can be found in Houston, *Charter* (1904), 557-562. The litigation dropped is listed in n. 27 above. Also see "Street Railway Suits," *Houston Post,* October 25, 1902.

38. *Houston Water Company v. City of Houston,* no. 32098, 11th District Court (1902); ibid., no. 50 or 56? (Equity), U. S. Circuit Court, Southern District of Texas (Houston, 1903); *City of Houston v. Houston Water Company* no. 32446, 11th District Court, (1902); and ibid., no. 33680 (1903). Also involved was *City of Houston v. Hartford Insurance Company,* 102 Texas 273 (1909). For the terms of the purchase and history of the work's modernization, see Houston, *Annual Report of 1912,* 18-43.

39. See above, n. 11. According to the U. S. Census Bureau (*Special Reports: 1906,* 282-284), Houston's real property was assessed at 50 percent of true value. The most striking feature of the report was that Houston maintained a per capita bonded debt of double the national average for cities of the same size. At the same time, it also provided services at similar levels. Houston's per capita tax burden of $13.93 was $2.50 above similar sized cities and $1.00 less than the national average of all cities. The statistics indicate that Houston taxpayers were willing to accept the costs of building an improved public sector.

40. "Mayor Holt's Message," *Houston Post,* January 27, 1904. Also see *Houston Post,* December 30, 1900; May 17, 1901; February 16, 1902. For similar views of other prominent Houstonians, as expressed in *Houston Post,* consult H. B. Rice, et al., "To Make a Greater Houston," January 4-9, 1901; and J. J. Pastorizza, "The Ideal City," September 25-26, 1903.

41. The reconciliation of Brashear's faction with Browne's was a well-kept secret that surprised both daily newspapers. The reasons are unclear, but perhaps Brashear's self-interest convinced him to join others in his social class. See *Houston Post,* February 16, 1904.

42. *City Directory* (1905), 8-19. The membership list establishes the importance of national influences present in Houston. A sketch of Johnson and his role in the Business League is provided in Carroll, *Standard History,* 217, 323-325. The League was not a closed elite group like Galveston's Deepwater Committee. See Rice, "The Galveston Plan," 380-388; and James Weinstein, "Organized Business and the City Commission and Manager Movements," *Journal of Southern History,* 28:2 (May, 1962), 166-182.

43. Ziegler, "Workingman in Houston," 203-226. The poll tax law and its impacts on Houston can be found in Texas, *Revised Civil Statutes, Supplement* (Herron, 1903), Title 36, c. 9; Houston, *Revised Ordinances* (1904), 456-470; Barr, *Reconstruction to Reform*, 193-208; "Some Election Records," *Houston Post*, April 5, 1902; *Houston Chronicle*, February 1, 1904; and U. S., Bureau of the Census, *Statistical Abstract of the United States: 1910*, 650. Local records and census data show that 10,500 of 13,800 eligible voters were registered in 1900, while only 5,700 of 17,300 could vote four years later. In 1904, Houston's total population was about 54,500. Similar results were recorded in other Southern and Texas cities. See above, n. 24, and Richard G. Miller, "Fort Worth and the Progressive Era: The Movement for Charter Revision, 1899-1907," *Essays on Urban America*, ed. Margaret Francine Morris and Elliot West (Austin, 1975), 89-124.

44. A copy of the charter and the defeated alternative of the council is found in "The Two Charters Compared," *Houston Post*, February 12, 19, 1905; and "The New Charter," *Houston Post*, January 20, 1905. In contrast to Galveston's commission members, who held equal power, Houston's system retained a separately elected mayor in addition to four commissioners. The mayor could veto the board's ordinances and resolutions (he could also vote on all issues). He possessed the exclusive authority to hire city employees and an independent power to fire them. According to a contemporary, "this so-called 'one-man' feature of the commission embodied its whole aim and intention . . . (see Carrol, *Standard History*, 100-108).

45. Since Rice's first term of 1896-1898, he had become a director of the street railway company and a vice-president of a national bank, a Kirby lumber concern, a large national brewery in Houston, and a cotton-processing firm (see *City Directory* [1905], 334). For Rice's reflections on the commission, see his 1910 speech to the Chicago Commercial Club, as reported in Carroll, *Standard History*, 97-99.

3. THE NEW METROPOLIS

1. For an overview of the annexation movement in the nineteenth and twentieth centuries, see Kenneth T. Jackson, "Metropolitan Government Versus Suburban Autonomy: Politics on the Crabgrass Frontier," in Jackson and Stanley K. Schultz, eds., *Cities in American History* (New York, 1972), 442-62. Cincinnati grew from 7 to 38 square miles between 1870 and 1900; Seattle, from 11 to 35; Minneapolis, from 5 to 53. The frequency of annexations also greatly increased in the late nineteenth and early twentieth centuries in many cities. Between 1801 and 1840, for example, Cincinnati had no annexations; Chicago and Cleveland averaged only 1 in 16.2 years. In the next forty-year period, the average for all three was 4.9; between 1881 and 1920, it fell to 1.7. (Data on sizes of cities is drawn from varied sources, including Jackson. Combined averages for Chicago, Cincinnati, and Cleveland are compiled from data in Chamber of Commerce of the United States, *Municipal Annexation of Land* [Washington, 1926], 11-12.)

2. For an analysis of all aspects of late nineteenth-century urban growth in an international perspective, see Eric E. Lampard, "The Urbanizing World," in H. J. Dyos and Michael Wolff, eds., *The Victorian City*, 2 vols. (London, 1973), 1:3-57.

3. General references for background and descriptive materials include Homer Hoyt, *One Hundred Years of Land Values in Chicago* (Chicago, 1933); Harold M. Mayer and Richard C. Wade, *Chicago: The Growth of a Metropolis* (Chicago, 1969); and Bessie Louise Pierce, *A History of Chicago, 1673-1893*, 3 vols. (New York, 1937-1957). For a succinct and gracefully written survey of Chicago from the 1860s to the early 1890s, see Louise C. Wade, *Graham Taylor: Pioneer for Social Justice, 1851-1938* (Chicago, 1964), 51-70.

4. For urban growth and transit developments in this period, see Hoyt, 128-148; also Mayer and Wade, 132-144, 154-174, for a good photographic survey of Chicago

suburbs. For the great increase in commuter steam rail trains serving both industrial and white-collar workers, see *Chicago Tribune*, June 12, 1887, 25. Many of the suburban working class, however, lived near their place of employment and did not commute; also, many were foreign-born and unskilled, especially in the steel mill district of Calumet, to indicate further the highly variegated residential patterns of suburbs in this example of the great "spread-cities" of the late nineteenth century. For comparable mixed suburban residential development in London, see H. J. Dyos, *Victorian Suburb: A Study of the Growth of Camberwell* (Leicester, 1961); also D. A. Reeder, "A Theatre of Suburbs: Some Patterns of Development in West London, 1801-1911," in H. J. Dyos, ed., *The Study of Urban History* (New York, 1968), 253-271.

5.   Helen Zatterberg, *An Historical Sketch of Ravenswood and Lake View* (Chicago, 1941), 1-5; Mayer and Wade, 157-58. For Cochran and Edgewater, see Marion A. White, *Book of the North Shore: Homes, Gardens, Landscapes, Highways and Byways, Past and Present* (Chicago, 1910), 104; John J. Flinn, *Chicago: The Marvelous City of the West: A History, an Encyclopedia and a Guide* (Chicago, 1892), 446; *Chicago and its Environs: A Complete Guide to the City and the World's Fair* (Chicago, 1893), 418-419; also, vol. 2, doc. 11 in "Documents, History of [Chicago] Communities," 6 vols., typescript, prepared for the Chicago Historical Society and the Local Community Research Committee, University of Chicago, (Chicago, 1925-30), Chicago Historical Society Library.

6.   *Chicago Tribune*, June 23, 1889, 3. For typical city and suburban arguments for annexation, see also *Chicago Daily News*, Nov. 5, 1887, 3; *Chicago Inter-Ocean*, June 27, 1889, 1, and the Chicago Real Estate Board's *The Call Board Bulletin*, 3 (July 5, 1889), 202.

7.   For a detailed account of the League's founding and activities in the 1890s, see Sidney J. Roberts, "The Municipal Voters' League and Chicago's Boodlers," *Journal of the Illinois State Historical Society*, 53:2 (Summer, 1960), 117-148. Contemporary sources include Edwin Burritt Smith, "The Municipal Voters' League of Chicago," *Atlantic Monthly*, 85 (June, 1900), 834-839; Frank H. Scott, "The Municipal Situation in Chicago," *Proceedings of the National Conference for Good City Government* (1903), 147-156; also Frederic C. Howe, "The Municipal Character and Achievements of Chicago," *World's Work*, 5 (March, 1903), 3241-3246.

8.   For an ethnocultural interpretation of the League, with its leaders as middle-class, native Americans opposing the values and politics of the immigrant working class, see Joel A. Tarr, *A Study in Boss Politics: William Lorimer of Chicago* (Urbana, 1971), 37-47; also John D. Buenker, "Dynamics of Chicago Ethnic Politics, 1900-1930," *Journal of the Illinois State Historical Society*, 67:2 (April, 1974), 187-190. The League is also cited in this context in Samuel P. Hays, "Political Parties and the Community-Society Continuum," in William Nisbet Chambers and Walter Dean Burnham, eds., *The American Party System: Stages of Political Development*, 2d. ed. (New York, 1975), 172; and Hays, "The Changing Political Structure of the City in Industrial America," *Journal of Urban History*, 1:1 (November, 1974), 23.

9.   In 1890, in the Twenty-fifth Ward in Lake View, for example, 77.3 percent of the total population were foreign-born or of mixed or foreign parentage. By 1910, the figure had dropped to 65.7 percent, still high for a residential area usually characterized as "old stock" in the literature of municipal reform.

10.   For a similar view of progressive leadership, see David P. Thelen, *The New Citizenship: Origins of Progressivism in Wisconsin, 1885-1900* (Columbia, Mo., 1972), 2-3. Thelen views the depression as the single force creating the broad support for reform. He does not discuss metropolitan growth or the annexation movement. For a summary of his views on the impact of the depression, see 55-56.

11.   Tarr, in *A Study in Boss Politics*, 76, cites the reform rhetoric of Fisher and Kent against two of Lorimer's business friends as proof of anti-Catholic nativism, which is unsupported by other evidence. Although Kent believed in "the civic and

economic necessity of carefully selecting our future citizenship," he told a Lake Forest College audience, "Don't for a moment be deluded into the belief that the problems of a great city are hopeless on account of the vast number of foreigners. Some of these foreigners, it is true, are hard to assimilate. . . . But you must realize that the most desperate crimes are committed by well-to-do Americans; that the purchase of legislation is worse than the murder of a legislator" (Kent, *Municipal Citizenship: An Address Delivered to the Students of Lake Forest College on the Occasion of Washington's Birthday, 1905* [Chicago, 1905], p. 11; also Kent folder, Papers of Graham Taylor, Newberry Library, Chicago). For the influence of Jenkin Lloyd Jones and Jane Addams on Kent, see Robert L. Woodbury, "William Kent: Progressive Gadfly, 1864-1928" (Ph.D. diss., Yale University, 1967); also Kent to Taylor, Jan. 6, 1927, Taylor Papers.

12.   In its 1898 Final Report, for example, the League said the following about its choice in the Seventh Ward: "Henry Fick, Jr.—Democrat, saloonkeeper, was Democratic candidate in 1897 and counted out by Brenner and others; born in Chicago and lived in ward all his life; personal and business standing good; will make good representative of the ward; endorsed by League" (*Chicago Tribune*, April 4, 1898, 7). The League was far more broad-minded in its recommendations than either Tarr or Hays suggests. Both cite a 1966 Roosevelt University M. A. thesis by Joan Miller ("The Politics of Municipal Reform in Chicago during the Progressive Era: The Municipal Voters' League as a Test Case, 1896-1920"), which was quite selective in its data.

13.   Recent studies have indicated, however, that high residential turnover is not characteristic of inner-city neighborhoods alone. See, for example, Howard P. Chudacoff, *Mobile Americans: Residential and Social Mobility in Omaha, 1880-1920* (New York, 1972), and Stephan Thernstrom, *The Other Bostonians: Poverty and Progress in the American Metropolis, 1880-1970* (Cambridge, Mass., 1973).

14.   Even the genial boss of the Seventeenth Ward, Johnny Powers, was not above threatening retaliation against small businessmen who dared to oppose him; see Allen F. Davis, "Jane Addams Versus the Ward Boss," *Journal of the Illinois State Historical Society* 53:3 (Autumn, 1960), 263.

15.   For a discussion of the limits of quantification, see Eric E. Lampard, "Two Cheers for Quantitative History: An Agnostic Forward," in Leo Schnore, ed., *New Urban History* (Princeton, 1974), 12-48. For annexation and council reform in England, see H. Keeble Hawson, *Sheffield: The Growth of a City, 1893-1926* (Sheffield, 1968), 288; also R. Newton, "Society and Politics in Exeter, 1839-1914," in Dyos, ed., *Study of Urban History*, 303, 311; for comparable developments in London, see William A. Robson, *The Government and Misgovernment of London* (London, 1939), 80-92.

16.   Between 1880 and 1920, foreign-born in Chicago from central Europe (excluding Germany), eastern and southern Europe jumped from 10.5 percent to 56.6 percent. Many arrived in the early 1900s; in fact 48.9 percent of the foreign-born living in Chicago in 1920 arrived between 1901 and 1914. By 1920, Poles were the largest group of foreign-born (137,611), Germans second (112,288), Russians third (102,095), and Italians fourth (59,215), ahead of the Swedish and Irish (58,563 and 56,786), respectively. Between 1880 and 1920, black population rose from 6,480 to 109,450 and would double in the next decade (data from Ernest W. Burgess and Charles S. Newcomb, *Census Data for the City of Chicago, 1920, 1930* [Chicago, 1931, 1933]).

17.   Housing data from the Chicago Land Use Survey, conducted by the Works Progress Administration in 1939-41, directed and published by the Chicago Plan Commission as *Residential Chicago*, 2 vols. (1943); for summary tables on housing, see vol. 1, Appendix, 4-72. The high percentage of single-family housing in these areas indicates that the worker's "cottage" by no means disappeared, as Sam B. Warner, Jr., suggests in his sketch of Chicago in *The Urban Wilderness* (New York, 1972), 109.

18. For an account of the election, see Lloyd Wendt and Herman Kogan, *Big Bill of Chicago* (Indianapolis, 1953), 89-115.

4. URBAN REFORM AND VOLUNTARY ASSOCIATION

1. Michael H. Frisch, *Town Into City: Springfield, Massachusetts, and the Meaning of Community, 1840-1880* (Cambridge, Mass., 1972), 39; Robert L. Buroker, "From Voluntary Association to Welfare State: The Illinois Immigrants' Protective League, 1908-1926," *Journal of American History*, 58:3 (December, 1971), 643-660. Buroker maintains that voluntary associations provided the foundation for development of the welfare state and modern public bureaucracies. See Arthur M. Schlesinger, Sr., "Biography of a Nation of Joiners," *American Historical Review*, 50:1 (October, 1944), 1-25, for a pioneering essay on the role of voluntary associations in American society.

2. George E. Mowry, "Social Democracy, 1900-1918," in *The Comparative Approach to American History*, ed. C. Vann Woodward (New York, 1968), 271-284; Seattle *Municipal News*, June 1, 1912 (available in Seattle Public Library). The *Municipal News* contains abundant examples of the League's awareness of other progressive experiments.

3. David M. Kennedy, "Overview: The Progressive Era," *The Historian*, 37:3 (May, 1975), 453-468 offers some suggestive new approaches to the debate.

4. Otis Pease, "Urban Reformers in the Progressive Era: A Reassessment" *Pacific Northwest Quarterly*, 62:2 (April, 1971), 50; David P. Thelen, "Social Tensions and the Origins of Progressivism," *Journal of American History*, 56:2 (September, 1969), 323-341, and his essay on progressivism in *Main Problems in American History*, ed. Howard H. Quint, Dean Albertson, and Milton Cantor, vol. 2, 3d ed. (Homewood, Ill., 1972), 149-158.

5. Gabriel Kolko, *The Triumph of Conservatism: A Reinterpretation of American History, 1900-1916* (New York, 1963), and *Railroads and Regulation, 1877-1916* (Princeton, 1965); Robert H. Wiebe, *Businessmen and Reform: A Study of the Progressive Movement* (Cambridge, Mass., 1962).

6. Robert H. Wiebe, *The Search for Order, 1877-1920* (New York, 1967); Samuel P. Hays, "The Politics of Reform in Municipal Government in the Progressive Era," *Pacific Northwest Quarterly*, 55:4 (October, 1964), 157-169.

7. George E. Mowry, *Theodore Roosevelt and the Progressive Movement* (Madison, 1946) and *The California Progressives* (Berkeley, 1951); Richard Hofstadter, *The Age of Reform: From Bryan to F. D. R.* (New York, 1955); Arthur Mann, *Yankee Reformers in the Urban Age* (Cambridge, Mass., 1954).

8. Alexander B. Callow, Jr., made one of the pioneering efforts to examine some of these questions in *The Tweed Ring* (New York, 1966), 253-278, 298-300.

9. Calvin F. Schmid, *Social Trends in Seattle* (Seattle, 1944), 98-99, 131-147; Janice Reiff Webster, "Seattle: The First Fifty-five Years: A Study in Urban Growth" (M. A. thesis, University of Washington, 1973), 78, 88. Consult Webster, 88, for chart comparing home ownership in selected eastern and western cities.

10. C. Edward White's "The Social Values of the Progressives: Some New Perspectives," *South Atlantic Quarterly*, 70:1 (Winter, 1971), 62-76, is suggestive. See Lee F. Pendergrass, "The Formation of a Municipal Reform Movement: The Municipal League of Seattle," *Pacific Northwest Quarterly*, 66:1 (January, 1975), 13-25, for further detail on the League's sociological profile and tactics.

11. Mansel Blackford, "Reform Politics in Seattle During the Progressive Era, 1902-1916," *Pacific Northwest Quarterly*, 59:4 (October, 1968), 177; Warren B. Johnson, "Muckraking in the Northwest: Joe Smith and Seattle Reform," *Pacific Historical Review*, 40:4 (November, 1971), 482; Kennedy, "Overview."

12. Mugwumps were political mavericks with long-established backgrounds, excellent education, and Anglo-Saxon blood who emphasized moral reform and their

inherited right to lead the country. Corruption and machine politics attracted their special attention. They were also antiexpansionists. See Hofstadter's *Age of Reform*, 131-172, and Robert L. Beisner, *Twelve Against Empire: The Anti-Imperialists, 1898-1900* (New York, 1968), 5-17, for definitions of Mugwumpery.

13. For the sake of clarity and convenience, I have adopted the classifications used by Melvin G. Holli in *Reform in Detroit: Hazen S. Pingree and Urban Politics* (New York, 1968). In some cases the boundaries were not as rigid as Holli's categorization implies. Leaguers such as Austin Griffiths engaged in both social and structural reform. See Richard M. Bernard and Bradley R. Rice, "Political Environment and the Adoption of Progressive Municipal Reform," *Journal of Urban History*, 1:2 (February, 1975), 170, for the view that social and structural reform had different constituencies.

14. Thelen, "Social Tensions and the Origins of Progressivism," 323-341, and *The New Citizenship: Origins of Progressivism in Wisconsin, 1885-1900* (Columbia, Mo., 1972); Stanley P. Caine, "The Origins of Progressivism," in *The Progressive Era*, ed. Lewis Gould (Syracuse, 1974), 30-32. According to Thelen, the significant issue in progressivism is not what separated groups but what drove them together.

15. Austin E. Griffiths, "Great Faith: Autobiography of an English Immigrant Boy in America, 1863-1950" (typed manuscript, University of Washington, n.d.), 180-181; Margaret Sherlock "The Recall of Mayor Gill," *Pacific Monthly*, 26 (August, 1911), 120; John C. Bollens, "The Municipal League of Seattle: An Analysis of a Citizen Supported Local Governmental Research Organization" (typescript, University of Washington, May, 1947), 14.

16. *Municipal News*, June 24, 1911; July 8, October 21, and December 2, 1911; January 27, 1912; Burton J. Hendrick, "The Recall in Seattle," *McClure's*, 37 (October, 1911), 647-663; Sherlock, "The Recall of Mayor Gill," 120. Similar ideas were common in other cities. See Norman H. Clark, *The Dry Years: Prohibition and Social Change in Washington* (Seattle, 1965), 45; Laurence Veysey, ed., *Law and Resistance: American Attitudes Toward Authority* (New York, 1970), 210-211. See Murray Morgan's *Skid Road: An Informal Portrait of Seattle*, rev. ed. (New York, 1960), 169-187, for a lively account of the more colorful aspects of the recall.

17. Quoted in Roger Sale, "Seattle's Crisis, 1914-1919," *American Studies*, 14:1 (Spring, 1973), 32.

18. Wesley Dick, "The Genesis of Seattle City Light" (M. A. thesis, University of Washington, 1965), 98-100; Hendrick, "The Recall in Seattle," 657, 660. The *Star*'s opinions are quoted in Dick. By law, 10,000 signatures were required to hold such an election.

19. Morgan, *Skid Road*, 179.

20. Griffiths, "Great Faith," 180-181, 184, documents this awareness.

21. Dick, "The Genesis of Seattle City Light," 103-106; *Municipal News*, December 7, 1912; John Kingsbury, "Democracy Tested in Seattle," *The American City*, 6 (July, 1912), 635. See Blackford, "Reform Politics in Seattle," 183, for information on the role of women's suffrage in the election.

22. Virgil Bogue, *Plan of Seattle* (Seattle, 1911), 15, 18, 20, 26-28; *Municipal News*, October 21, 1911; Dorothy O. Johansen and Charles Gates, *Empire of the Columbia: A History of the Pacific Northwest*, 2d ed. (New York, 1967), 421; Mel Scott, *American City Planning Since 1890* (Berkeley, 1969), 126-127. See Kenneth T. Jackson, "The Crabgrass Frontier: 150 Years of Suburban Growth in America," in *The Urban Experience: Themes in American History*, ed. Raymond A. Mohl and James F. Richardson (Belmont, Cal., 1973), 196-221 for some intriguing similarities between this issue and later fights over the construction of suburban shopping centers in the 1920s.

23. *Municipal News*, January 20, 27, February 10, 24, and November 2, 1912. Homer Hoyt's *One Hundred Years of Land Values in Chicago* (Chicago, 1933) and

Walter Firey's *Land Use in Central Boston* (Cambridge, Mass., 1947) are pioneering studies of urban land use.

24.   Grant Redford, ed., *That Man Thomson* (Seattle, 1950), 53–56; Charles Gates, "Boom Stages in American Expansion," *Business History Review,* 33:1 (Spring, 1959), 34–42; Norbert MacDonald, "The Business Leaders of Seattle, 1880–1912," *Pacific Northwest Quarterly,* 50:1 (January, 1959), 7–10. Quotes from Gates. Robert Nesbit's *"He Built Seattle": A Biography of Judge Thomas Burke* (Seattle, 1961) is an exhaustive and excellent account.

25.   Interview, December 2, 1971, with Henry Broderick, a well-to-do businessman who knew many of the older capitalists.

26.   *Municipal News,* January 20 and January 29, 1912; Griffiths, "Great Faith," 114–136, 140; Erastus Brainerd Correspondence, Griffiths to Brainerd, December, 27, 1911, Box 3, Folder 8, University of Washington Archives; interviews with Broderick, December 2, 1971, and Mary Nelson and Louis John Inkster, March 19, 1971. All three knew Leaguers of the period.

27.   Seattle *Times,* March 5, 1912; *Post-Intelligencer,* February 27, 1912; Seattle *Star,* February 28, 1912; Seattle *Union-Record,* February 24, 1912. While civic centers were frequently proposed and discussed, by 1920 only six cities were in the process of building them. See Ernest S. Griffith, *A History of American City Government: The Progressive Years and Their Aftermath, 1900–1920* (New York, 1974), 201–202.

28.   Proceedings of the City Council, March 5, 1912, City Clerk's Office, Seattle Municipal Building. Ironically, the city in later years based its development of the arterial highway network, the park system, and part of the waterfront upon Bogue's proposals. See Scott, 127.

29.   Johansen and Gates, *Empire of the Columbia,* 440–441. The considerably high cost of Seattle government is documented in Melvin G. Holli, "Urban Reform in the Progressive Era," in *The Progressive Era,* ed. Gould, 150–151.

30.   *Post-Intelligencer,* August 7, September 5, September 8, September 18, and October 15, 1913; *Municipal News,* August 2, August 9, August 16, and November 1, 1913; C. K. Yearley, *The Money Machines: The Breakdown and Reform of Governmental and Party Finance in the North, 1860–1920* (Albany, N. Y., 1970), 13–14, 16–17, 25–26; Frisch, *Town Into City,* 96.

31.   *Municipal News,* December 27, 1913; Sydney Strong Scrapbooks, vol. 3, 1, 3, 6, 8–9, 12–13, 23, University of Washington Northwest Collection; Samuel Koch Scrapbooks, n.p., University of Washington Archives; *Union-Record,* July 12 and October 18, 1913. Allen F. Davis in *Spearheads for Reform: The Social Settlements and the Progressive Movement, 1890–1914* (New York, 1967) noted a similar change among settlement workers, but only during World War I. Obviously, these were exceptions to Frederick Jackson Turner's argument that the frontier had closed twenty years earlier.

32.   *Union-Record,* June 21, 1913, April 4, 1914; Koch Scrapbooks, n.p.; Seattle *Times,* December 8 and December 27, 1913; Kenneth L. Kusmer, "The Functions of Organized Charity in the Progressive Era: Chicago as a Case Study," *Journal of American History,* 60:3 (December, 1973), 657–678; Davis, *Spearheads for Reform,* 13; Buroker, 646; Strong Scrapbooks, vol. 3, 12–13; Egal Feldman, "Prostitution, the Alien Woman and the Progressive Imagination, 1910–1915," *American Quarterly,* 19:2 (Summer, 1967), 192–206.

33.   Blackford, "Reform Politics in Seattle," 183; *Union-Record,* August 9, October 11, November 1, November 8, December 20, and December 27, 1913; January 17 and April 11, 1914. The best book to consult on the IWW is Melvyn Dubofsky's *We Shall Be All: A History of the Industrial Workers of the World* (Chicago, 1969).

34.   Robert D. Saltvig, "The Progressive Movement in Washington" (Ph.D. diss., University of Washington, 1966), 419.

35.   Holli, "Urban Reform in the Progressive Era," 150–151; Blackford, "Reform Politics in Seattle," 184. For more detail on the efficiency side of progressivism,

see Samuel P. Hays, *Conservation and the Gospel of Efficiency: The Progressives and the Conservation Movement, 1890-1920* (Cambridge, Mass., 1959); Samuel Haber, *Efficiency and Uplift: Scientific Management in the Progressive Era, 1890-1920* (Chicago, 1962); Wiebe, *Search for Order.*

36.   Samuel P. Hays, "The Changing Political Structure of the City in Industrial America," *Journal of Urban History,* 1:1 (November, 1974), 23; Hays, "The Politics of Reform," 157-169; Saltvig, 196-198; Johnson, "Muckraking in the Northwest," 495. Relying upon census tracts and real estate atlases, Blackford describes how workers were scattered over the city's fourteen precincts. See his M. A. thesis, "Sources of Support for Reform Candidates and Issues in Seattle Politics, 1902-1916" (University of Washington, 1967).

37.   Hays, "The Changing Political Structure of the City," 6-38; Bernard and Rice, "Political Environment," 149-171; Holli, "Urban Reform in the Progressive Era," 150-151; Blackford, "Sources of Support," 82, 91-92; *Union-Record,* September 26, November 28, 1914; Morgan, 196; Saltvig, 420-421.

38.   Donald A. Ritchie, "The Gary Committee: Businessmen, Progressives and Unemployment in New York City, 1914-1915," *New-York Historical Society Quarterly,* 57:4 (October, 1973), 327-347; *Municipal News,* February 6, 1915. Similar problems were encountered in many other cities, but they did not necessarily correspond with an economic downswing. See Blake McKelvey, "Cities in the Progressive Movement," in *The City in American History* (New York, 1969), 74.

39.   Everett *Morning Tribune,* June 10, 1915; *Union-Record,* March 27, April 10, May 8, June 12, and August 21, 1915; January 29, February 19, February 27, March 25, April 1, June 24, July 1, July 15, July 29, and August 19, 1916; *Municipal News,* July 1, July 15, July 22, August 12, August 26, September 23, and October 7, 1916; Saltvig, 423-426. See Norman H. Clark, *Mill Town: A Social History of Everett, Washington, From Its Earliest Beginnings on the Shores of Puget Sound to the Tragic and Infamous Event Known as the Everett Massacre* (Seattle, 1970) for an excellent discussion of events leading to the Everett massacre.

40.   Hofstadter, *Age of Reform,* 131-172. Richard Wade suggests that urban reform and the political patterns of the Progressive Era were an integral part of a dichotomy between the central city and the suburbs. See Wade's "An Agenda for Urban History," in *American History: Retrospect and Prospect,* ed. George Athan Billias and Gerald N. Grob (New York, 1971), 387-398, and his "Urbanization," in *The Comparative Approach to American History,* ed., C. Vann Woodward, (New York, 1968), 187-205.

41.   Holli, "Urban Reform in the Progressive Era," 142, based on Hays's analysis in "Reform in Municipal Government." Besides Dilling, George Cotterill, who succeeded Dilling as mayor, was also a member of the Municipal League. Robert Hesketh, another member, was president of the city council in 1913. See *Post-Intelligencer,* December 17, 1913; also Pendergrass, "Formation of a Municipal Reform Movement."

42.   Blackford, "Reform Politics in Seattle," 184-185.

43.   See Lee F. Pendergrass, "Urban Reform and Voluntary Association: A Case Study of the Seattle Municipal League, 1910-1929" (Ph. D. diss., University of Washington, 1972), 70-95, for more information on this issue.

5. THE IMPACT OF REFORM IDEOLOGY

The author wishes to thank Robert H. Wiebe of Northwestern University for first suggesting to him the importance of the progressives' views of government and society for an understanding of their reform efforts.

1.   Robert H. Wiebe, "The Progressive Years, 1900-1917," in *The Reinterpretation of American History and Culture,* ed. William H. Cartwright and Richard L.

Watson, Jr. (Washington, D. C., 1973), 425–427, 434–436; Wiebe, *The Search for Order* (New York, 1967), 111–132, 159–176; Samuel P.

Hays, "The Politics of Reform in Municipal Government in the Progressive Era," *Pacific Northwest Quarterly* 55:4 (October, 1964), 157–169, and "The Changing Political Structure of the City in Industrial America," *Journal of Urban History* 1:1 (November, 1974), 6–25; Otis A. Pease, "Urban Reformers in the Progressive Era: A Reassessment" *Pacific Northwest Quarterly*, 62:2 (April, 1971), 49–58.

2.   Lawrence Veiller, "Housing as a Factor in Health Progress in the Past Fifty Years," in *A Half Century of Public Health*, ed. Mazyck Porcher Ravenel (New York, reprint ed., 1970), 323–334; Roy Lubove, *The Progressives and the Slums: Tenement House Reform in New York City, 1890-1917* (Pittsburgh, 1962), 1–115. For a recent survey that integrates urban health and housing reform, see Sam Bass Warner, Jr., *The Urban Wilderness: A History of the American City* (New York, 1972), 198–266.

3.   Lawrence Veiller, *Oral History Memoir*, 1:3, Oral History Collection, Columbia University (all *Oral History Memoirs* cited in this article are from the collection at Columbia University); Lawson Purdy, *Oral History Memoir*, 35.

4.   Veiller, *Oral History Memoir*, 1:5–8; Veiller, "Tenement House Reform in New York City, 1834-1900," in *The Tenement House Problem*, ed. Robert W. deForest and Lawrence Veiller, 2 vols. (New York, 1903), 1:71–116; Lawrence Veiller, "A History of Tenement House Legislation in New York, 1852-1900," Appendix 4 in *Tenement House Problem*, 2:201–345.

5.   Veiller, *Oral History Memoir*, 1:5–9, 11–36; draft of a proposal "to establish a permanent Tenement House Commission, or Society, as a new philanthropic body," April 20, 1898, 1–5. Papers of Lawrence Veiller, Columbia University; Veiller, "Tenement House Reform," 110–116, and "Prospectus of Tenement House Exhibition," July 19, 1899, Veiller Papers. For a detailed history of the housing movement and the tenement commission's reports, see deForest and Veiller, eds., *The Tenement House Problem;* also "Skeleton Outline of a Plan for a New Tenement House Department," enclosed with letter from Veiller to deForest, October 17, 1900, Veiller Papers; G. Wallace Chessman, *Governor Theodore Roosevelt: The Albany Apprenticeship, 1898-1900* (Cambridge, 1965), 231–233; Lubove, *Progressives and the Slums*, 117–149.

6.   Lawrence Veiller, *Housing Reform: A Hand-book for Practical Use in American Cities* (New York, 1911), 3–7; Veiller, "The Housing Problem in American Cities," *The Annals of the American Academy of Political and Social Science*, 25 (1905), 48–54; Veiller to H. H. Hart, Secretary, National Conference of Charities and Corrections, May 6, 1899, Veiller Papers. See also Lubove, *Progressives and the Slums*, 127–132.

7.   Robert W. deForest and Lawrence Veiller, "The Tenement House Problem (Being the general report of the Commission)," in deForest and Veiller, eds., *The Tenement House Problem*, 1:3–24; deForest, "Introduction: Tenement Reform in New York Since 1901," in ibid., xiv–xix.

8.   DeForest and Veiller, "Tenement House Problem," 11, 25–30; Veiller, "Housing Problem in Cities," 63–70; Veiller, *Hand-book*, 44–46.

9.   DeForest and Veiller, "Tenement House Problem," 29.

10.   Lubove, *Progressives and the Slums*, 175–177; Veiller, "Housing Problem in Cities," 55; also see Veiller, *Hand-book*, 83–86.

11.   Veiller, "Housing Problem in Cities," 56–57.

12.   Veiller, *Hand-book*, 77–86; Veiller, *Oral History Memoir*, 1:38–84; "Memorandum in Regard to Tenement House Department Administration," December 24, 1904, Veiller Papers; deForest, "Introduction," xii–xiv; deForest, "Recent Progress in Tenement-House Reform," *Annals*, 23 (1904), 297–310; Lubove, *Progressives and the Slums*, 153–174, 179–184.

13.   Veiller, "Housing as a Factor in Health Progress"; Hermann M. Biggs, "Tuberculosis and the Tenement House Problem," in deForest and Veiller, eds., *The Tene-*

ment House Problem, 1:447–458; Lubove, *Progressives and the Slums,* 11–23, 83–88; Charles V. Chapin, "History of State and Municipal Control of Disease," in Ravenel, ed., *Half Century of Public Health,* 133–136; George Rosen, *A History of Public Health* (New York, 1958), 233–241.
14. Lubove, *Progressives and the Slums,* 15–25.
15. John Duffy, *A History of Public Health in New York City, 1866-1966* (New York, 1974), 48–91.
16. Charles-Edward A. Winslow, *The Life of Hermann M. Biggs, Physician and Statesman of the Public Health* (Philadelphia, 1929), 1–152; Winslow, "The Contribution of Hermann Biggs to Public Health," reprinted by The New York Tuberculosis and Health Association from *The American Review of Tuberculosis* 20:1 (July, 1929), 2–15; Duffy, *Public Health in New York,* 94–110, 238–252.
17. Quoted in Winslow, "Contribution of Hermann Biggs," 16–17.
18. Ibid., 15–16.
19. Winslow, "Contribution of Hermann Biggs," 17–21; Winslow, *Life of Biggs,* 185–250; Hermann M. Biggs, "To Rob Consumption of Its Terrors," *Forum,* 16 (Sept.–Feb., 1893–94), 759–766; Duffy, *Public Health in New York,* 252–265, an extremely detailed, almost year by year, history of the workings of the New York Health Department.
20. Duffy, *Public Health in New York,* 266–275.
21. Ibid., 276.
22. Augustus Cerillo, Jr., "Reform in New York City: A Study of Urban Progressivism" (Ph.D. diss., Northwestern University, 1969), 60–96, 138–140, provides a summary of the history of utility promotion and regulation to 1905.
23. Merchants' Association of New York, *Passenger Transportation Service in the City of New York* (New York, 1903), v–ix; Merchants' Association of New York, *Yearbook,* 1905, 45, 1907, 17; Merlo J. Pusey, *Charles Evans Hughes,* 2 vols. (New York, 1951), 1:74–82, 105–117, 132–139; Dexter Perkins, *Charles Evans Hughes and American Democratic Statesmanship* (Boston, 1956), xv–xvii; Robert F. Wesser, *Charles Evans Hughes: Politics and Reform in New York, 1905-1910* (Ithaca, 1967), 18–48; Henry C. Beerits, "The Gas and Insurance Investigations," 3–7, Box 165, Papers of Charles E. Hughes, Library of Congress; Burton J. Hendrick, "Governor Hughes," *McClure's Magazine,* 30 (March, 1908), 530–531; *New York Times,* April 22, 1905; *Annual Report of the City Club of New York,* 1905, 56–57; *New York World,* March 31, April 29, 30, May 5, 1905; "First Annual Report of the Commission of Gas and Electricity of the State of New York," *New York State Senate Documents,* No. 15, VIII (129 Sess.), 1906, 64–73.
24. William A. Prendergast, *Oral History Memoir,* 2:226.
25. Wesser, *Charles Evans Hughes,* 49–101, the quote is from 88; also see Irwin Yellowitz, *Labor and the Progressive Movement in New York State, 1897-1916* (Ithaca, 1965), 203–215.
26. *Public Papers of Charles Evans Hughes,* 1907 (Albany, 1908), 7; *New York Times,* March 1, 1907; Charles E. Hughes, *Conditions of Progress in Democratic Government* (New Haven, 1910), 6–20, 34–39.
27. Wesser, *Charles Evans Hughes,* 346.
28. Ibid., 302–339; see also Walter I. Trattner, *Homer Folks: Pioneer in Social Welfare* (New York, 1968).
29. Seth Low to Hughes, May 23, 1907, Hughes Papers; *Public Papers of Hughes,* 1907, 29–35; Henry C. Beerits, "First Term as Governor," 23–24, Memorandum, Hughes Papers; "Annual Report of the Public Service Commission, First District, 1907," *New York State Senate Documents,* No. 20, IV (131 Sess.), 1908, 7–9; Veiller, *Oral History Memoir,* 1:149–50; "Public Service Commission," 1–5, Box 166, Hughes Papers; *New York Times,* March 6, 1907; Wesser, *Charles Evans Hughes,* 102–181.
30. *Public Papers of Hughes,* 1907, 32–33.

31.   Ibid., 29; *New York Times*, April 21, 1907; "Speech of Governor Hughes at banquet of the Utica Chamber of Commerce," April 1, 1907, Box 181E, Hughes Papers.

32.   *New York Times*, April 2, 1907; Henry Bruère, "Public Utilities Regulation in New York," *Annals*, 31 (May, 1908), 17.

33.   State of New York, *Annual Report of the Public Service Commission, First District*, 1907 (Albany, 1908), I, 20–26, 127–132; 1908 (Albany, 1909), I, 9–10, 14–22, 135–140, 144–147, 157–166; 1909 (Albany, 1910), I, 8–10, 112–116; 1910 (Albany, 1911), I, 7–8, 21; 1911 (Albany, 1912), I, 9–12 (hereafter cited *PSC Report*); Milo R. Maltbie, "The Fruits of Public Regulation in New York," *Annals*, 37 (January, 1911), 173–184; Bruère, "Public Utilities Regulation," 14–17.

34.   *PSC Report*, 1908, I, 14, 143; Maltbie, "Fruits of Public Regulation," 178; Lyman Beecher Stowe, "How New York Deals with Her Public Service Companies," *American Review of Reviews*, 42 (August, 1910), 211–213; Bruère, "Public Utilities Regulation," 10; John S. Kennedy, "The New York Public Service Commissions," *Forum*, 48 (November, 1912), 585–586; Edward A. Fitzpatrick, ed., *Experts in City Government* (New York, 1919), 31; Delos F. Wilcox, "The Crisis in Public Service Regulation in New York," *National Municipal Review*, 4 (October, 1915), 553.

35.   The details and politics of the dual subway contracts negotiation can be found in Cerillo, "Reform in New York City," 240–246.

36.   Wilcox, "Crisis in Regulation," 547–563; Stiles P. Jones, "State Versus Local Regulation," *Annals*, 53 (May, 1914), 94.

37.   "Complete Report of the Joint Legislative Committee Appointed to Investigate the Public Service Commissions," *New York State Senate Documents*, No. 41, XXI (140 Sess.), 1917, 9–84, 103–149, 285–313.

38.   Ibid., 12.

39.   See Cerillo, "Reform in New York City," 248–253.

40.   Jane S. Dahlberg, *The New York Bureau of Municipal Research* (New York, 1966), 3–6; Robert A. Caro, *The Power Broker: Robert Moses and the Fall of New York* (New York, 1974), 59–61; Charles A. Beard, *American City Government* (New York, 1912), 3–30; Augustus Cerillo, Jr., "The Reform of Municipal Government in New York City: From Seth Low to John Purroy Mitchel," *The New-York Historical Society Quarterly*, 57:1 (January, 1973), 52–57.

41.   William H. Allen, *Oral History Memoir*, 1:92–93, 100; Bruère, *Oral History Memoir*, 3–18, 23–36, 42; Allen, "A Proposed Institute for Municipal Research," December 1906, George McAneny Papers, Princeton University; Dahlberg, *New York Bureau of Municipal Research*, 7–16; Norman Gill, *Municipal Research Bureaus* (Washington, D. C., 1944), 14–15, n. 11.

42.   Henry Bruère, *The New City Government* (New York, 1912), 1–8, 100; Frederick A. Cleveland, *Organized Democracy* (New York, 1913), 447–451; William H. Allen, *Efficient Democracy* (New York, 1908), 72–74.

43.   Bruère, *New City Government*, 2.

44.   Allen, *Efficient Democracy*, 343–344.

45.   Bruère, *New City Government*, 2, 8.

46.   Cleveland, *Organized Democracy*, 451; see also Frederick A. Cleveland, *Chapters on Municipal Administration and Accounting* (New York, 1909), 10, 102–104, 351, 357.

47.   Bruère, *New City Government*, 106–124.

48.   Allen, *Oral History Memoir*, 2:159; Bruère, *New City Government*, 100, 106.

49.   Cerillo, "Reform of Municipal Government," 60–70; Edwin R. Lewinson, *John Purroy Mitchel: The Boy Mayor of New York* (New York, 1965), 51–53; Caro, *The Power Broker*, 61–63; Dahlberg, *New York Bureau of Municipal Research*, 7, 11–14, 17–20, 57–60, 78–80, 149–182, 209–220.

50.   Caro, *The Power Broker*, 63; Dahlberg, *New York Bureau of Municipal Research*, 35–36, 203–206.

51. Dahlberg, *New York Bureau of Municipal Research,* 115-142; Caro, *The Power Broker,* 63-64.
52. Bruère, *New City Government,* 107.
53. Lewinson, *John Purroy Mitchel,* 126-127, 129, 150-169, 170-188; William A. Prendergast, "Why New York City Needs a New School Plan," *American Review of Reviews,* 52 (November, 1915), 588; Bruère, "Mayor Mitchel's Administration of the City of New York," *National Municipal Review,* 5 (January, 1916), 24-37; Albert Shaw, "New York's Government by Experts," *American Review of Reviews,* 29 (February, 1914), 173-178; Sol Cohen, *Progressives and Urban School Reform: The Public Education Association of New York City, 1895-1954* (New York, 1964), 87, 94-95.
54. Lewinson, *John Purroy Mitchel,* 245.
55. Caro, *The Power Broker,* 83.

6. REDEFINING THE SUCCESS ETHIC FOR URBAN REFORM MAYORS

This paper was originally delivered at the Richmond American History Seminar in November 1975, where Edward J. Kopf, Virginia Commonwealth University, provided a most constructive critique. In its final form it was presented to the Columbia University Seminar on The City in October 1976. An earlier version was also read by Neil K. Basen, University of Iowa, whose suggestions were illuminating. Colleagues at Lake Forest College—Joseph Carens, Jonathan F. Galloway, D. L. LeMahieu, and Arthur Zilversmit—have offered helpful comments; so have Norman Blume, University of Toledo, Kenneth T. Jackson, Columbia University, Robert M. Saunders, Christopher Newport College, and Bruce M. Stave, University of Connecticut. Two valued friends, both scholars of the Progressive Era, William H. Harbaugh, my mentor at the University of Virginia, and Eugene M. Tobin, my coeditor, have taken time from their respective work to read virtually every draft of this essay—to my inestimable benefit.

1. Russell McCulloch Story, "The American Municipal Executive," *University of Illinois Studies in the Social Sciences,* 7:3 (September, 1918), 24-31; Richard M. Bernard and Bradley R. Rice, "Political Environment and the Adoption of Progressive Municipal Reform," *Journal of Urban History,* 1:2 (February, 1975), 154; and Jon C. Teaford, *The Municipal Revolution in America: Origins of Modern Urban Government, 1650-1825* (Chicago, 1975), 129, n. 6.
2. Samuel P. Hays, "The Changing Political Structure of the City in Industrial America," *Journal of Urban History,* 1:1 (November, 1974), 16-25.
3. Harlan Hahn, "The American Mayor: Retrospect and Prospect," *Urban Affairs Quarterly,* 11:2 (December, 1975), 276-288 offers a review of recent social science literature. I have derived great benefit from Charles H. Levine, *Racial Conflict and the American Mayor: Power, Polarization, and Performance* (Lexington, Mass., 1974), passim—a critique of the pluralistic model of urban leadership.
4. *Passaic Daily Herald,* November 16, 1908, and September 29, 1909. It should be clarified, regarding the denial for renomination, that in 1893 an incumbent Republican failed to win redesignation by his party but subsequently stood successfully for reelection on a coalition ticket.
5. Ernest S. Griffith, *A History of American City Government: The Conspicuous Failure, 1870-1900* (New York, 1974), 270; Stanley H. Friedelbaum, *Municipal Government in New Jersey* (New Brunswick, N. J., 1954), 9f.; and Thomas M. Moore, comp., *City of Passaic, Charter and Ordinances* (Trenton, 1895), 11-20.
6. Michael H. Ebner, "Passaic, New Jersey, 1855-1912: City-Building in Post-Civil War America" (Ph.D. diss., University of Virginia, 1974), 34-123; and Ebner, "The Historian's Passaic, 1855-1912: A Research Model for New Jersey's Urban

Past," in *New Jersey since 1860: New Findings and Interpretations*, ed. William C. Wright (Trenton, 1972), 10–35.

7. William W. Scott, *History of Passaic and Its Environs*, vol. 1 (New York and Chicago, 1922), chap. 33, provides general background on the mayors, although scattered details also have been culled from the press.

8. *Power* (February, 1936), 57f., provides the most complete biographical sketch, published on the occasion of Low's death on January 22 of that year; Monte A. Calvert, "The Search for Engineering Unity: The Professionalization of Special Interest," in *Building the Organizational Society: Essays on Associational Activities in Modern America*, ed. Jerry Israel (New York, 1972), 42–54; and Edwin T. Layton, Jr., *The Revolt of the Engineers: Social Responsibility and the American Engineering Profession* (Cleveland, 1971), passim, all study the milieu in which Low functioned.

9. *Power* (February 9, 1909), 308, and *Passaic Daily Herald*, February 25, 1909; also consult *Power* (December 29, 1908), 1044f., and *Passaic Daily News*, March 29, 1909.

10. Suggestive of Low's career as engineer-journalist and politician is the notable case of Herbert Hoover, especially in the years prior to World War I; see David Burner and Thomas R. West, "A Technocrat's Morality: Conservatism and Hoover the Engineer," in *The Hofstadter Aegis: A Memorial*, ed. Stanley Elkins and Eric McKitrick (New York, 1974), 235–256; and Joan Hoff Wilson, *Herbert Hoover: Forgotten Progressive* (Boston, 1975), 31–53.

11. *Passaic Daily News*, March 17, 26, 27, 29, April 11, 1900; August 1, 3, 15, September 9, 16, 28, 1903.

12. David P. Thelen, "Progressivism as a Radical Movement," in *Main Problems in American History*, ed. Howard H. Quint et al., II (Homewood, Ill., 1972), 157, is the source for the concept "issue-oriented mass educator." For an elaboration consult Thelen, *Robert M. LaFollette and the Insurgent Spirit* (Boston, 1976), passim.

13. The role of Spencer in the Public Service dispute is best recounted in a comprehensive biography written by journalist George Montgomery Hartt that appeared as an obituary (*Passaic Daily News*, July 29, 1931) the day after the former mayor's death; Ebner, "Passaic, New Jersey," 174–176, should also be consulted. Ransom E. Noble, Jr., *New Jersey Progressivism before Wilson* (Princeton, 1946), 34ff., deals with the linkage between Public Service and Republican politicians elsewhere in the state.

14. Eugene M. Tobin, "The Progressive as Politician: Jersey City, 1896-1907," *New Jersey History*, 91:1 (Spring, 1973), 5–23; and Tobin, "The Progressive as Single Taxer: Mark Fagan and the Jersey City Experience, 1900-1917," *American Journal of Economics and Sociology*, 33:3 (July, 1974), 287–297. Of course, Noble, *New Jersey Progressivism before Wilson*, 1–42, must also be consulted.

15. *Passaic Daily News*, August 17, 26, 30, September 6, 1907; *Passaic Daily Herald*, September 11, 1907. After losing the nomination, Spencer severed his connection with Public Service. A report in the *Newark News*, November 25, 1907, and implicitly corroborated in the *Passaic Daily Herald* of the same day, suggests that he was at odds with the management of the firm.

16. Table 6-1 provides a more thorough review of Low's political strength in the city's four wards.

17. *Passaic Daily Herald*, August 10, 20, 24, September 3-6, 9-11, 14, 21, October 7, November 2, 4, 1907; *Passaic Daily News*, September 4, 5, 9, October 7, November 2, 4, 1907.

18. *Passaic Daily News*, August 26, 1907, and *Passaic Daily Herald*, October 12, 1907, January 7, 1908; Melvin G. Holli, *Reform in Detroit, Hazen S. Pingree and Urban Politics* (New York, 1969), 163, presents a thorough analysis of "structural" and "social reform" concepts of change.

19. Ernest S. Griffith, *A History of American City Government: The Progressive Years, and Their Aftermath, 1900-1920* (New York, 1974), 198f., is insightful on the issue of physical development.

20. Ronald M. Zarychta, "Municipal Reorganization: The Pittsburgh Fire Department as a Case Study," *Western Pennyslvania History Magazine,* 58:4 (October, 1975), 471-486, is insightful on the range of issues involved.

21. Eugene M. Tobin, "The Progressive as Humanitarian: Jersey City's Search for Social Justice, 1890-1917," *New Jersey History,* 93:3-4 (Autumn-Winter, 1975), 77-98, affords a superb perspective on the political implications of reform in another setting.

22. Hays, "The Changing Political Structure of the City in Industrial America," 16-25.

23. *Passaic Daily Herald,* December 4, 24, 26-28, 30, 1907; January 3, 4, 6-8, 13-18, 21-23, 28, 30, February 10, 14, 20, March 2, 3, 5, 20, 25, June 6, 1908; *Passaic Daily News,* December 31, 1907; January 3, June 6, 1908. Theodore J. Lowi, *At the Pleasure of the Mayor: Patronage and Power in New York City, 1898-1958* (New York, 1964), 61ff., is suggestive on the matter of mayoral appointments.

24. *Passaic Daily News,* March 26, 27, 1900; August 19, 20, 26, September 19, October 7, 12, November 23, December 21, 1907; January 17, 22, March 26-28, 31, 1908; September 9, 1909; *Passaic Daily Herald,* August 7, 20, October 2, 6, 7, 12, December 17, 24, 1907; January 17, February 7, 8, 14, 15, 18, 24, March 14, 23, 25-28, 30, 31, 1908; May 5, June 30, October 4, November 30, 1909. Joseph A. Miri, "The Politics of Water Supply in Northern New Jersey: Regional and Institutional Cleavages in a Metropolitan Area" (Ph.D. diss., Rutgers University, 1971), 50-74, and Eugene M. Tobin, "Mark Fagan and the Politics of Urban Reform: Jersey City, 1900-1917" (Ph.D. diss., Brandeis University, 1972), 272-278, are essential to understanding the multitude of legal questions shrouded in the water supply control issue.

25. Table 6-1 ("Election Analysis") includes complete ward data on the referenda in 1908. Actually, initially it was reported that the school board proposition also was defeated, but an investigation in the spring of 1909 proved that the ballot count had been fraudulent.

26. *Passaic Daily Herald,* December 7, 1907, and January 25, March 25, 26, May 5, 29, 1908; *Passaic Daily News,* April 16, May 5, 15, 29, 1908. Low's dismay with public safety administration dated back to his term as councilman-at-large, when he chaired the police committee. James F. Richardson, *Urban Police in the United States* (Port Washington, N. Y., 1974), 62-85, offers good perspective.

27. *Passaic Daily Herald,* November 26, 1907; August 5, October 20, November 2, 1908; *Passaic Daily News,* October 21, 29-31, 1908; Leonard P. Ayres, *Laggards in Our Schools: A Study in Retardation and Elimination in City School Systems* (New York, 1909), Tables 100 and 101. On local reaction to the report, see *Passaic Daily Herald,* June 22, 23, 1909; for national perspective refer to David B. Tyack, *The One Best System: A History of American Urban Education* (Cambridge, 1974), 147-160.

28. *Passaic Daily Herald,* January 18, 28, 30, February 19, March 24, 28, April 9, 10, 17, May 11, 13, 21, 28, 29, June 2, 3, 5, 1908; *Passaic Daily News,* April 20, 25, 27, May 5, 13, 19, 23, 26, June 3, 1908. As a last minute ploy, seemingly for the purpose of achieving an electoral "coat-tails" effect, Low successfully tacked onto the public safety referendum a proposition on municipal lighting. This nonbinding question carried with 80.1 percent.

29. Spencer claimed that if Low wanted to influence public safety administration he could do so under the existing charter. Instances of Low's subsequent efforts to do just that can be found throughout the remainder of his term, but his every effort, even when successful, remained subject to public scrutiny and doubt. His political rivals on the council brought forth an unending barrage of procedural,

jurisdictional, and substantive questions. For evidence, consult *Passaic Daily Herald,* July 13-16, 20, 25, 27, 30, September 26, 1908; *Passaic Daily News,* July 14, 15, 20, 21, 1908—dealing with Low's successful order to change patrol assignments. 30. *Passaic Daily News,* October 31, 1908, and June 8, 1909; *Passaic Daily Herald,* May 7, June 7, 8, 11, 14, 15, 1909, on Levendusky. Ironically, in 1911, when Passaic adopted the commission format of municipal government, with five members to be elected in a nonpartisan city-wide contest, Levendusky placed sixth in a field of sixty-two. Actually, no resident of the First Ward, much less a citzen of Slavonic heritage—Passaic's largest ethnic group—was elected.

31. Melvin G. Holli, "Urban Reform in the Progressive Era," in *The Progressive Era,* ed. Lewis L. Gould (Syracuse, 1974), 143-151, is illuminating on the symbolism of such terms as "efficiency" and "economy" as applied to urban political reform. His essay must be supplemented by J. Rogers Hollingsworth and Ellen Jane Hollingsworth, "Expenditures in American Cities," in *The Dimensions of Quantitative Research in History,* ed. William O. Aydelotte et al. (Princeton, 1972), 347-389. For illustrations of Low's expressions on efficiency in an engineering context, see *Power,* September, 1907, 639; May 12, 1908, 756; August 11, 1908, 251; August 25, 1903, 334; September 8, 1908, 420f.; November 10, 1908, 808f.; and December 15, 1908, 1018f.

32. *Passaic Daily Herald,* June 6, 8, 9, 11, September 1, 1908; Department of Commerce and Labor, Bureau of the Census, *Special Reports: Statistics of Cities Having a Population of Over 30,000, 1908* (Washington, 1910), 302, 306, 348; and Department of Commerce and Labor, Bureau of the Census, *Special Reports: Financial Statistics of Cities Having a Population of Over 30,000, 1909* (Washington, 1913), 216-218. See Table 6-2 for comparative data on municipal taxation and expenditures.

33. Samuel P. Hays, "The Politics of Reform in Municipal Government in the Progressive Era," *Pacific Northwest Quarterly,* 55:4 (October, 1964), 157-169, is the classic statement on the primacy of efficiency amongst urban reformers.

34. *Passaic Daily Herald,* June 29, 30, July 13, August 31, September 1, 4, 1909.

35. Department of Commerce and Labor, Bureau of the Census, *Special Reports: Financial Statistics of Cities Having a Population of Over 30,000, 1910* (Washington, 1913), 222-226; and *Passaic Daily News,* August 31, 1909. See Table 6-2 for further comparisons.

36. Eugene M. Tobin, "In Pursuit of Equal Taxation: Jersey City's Struggle Against Corporate Arrogance and Tax-Dodging by the Railroad Trust," *American Journal of Economics and Sociology,* 34:2 (April, 1975), 219-222; *Passaic Daily Herald,* January 7, May 7, 8, July 16, 20, August 6, 1908; January 5, 21, 1909; *Passaic Daily News,* May 6, July 18, 21, 1908; January 5, March 30, 1909. Essential to understanding municipal taxation in this period is C. K. Yearley, *The Money Machines: The Breakdown and Reform of Government and Party Finance in the North, 1860-1920* (Albany, N. Y., 1970), 137-281.

37. *Passaic Daily Herald,* July 3, August 7, September 1, 1909; Department of Commerce and Labor, *Special Reports: Financial Statistics of Cities . . . 1909,* 242-248; and idem., *Special Reports: Financial Statistics of Cities . . . 1910,* 234-240.

38. Adding to Low's predicament was the fact that the city lost state school funds of $33,709 for the new fiscal year, as reported in *Passaic Daily News,* June 29, 1909, and *Passaic Daily Herald,* September 1, 2, 1909.

39. *Passaic Daily Herald,* June 29, August 5-7, 9, 1909; *Passaic Daily News,* August 6, 1909.

40. *Passaic Daily Herald,* January 5, April 21, 1909; *Passaic Daily News,* April 14, 1909; Thelen, "Progressivism as a Radical Movement," 150; Tobin, "The Progressive as Single Taxer," 297f.; and Jack Tager, *The Intellectual as Urban Reformer: Brand Whitlock and the Progressive Movement* (Cleveland, 1968), 107-112.

41.   Holli, *Reform in Detroit*, 157-181, distinguishes this group of progressive mayors from their counterparts of more traditional orientation. And while Governor Hughes never served as mayor, his performance in New York State, while certainly not devoid of concern for social justice, proved relatively normative by comparison—although Robert F. Wesser, *Charles Evans Hughes: Politics and Reform in New York* (Ithaca, 1967), offers a sympathetic portrait.

42.   *Passaic Daily Herald*, May 10, 19, September 7, 1909; *Passaic Daily News*, May 11, August 13, 31, 1909.

43.   *Passaic Daily News*, August 31, 1909, and Table 6-1.

44.   Roy Lubove, "The Twentieth Century City: The Progressive as Municipal Reformer," *Mid-America*, 41:4 (October, 1959), 195-207; and *Passaic Daily Herald*, November 16, 1908, and July 6, 1909. For a later perspective of Low's thinking, see his speech to a civic meeting as published in *Passaic Daily News*, June 16, 1916. It should also be noted that during a wave of local antiradical hysteria following the First World War, Low stated his total opposition to an ordinance requiring permits to be obtained from the police department prior to conducting public meetings; see *Passaic Daily News*, March 29, 1920.

45.   *Passaic Daily Herald*, May 4, 6, June 15, 23, July 27, 28, 30, August 8, September 10, 29, 1908; March 15, 17, 23, May 12, September 21, 1909; *Passaic Daily News*, June 15, September 22, 1908; June 2, September 21, 1909.

46.   Theodore Roosevelt, "Practical Work in Politics," National Conference for Good Government, *Proceedings* (Philadelphia, 1894), 299; Lyle W. Dorsett, "The City Boss and the Reformer," *Pacific Northwest Quarterly*, 63:4 (October, 1972), 150-154; and John D. Buenker, *Urban Liberalism and Progressive Reform* (New York, 1973), passim.

47.   Melvin G. Holli, "Mayor Pingree Campaigns for the Governorship," *Michigan History*, 52:3 (Summer, 1973), 151-173, and idem., *Reform in Detroit*, 125-181. The only pre-World War I urban progressive to match Pingree's feat was Edward F. Dunne (see John D. Beunker, "Edward F. Dunne: The Urban New Stock Democrat as Progressive," *Mid-America*, 50:1 [January, 1968], 3-21), who went from Chicago's mayoralty (1905-1907) to the governorship of Illinois (1913-1917). Martin J. Schiesl, "Progressive Reform in Los Angeles Under Mayor Alexander, 1909-1913," *California Historical Quarterly*, 54:1 (Spring, 1975), 52f., is enlightening on the causes of "failure" among reform types. Anthony R. Travis, "Mayor George Ellis: Grand Rapids Political Boss and Progressive Reformer," *Michigan History*, 50:2 (Summer, 1972), 101-130, is an outstanding analysis of governance in the Pingree tradition.

48.   Allan Nevins, *Grover Cleveland: A Study in Courage* (New York, 1933), 79-93, 114-118, and Horace Samuel Merrill, *Bourbon Leader: Grover Cleveland* (Boston, 1957), 27-31.

49.   *Power* (May 11, 1909), 863.

50.   Michael H. Ebner, "Socialism and Progressive Political Reform: The 1911 Change-of-Government in Passaic, New Jersey," in *Socialism and the Cities*, ed. Bruce M. Stave (Port Washington, N. Y., 1975), 116-140, examines how municipal government in the city was subsequently "reformed" by some of the very individuals and interest groups whom Fred Low had opposed. Low took no role in the campaign to implement a five-member, at-large, nonpartisan government.

7. POLITICIANS IN DISGUISE

1.   Samuel P. Hays, "The Politics of Reform in Municipal Government in the Progressive Era," *Pacific Northwest Quarterly*, 55:4 (October, 1964), 157-169. See also Hays, "The Changing Political Structure of the City in Industrial America," *Journal of Urban History*, 1:1 (November, 1974), 16-25; James Weinstein, *The*

Corporate Ideal in the Liberal State: 1900-1918 (Boston, 1968), 92-116; Melvin G. Holli, *Reform in Detroit: Hazen S. Pingree and Urban Politics* (New York, 1969), 178-180. Holli sees Pingree as the prototype of a group of "social reform" mayors who attacked the privileges of "structural reformers" in the business community and worked to distribute more welfare services to the lower classes (*Reform in Detroit*, 157-161, 169-171). For evidence that progressivism was not exclusively an upper-middle-class movement and had an important urban wing of working-class people, see John D. Buenker, *Urban Liberalism and Progressive Reform* (New York, 1973), especially 42-117.

2.   Ernest S. Griffith, *A History of American City Government: The Progressive Years and Their Aftermath, 1900-1920* (New York, 1974), 50. See also Otis A. Pease, "Urban Reformers in the Progressive Era: A Reassessment," *Pacific Northwest Quarterly*, 62:2 (April, 1971), 53-54.

3.   Robert M. Fogelson, *The Fragmented Metropolis: Los Angeles, 1850-1930* (Cambridge, Mass., 1967), 205-209.

4.   Los Angeles *Times*, November 17, 19, 1901, February 4, 1902; Vincent Ostrom, *Water and Politics: A Study of Water Policies and Administration in the Development of Los Angeles* (Los Angeles, 1953), 52-54, 92.

5.   "Water Commissioners," *Annual Report of the Auditor of the City of Los Angeles for the Year Ending November 30, 1903*, 215-217.

6.   Municipal League of Los Angeles, *Civil Service Reform in the City of Los Angeles* (pamphlet, 1902); *Charter of the City of Los Angeles 1889-1913*, 184-195.

7.   Los Angeles *Herald*, January 25, 1903; "Civil Service Commission: First Annual Report," *Annual Report of the Auditor . . . November 30, 1903*, 50.

8.   "Mayor's Annual Message," *Annual Report of the Auditor of the City of Los Angeles for the Year Ending November 30, 1904*, 10.

9.   "Civil Service Commission: Second Annual Report," *Annual Report of the Auditor . . . November 30, 1904*, 104.

10.   "Civil Service Commission," *Annual Report of the Auditor of the City of Los Angeles for the Year Ending November 30, 1905*, 116-118.

11.   *Charter of the City of Los Angeles 1889-1913*, 83-90.

12.   Editor, "What the 'Cranks' Have Done: Beginnings of the Movement for Better City Government," *Pacific Outlook*, 2 (May 25, 1907), 10-11; Los Angeles *Examiner*, December 9, 1907.

13.   Los Angeles *Examiner*, December 6, 1906.

14.   Los Angeles *Times*, December 31, 1906; *Pacific Outlook*, 2 (April 6, 1907) 3-4; ibid. (June 22, 1907), 3-4; ibid. (June 29, 1907), 3-4; Los Angeles *Examiner*, December 9, 1907.

15.   *Pacific Outlook*, 4 (June 6, 1908), 3-4; Albert H. Clodius, "The Quest for Good Government in Los Angeles," 0161-0681 (Ph.D. diss., Claremont Graduate School, 1953), 244.

16.   Pease, "Urban Reformers in the Progressive Era," 53-54.

17.   Marshall Stimson, "Fun, Fights, and Fiestas in Old Los Angeles: An Autobiography," Marshall Stimson Papers, Henry E. Huntington Library, San Marino, California, 172; *Charter of the City of Los Angeles 1889-1913*, 157-167.

18.   Hays, "Changing Political Structure of the City," 22-25.

19.   Los Angeles *Herald*, January 25, 1909.

20.   Meyer Lissner to Francis J. Heney, February 2, 1909, box 2, Meyer Lissner Papers, Borel Collection, Stanford University Libraries; "Petition for the Recall of Mayor Harper" (1909), John Randolph Haynes Papers, University Research Library, University of California, Los Angeles.

21.   Los Angeles *Express*, March 12, 25, 27, 1909; Grace Heilman Stimson, *Rise of the Labor Movement in Los Angeles* (Berkeley, 1955), 324-325.

22.   Los Angeles *Examiner*, March 30, 1909.

23.   Los Angeles *Examiner*, March 30, April 1, 6, 23, 1909; Los Angeles *Express*, April 4, 23, 1909.
24.   Los Angeles *Times*, April 28, May 19, 1909.
25.   Los Angeles *Examiner*, December 6, 1909.
26.   Fogelson, *Fragmented Metropolis*, 68–73, 78.
27.   Griffith, *American City Government*, 195.
28.   "Six Months of Good Government Administration," *Pacific Outlook*, 8 (June 25, 1910), 2–3; *Annual Report of the Mayor, July 31, 1911*, 7–12, 14–16; Los Angeles *Examiner*, July 5, 1912. See also Martin J. Schiesl, "Progressive Reform in Los Angeles under Mayor Alexander, 1909–1913," *California Historical Quarterly*, 54:1 (Spring, 1975), 44, 47, 50.
29.   Police official to John R. Haynes, July 9, 1908, Haynes Papers; Los Angeles *Times*, April 11, 1909. See also Clodius, "Quest for Good Government," 218–219.
30.   *Annual Report of the Police Department of the City of Los Angeles, California, for the Year Ending June 30, 1912*, 4–5, 7, 10, 14–15; *Annual Report of the Police Department . . . June 30, 1913*, 4–5, 8–10, 13–14.
31.   Los Angeles *Herald*, October 20, 30, 1909; *First Annual Report of the Board of Public Utilities of the City of Los Angeles, June 30, 1910*, 1, 6–8, 32–33.
32.   *Second and Third Annual Report of the Board of Public Utilities, Los Angeles, California, July 1, 1910–June 30, 1912*, 87–88, 115–118; Los Angeles *Express*, June 30, 1911.
33.   Lewis R. Works to T. Perceval Gerson, July 10, 1911, box 1, Theodore Perceval Gerson Papers, University Research Library, University of California, Los Angeles.
34.   *Pacific Outlook*, 6 (June 26, 1909), 7.
35.   *Fourteenth Annual Report of the Board of Public Service Commissioners of the City of Los Angeles for the Year Ending June 30, 1915*, 55–56; Ostrom, *Water and Politics*, 55.
36.   Los Angeles *Examiner*, June 9, 24, July 12, 1912.
37.   *Eleventh Annual Report of the Board of Public Service Commissioners of the City of Los Angeles, California, for the Year Ending June 30, 1912*, 6.
38.   Los Angeles *Examiner*, April 9, 16, 1913; Los Angeles *Record*, April 14, 16, 1913.
39.   Believing that Mayor Alexander represented civic organizations unsympathetic to workers, the Union Labor Political Club and the Socialist Party nominated attorney Job Harriman for the mayoralty. Harriman conducted a strong primary campaign, in which he emphasized the Socialist commitment to efficient administration and welfare programs. His ticket won a plurality of votes. In the fear that the city might come under a labor administration, the progressives joined forces with party regulars and campaigned vigorously for Alexander's reelection. Shortly before the final election, two labor organizers confessed to the crime of dynamiting the Los Angeles *Times* building on October 1, 1910, in which twenty-one persons died. Harriman lost considerable support from lower-middle-class elements, and Alexander defeated him by a wide margin. See Stimson, "Fun, Fights, and Fiestas," 215; Los Angeles *Examiner*, November 7, 16, 19, December 5, 6, 1911.
40.   Marshall Stimson to E. A. Dickson, March 31, 1913, box 2, Edward A. Dickson Papers, University Research Library, University of California, Los Angeles; Los Angeles *Express*, April 23, 26, 1913.
41.   Meyer Lissner to Members of the Municipal Conference, May 1, 1913, box 21, Lissner Papers; Los Angeles *Examiner*, May 28, June 2, 4, 1913.
42.   Fogelson, *Fragmented Metropolis*, 217.
43.   *Fiscal Year Report and First Annual Message of Mayor H. H. Rose, July 1, 1914*, 1–7.
44.   Fred W. Riggs, "Bureaucratic Politics in Comparative Perspective," in Fred W. Riggs, ed., *Frontiers of Development Administration* (Durham, 1971), 406–410.

45. *Twelfth Annual Report of the Board of Civil Service Commissioners of Los Angeles, California, with Charter Provisions, July 1, 1913 to June 30, 1914*, 4–5.
46. Efficiency Committee of the Municipal League, "Efficiency in Los Angeles City Government" (1913), Haynes Papers, 1, 5; Efficiency Department of Los Angeles, *The City Government of Los Angeles, California: Organization and Charts* (pamphlet 1914).
47. Jesse D. Burks, "A Business Re-organization for Los Angeles," *California Outlook*, 17 (November 28, 1914), 13–14.
48. Lorin A. Handley, "One-Man Administration," *California Outlook*, 17 (December 19, 1914), 13. Handley was president of the city's Board of Public Works.
49. "The Proposed New Charter for Los Angeles, Statement of the Board of Freeholders," *Pacific Municipalities*, 30 (April, 1916), 141–143; Citizens New Charter Committee, "The New Charter or the Old" (1916), Haynes Papers.
50. Los Angeles *Times*, May 14, 16, June 4, 16, 1916. See also Burton L. Hunter, *The Evolution of Municipal Organization and Administrative Practice in the City of Los Angeles* (Los Angeles, 1933), 155–156.
51. Los Angeles *Tribune*, April 29, May 1, 1917.
52. William T. Craig to John R. Haynes, October 29, 1917. Haynes Papers. Craig was a member of the Los Angeles Board of Civil Service Commissioners.
53. Jesse D. Burks, "The Efficiency Program of Los Angeles," *California Outlook*, 19 (July 3, 1915), 9–10; Hunter, *Municipal Organization and Administrative Practice*, 145–146, 166–167.
54. "Report of the Efficiency Commission to the City Council, December 10, 1916," Haynes Papers, 1.
55. "Report of the Efficiency Commission . . . December 10, 1916," Haynes Papers, 1–3; *Annual Message of Mayor Frederic T. Woodman, Los Angeles, California, January 2, 1918*, 30, 33–34, 38–41; *Annual Message of Mayor Frederic T. Woodman . . . January 2, 1919*, 7–9.
56. Melvin G. Holli, "Urban Reform in the Progressive Era," in Lewis L. Gould, ed., *The Progressive Era* (Syracuse, 1974), 142–147.
57. Fogelson, *Fragmented Metropolis*, 75–79. Several unincorporated districts joined the metropolis between 1915 and 1920, and Los Angeles expanded from 115 to 364 square miles (*Fragmented Metropolis*, 226).
58. *Annual Report of the Police Department, City of Los Angeles, California, for the Year Ending June 30, 1917*, 3, 5–8, 17–18; *Annual Report of the Police Department . . . June 30, 1918*, 6–9, 12–13. For similar police reform in other cities, see Griffith, *American City Government*, 213–215.
59. *Annual Report of the Social Service Commission, City of Los Angeles, California, July 1, 1916–July 1, 1917*, 8–11; *Annual Report of the Social Service Commission . . . July 1, 1918–July 1, 1919*, 3–4, 26–27.
60. *Annual Message of Mayor Frederic T. Woodman . . . January 2, 1918*, 4–5, 14–15, 41–43, 50–54; *Annual Message of Mayor Frederic T. Woodman . . . January 2, 1919*, 19–20, 29–33, 41–43, 50–52; Mary Chaffee, "Social Work as a Profession in Los Angeles," *Studies in Sociology*, No. 9 (Los Angeles, 1918), 1–10.
61. *Annual Report of the Department of Health of the City of Los Angeles, California, for the Year Ending June 30, 1917*, 109–120; *Annual Report of the Department of Health . . . June 30, 1919*, 100–105.
62. *Eighteenth Annual Report of the Board of Public Service Commissioners of the City of Los Angeles, California, for the Year Ending June 30, 1919*, 6, 31; Ostrom, *Water and Politics*, 59–61.

8. DISINFECTING THE INDUSTRIAL CITY

1. Samuel Haber, *Efficiency and Uplift: Scientific Management in the Progressive Era, 1890-1920* (Chicago, 1964), x–xi, 112, 134. See Samuel P. Hays,

Conservation and the Gospel of Efficiency: The Progressive Conservation Movement, 1890-1920 (Cambridge, 1959); Robert H. Wiebe, The Search for Order: 1877-1920 (New York, 1967), 111-196; Roy Lubove, The Professional Altruist: The Emergence of Social Work as a Career, 1880-1930 (Cambridge, 1965); James H. Timberlake, Prohibition and the Progressive Movement, 1900-1920 (New York, 1970); John D. Buenker, Urban Liberalism and Progressive Reform (New York, 1973); see also Zane L. Miller, Boss Cox's Cincinnati: Urban Politics in the Progressive Era (New York, 1968), 146-160.

2. Roy Lubove, The Progressives and the Slums: Tenement House Reform in New York, 1890-1917 (Pittsburgh, 1962), 151-184.

3. Lubove, The Progressives and the Slums, 174f.

4. On the Octavia Hill Society, see John F. Sutherland, "The Origins of Philadelphia's Octavia Hill Society: Social Reform in the Contented City," Pennsylvania Magazine of History and Biography, 99:1 (January, 1975), 20-44. On the Whittier Center, see Harry Moul, The Work of the Whittier Center, 1893-1927 (Whittier Center, 1927), Housing Association of Delaware Valley Records, Temple University Urban Archives, Temple University, Philadelphia (hereinafter, HAR).

5. On modernization, see Gino Germani, "Urbanization, Social Change, and the Great Transformation," in Gino Germani, ed., Modernization, Urbanization, and the Urban Crisis (Boston, 1973), 3-27. On the "distended society," see Wiebe, The Search for Order, 11-110.

6. Germani, "Urbanization, Social Change, and the Great Transformation," 7-20. David P. Thelen discusses the social gestation of the period and stresses the depression of 1893 in "Social Tensions and the Origins of Progressivism," Journal of American History, 56:2 (September, 1969), 323-341.

7. Wiebe, Search for Order, 160; Allen F. Davis, Spearheads for Reform: The Social Settlement and the Progressive Movement (New York, 1967), 66-67.

8. Jacob A. Riis, How the Other Half Lives: Studies Among the Tenements of New York (New York, 1957 ed.), passim.

9. Lubove, The Progressives and the Slums, 65.

10. Leah Hannah Feder, Unemployment Relief in Periods of Depression: A Study of Measures Adopted in Certain American Cities, 1857 through 1922 (New York, 1936), 47, 247-248; Lubove, Professional Altruist, 46.

11. Mel Scott, American City Planning since 1890 (Berkeley, 1969), 58-60; Donald W. Disbrow, "The Progressive Movement in Philadelphia, 1910-1916" (Ph. D. diss., University of Rochester, 1956), 77-78; and Disbrow, "Reform in Philadelphia Under Mayor Blankenburg, 1912-1916," Pennsylvania History, 27:4 (October, 1960), 379-380. Melvin G. Holli provides the classic case of structural reform in Reform in Detroit: Hazen S. Pingree and Urban Politics (New York, 1969).

12. Haber, Efficiency and Uplift, 108-111; Edwin T. Layton, Jr., "Engineers in Revolt," in Edwin T. Layton, ed., Technology and Social Change in America (New York, 1973), 149-150.

13. Disbrow, "The Progressive Movement in Philadelphia," 21-26; Samuel P. Hays, "The Politics of Reform in Municipal Government in the Progressive Era," Pacific Northwest Quarterly, 55:4 (October, 1964), 157-169.

14. John Sutherland, "A City of Homes: Philadelphia Slums and Reformers, 1880-1918," (Ph.D. diss., Temple University, 1973), 158; "Address Made by Mr. Weber," mimeographed, n.d. (circa December, 1909), in URB 3/1/122 HAR.

15. Joseph Neff to Gustavus Weber, 27 August 1909, URB 3/1/119, HAR; see also draft proposal for a housing commission bearing the heading "Octavia Hill Association," URB 3/1/122, HAR; Bernard Newman to Elmer S. Forbes, 26 July 1911, HAR; Jesse D. Burks, Director of the Philadelphia BMR, to Newman, 1 October 1913, URB 3/1/187, HAR.

16. Note Joseph Neff's minutes of the conference founding the Philadelphia Housing Commission, 8 September 1909, in URB 29, Box 3, HAR.

17. On the purpose of the Commission, see "Notes for Committee on Permanent

Organization," URB 3/1/112, *HAR;* my list of eighteen persons was compiled by making a record of the names that appeared most frequently on the Commission's schedules of officers, board members and committee members, 1909-1915; see "Memorandum: Chief Characteristics and Results of Dr. Neff's Administration" mimeographed, n.d., URB 3/1/113, *HAR;* on Porter Lee, see Lee to Newman, 30 October 1911, URB 3/1/93, *HAR;* on Solenberger, see Solenberger to Newman, 25 October 1911, URB 3/1/19, *HAR.*

18. Richard Waterman, Secretary of the City Club, to Gustavus Weber, 28 August 1909, URB 3/1/88A, *HAR;* on Norris, see Disbrow, "Progressive Movement in Philadelphia," 71.

19. See "Minutes of the Meeting of the Committee on Investigations of the Philadelphia Housing Commission," URB 29, Box 33, *HAR;* also Newman to Mrs. Blade of the Society to Protect Children from Cruelty, 20 June 1911, URB 3/1/9, *HAR.*

20. On meeting in Mayor Reyburn's office and Veiller's speech, see "Minutes of a Public Meeting of the Philadelphia Housing Commission in the Mayor's Reception Room, December 14, 1910, at 4 P.M.," in URB 29, Box 3, *HAR.*

21. Veiller to Helen Parrish, 3 March 1911, URB 3/1/93, *HAR;* Alfred T. White to S. Burns Weston, 7 March 1911, URB 3/1/93, *HAR;* Newman to Helen Parrish [*sic*], 1 March 1911, URB 3/1/93, *HAR;* and "copy of sketch sent to 'Who's Who in America,'" 21 January 1931, in URB 3/1/93, *HAR.*

22. Newman, "Town Planning and Public Health," mimeographed, n.d., URB 3/1/11, *HAR;* also Newman to Elmer S. Forbes, Director of Social Services, Boston, Mass., 26 July 1911, *HAR;* and Newman to Sigurd Anderson, a friend of Newman and inmate in Fort Leavenworth Federal Prison, 23 June 1911, *HAR.*

23. Newman to Dr. Carl Kelsey, an economist at the University of Pennsylvania, 4 May 1914, URB 3/1/91, *HAR;* "Minutes of the Executive Board," 19 April 1911, URB 29, Box 3, *HAR.*

24. Newman to Miss Emma Hunt, 22 March 1912, *HAR.*

25. Newman to M. B. Reinhardt, 28 July 1911, *HAR;* Newman to Henry C. Morris, a Philadelphia engineer, 21 March 1912, URB 3/1/97, *HAR.*

26. Newman to Dean John Holdsworth, University of Pittsburgh, 26 December 1911, URB 3/1/75, *HAR;* "Report of Committee on Publicity," URB 29, Box 3, *HAR;* on housing tours, see Jacob Riis, "The Nation-Wide Battle Against the Slum," *Survey,* 29 (December 21, 1912), 349-352.

27. Newman to Elmer S. Forbes, 31 July 1911, *HAR;* Newman to George W. Norris, 24 April 1913, URB 3/1/11, *HAR.*

28. See Newman's "Report of the Executive Board of the Philadelphia Housing Commission for the Year Ending December 21, 1912," *HAR.*

29. Ibid. Newman discusses the "dog pure" problem in a letter to Alexander Wilson, 20 May 1912, *HAR.*

30. "The House as a Factor in the Evolution of Tuberculosis," mimeographed, n.d., URB 3/1/11, *HAR.*

31. Newman to Albert Smith Faught, a prominent Philadelphia reformer, 28 July 1911, *HAR;* edited copy, probably Newman, on "How to Prevent Congestion," n.d., *HAR.* For an excellent treatment of the "boarder problem" in urban America, see John Modell and Tamara Hareven, "Urbanization and the Malleable Household: An Examination of Boarding and Lodging in American Families," *Journal of Marriage and the Family,* 35:3 (August, 1973), 467-479.

32. "The Housing Problem," mimeographed, n.d., *HAR.*

33. Disbrow, "Progressive Movement in Philadelphia," 188; on Heidinger housing bill, see Sutherland, "A City of Homes," 174-180; and "Fourth Annual Report of the Philadelphia Housing Commission," URB 3/1/3, *HAR.*

34. Newman to George W. Norris, 1 August 1913, URB 3/1/12, *HAR.*

35. J. D. Burns to Newman, 1 October 1913, URB 3/1/107, *HAR.*

36. *Minutes* Philadelphia Board of Trade, 15 April 1912, 16 December 1914, in the Historical Society of Pennsylvania, Philadelphia; also George Rowland of Fels and Company, to Newman, 31 December 1914, URB 3/1/13, *HAR;* and M. T. Rogers of Packard Motor Car Company of Philadelphia, to Newman, 23 October 1912, URB 3/1/159, *HAR.*

37. For an example of the analytical-empirical orientation to problems, see Newman to George W. Norris, 7 May 1912, *HAR.*

38. "Report of the Philadelphia Housing Commission for 1913," *HAR;* also, see Newman to Charles Hall, 26 April 1912, URB 3/1/13A, *HAR.* Newman discussed the compromise housing law in a four-page letter to Veiller, 15 May 1912, *HAR.*

39. Karl DeSchweinitz, "Philadelphia Striking a Balance between Boss and Business Rule," *Survey,* 31 (January 17, 1914), 458–462.

40. Ibid. Edward C. Banfield and James Q. Wilson in *City Politics* (Cambridge, 1963), passim, afford an extensive discussion of the relationship between middle-class values and urban reform.

9. PROGRESSIVE EDUCATION IN THE URBAN SOUTH

The author's interest in this topic was stimulated by the work of Hughie Majors and Elizabeth Jackson, graduate students at Georgia State University. Geraldine Clifford, Edgar Gumbert, and George Overholt helped the essay along through their careful and critical reading of an earlier version.

1. Lawrence A. Cremin, *The Transformation of the School* (New York, 1961). The reference here is mainly to part 1 of Cremin's book, which covers progressive reform from its beginnings to 1917.

2. Edward A. Krug, *The Shaping of the American High School 1880-1920* (New York, 1964), 249–283.

3. Raymond E. Callahan, *Education and the Cult of Efficiency* (Chicago, 1962), chapter 4.

4. In most respects, the Atlanta school reform was comparable to that in other cities. In terms of the politics of reform, however, Atlanta events were unique; they were understandable not as a part of city political battles, but rather as a piece of the statewide political picture. This uniqueness is explored further in the concluding section of this essay.

5. Biographical information on Guinn can be found in Melvin Ecke, *From Ivy Street to Kennedy Center: A Centennial History of the Atlanta Public Schools* (Atlanta, 1972), 83. Also consulted was the Robert J. Guinn scrapbook, a copy of which is available from Mr. Walter Bell, historian, Atlanta Public Schools.

6. Guinn scrapbook and *Atlanta Journal* (November 13, 1908) for Guinn's role in 1908 Atlanta mayoral election; *Atlanta Constitution,* (June 3, 1915) for his activity in 1914 U. S. Senate campaign.

7. Brittain, Parrish, Wardlaw, and Smith all had bachelor's degrees and had done extensive graduate work, including some at the University of Chicago. All but Parrish were rural or small-town Georgians; Parrish was from a small town in Virginia. It is noteworthy that when Parrish moved to Atlanta to take up her work as assistant to the state superintendent she resided, according to the 1912 Atlanta *City Directory,* at the home of Robert J. Guinn. For biographical information: on Brittain, see Dorothy Orr, *A History of Education in Georgia* (Chapel Hill, 1950), 387; on Parrish, see "Parrish, Celestia Susannah," in Dumas Malone, ed., *Dictionary of American Biography* (New York, 1943) vol. 14:257, and Charles E. Strickland, "Parrish, Celestia Susannah," in Edward T. James, ed., *Notable American Women* (Cambridge, 1971) vol. 3, part 2, 18–20; on Wardlaw, see Ecke, *Centennial History,* 107, and Fanny Spahr, "Superintendents of the Atlanta Schools,"

(M. A. thesis, Oglethorpe University, 1930), 30–33; and on Smith, see *Atlanta Journal,* June 8, 1915.

8. Strickland, "Parrish."
9. C. S. Parrish, *Survey of the Atlanta Schools* (Atlanta, 1914), reprinted in 1973 by the Board of Education, 13.
10. Ibid., 30–31, 18–20, 24–28.
11. Ecke, *Centennial History,* 111.
12. Ibid., 103–104; Krug, *Shaping of the American High School,* 276; and David B. Tyack, *The One Best System: A History of American Urban Education* (Cambridge, Mass., 1974), 191.
13. Ecke, *Centennial History,* 93–94 and 102–103.
14. Michael B. Katz, *Class, Bureaucracy and Schools* (New York, 1971), 118–125.
15. On teachers and reform, see Wayne J. Urban, "Teachers, Politics, and Progressivism: The Early Years of the Atlanta Public School Teachers' Association" (paper presented at History of Education Society meeting, Chicago, Illinois, October 24, 1973). On the Women's School Improvement Association, see Philip N. Racine, "Atlanta's Schools: A History of the Public School System, 1869–1955" (Ph.D. diss., Emory University, 1969), 167–168.
16. *Journal of Labor,* January 22, 1915, and *Atlanta Constitution,* February 5, 1915.
17. Urban, "Teachers, Politics, and Progressivism."
18. Ecke, *Centennial History,* 71–73, 104–105, 108.
19. Ibid., 118–119, and *Atlanta Constitution,* May 28, 1918.
20. "Evidence and Proceedings Before a Special Committee of Five, Appointed Under a Resolution of City Council," (1918), 152–160. My copy of this document was obtained from Professor Melvin Ecke, History Department, Georgia State University. A copy is also available from the Atlanta city council at the offices of the clerk.
21. Ibid.; *Journal of Labor* (March 18, 1921); and Urban, "Teachers, Politics, and Progressivism." On the Gary system, see Callahan, *Cult of Efficiency,* chapter 6.
22. *Atlanta Constitution,* June 2, 1915.
23. Ecke, *Centennial History,* 105, notes that the *Atlanta Journal* was the only local paper to back the firing of Slaton. Dewey W. Grantham, *Hoke Smith and the Politics of the New South* (Baton Rouge, 1958), chapter 9 and p. 268 describes the factions in the Democratic party and the election of 1914. Andrew J. Ritchie, *Sketches of Rabun County History, 1819–1948* (Clayton, Ga., 1948), 332–333, discusses the joint appearance of Hoke Smith and Celeste Parrish.
24. Mercer G. Evans, "A History of the Organized Labor Movement in Georgia" (Ph.D. diss., University of Chicago, 1929), 261, describes the relationship between Clark Howell and labor. On Mrs. Howell's participation in the Women's School Improvement Association, see Racine, "Atlanta's Schools," 137.
25. Grantham, *Hoke Smith,* passim, and 17–20, 131, 211, 371.
26. Ibid., 148–149, 285–291.
27. *Atlanta Constitution,* July 4, 6, 1918.
28. Ibid., August 10, 1918, and December 10, 1918.
29. David P. Thelen, "Social Tensions and the Origins of Progressivism," *Journal of American History,* 56:2 (September, 1969), 323–341, and *The New Citizenship: Origins of Progressivism in Wisconsin, 1885–1900* (Columbia, Mo., 1972). Thelen has recently labeled the democratic reformers "insurgents" and the interest-oriented reformers as "modernizers"; see his *Robert M. LaFollette and the Insurgent Spirit* (Boston, 1976), vii–viii.
30. Tyack, *One Best System,* 182–198.

31.   Samuel P. Hays, "The Politics of Reform in Municipal Government in the Progressive Era," *Pacific Northwest Quarterly* 55:4 (October, 1964), 157–169, and "The Changing Political Structure of the City in Industrial America," *Journal of Urban History,* 1:1 (November, 1974), 6–38.

32.   *Journal of Labor,* May 31, July 12, and August 23, 1918, all contain endorsements of Key, while no mention of the school investigation is made in the paper during the summer of 1918.

33.   John D. Buenker, "The Progressive Era: A Search for Synthesis," *Mid-America,* 51:3 (July, 1969), 175–193, and *Urban Liberalism and Progressive Reform* (New York, 1973).

34.   On Atlanta in this period, the major source is Thomas M. Deaton, "Atlanta During the Progressive Era" (Ph.D. diss., University of Georgia, 1969). Deaton struggles mightily throughout the study to fit the Atlanta events into a consistent political framework but fails to achieve this objective. For his comparison of Atlanta with other cities, see 410–418.

35.   On the prevalence of home-rule movements in other cities, see Buenker, *Urban Liberalism,* 135–139; James B. Crooks, *Politics and Progress: The Rise of Urban Progressivism in Baltimore, 1895 to 1911* (Baton Rouge, 1968), 48; and William D. Miller, *Memphis During the Progressive Era* (Memphis, 1957), 138–139.

36.   On the statewide influence of Atlanta's newspapers, see William Anderson, *The Wild Man from Sugar Creek* (Baton Rouge, 1975), 148.

10.   "ENGINES OF SALVATION" OR "SMOKING BLACK DEVILS"

My friend and co-editor, Michael H. Ebner, read many revisions of this article and provided a good deal of constructive criticism. His colleague at Lake Forest College, Charles A. Miller, read an earlier version and was especially helpful in clarifying late nineteenth-century legal developments. I would also like to acknowledge the assistance and encouragement of Jon A. Peterson of Queens College, CUNY, Stanley N. Katz of the University of Chicago Law School, Roger D. Simon of Lehigh University, Morton Keller of Brandeis University, and James Willard Hurst of the University of Wisconsin School of Law.

1.   Robert H. Wiebe, *Businessmen and Reform: A Study of the Progressive Movement* (Cambridge, 1962), and Samuel P. Hays, "The Politics of Reform in Municipal Government in the Progressive Era," *Pacific Northwest Quarterly,* 55:4 (October, 1964), 157–169.

2.   See in particular the following works: David P. Thelen, *The New Citizenship: Origins of Progressivism in Wisconsin, 1885-1900* (Columbia, Mo., 1972); Melvin. G. Holli, *Reform in Detroit: Hazen S. Pingree and Urban Politics* (New York, 1969); Hoyt L. Warner, *Progressivism in Ohio, 1897-1917* (Columbus, 1964); Gabriel Kolko, *Railroads and Regulation, 1877-1916* (Princeton, 1965); Robert W. Harbeson, "Railroads and Regulation, 1877-1916; Conspiracy or Public Interest?" *Journal of Economic History,* 27:2 (June, 1967), 230–242; and Stanley P. Caine, *The Myth of a Progressive Reform: Railroad Regulation in Wisconsin, 1903-1910* (Madison, 1970).

3.   Robert H. Wiebe, *The Segmented Society: An Introduction to the Meaning of America* (New York, 1975), 150–151.

4.   For example, of the 4,500 laws passed by the New Jersey (1895) Legislature and printed in the General Statutes of New Jersey, 1,141 dealt with municipal subjects (Harris I. Effross, "Comments," in *New Jersey History Since 1860: New Findings and Interpretations,* William C. Wright, ed., [Trenton, 1972], 94).

5.   The quotation is from Wiebe, *The Segmented Society*, 151. See also Arnold M. Paul, *Conservative Crisis and the Rule of Law: Attitudes of Bar and Bench, 1887-1895* (Ithaca, 1960), 1-18.

6.   , Ransom E. Noble, Jr., *New Jersey Progressivism Before Wilson* (Princeton, 1946), 4-11; S. McReynolds, "The Home of Trusts," *World's Work*, 4 (September, 1902), 2526-2532; and Lincoln Steffens, "New Jersey: A Traitor State," *McClure's Magazine*, 24 (April, 1905), 649-664, and 25 (May, 1905), 41-55.

7.   Robert W. Fogel, *Railroads and American Economic Growth: Essays in American Econometric History* (Baltimore, 1964), 7.

8.   In addition to the previously mentioned works by Kolko, Harbeson, and Caine, readers should consult the following: Albro Martin, *Enterprise Denied: Origins of the Decline of American Railroads, 1897-1917* (New York, 1971), and Robert H. Wiebe, *The Search For Order, 1877-1920* (New York, 1967).

9.   In 1903 the Interstate Commerce Commission disclosed that the gross earnings of railroads operating in New Jersey had risen 46 percent since 1890; yet, railroad taxes had increased only 16 percent over the same period. See Brief on Behalf of Jersey City, "In the Matter of Investigation of the System of Taxation in New Jersey" (Jersey City, 1904).

10.   Noble, *New Jersey Progressivism Before Wilson*, 6-7.

11.   See Eugene Tobin, "In Pursuit of Equal Taxation: Jersey City's Struggle Against Corporate Arrogance and Tax-Dodging by the Railroad Trust," *American Journal of Economics and Sociology*, 34:2 (April, 1975), 214.

12.   C. K. Yearley, *The Money Machines: The Breakdown and Reform of Governmental and Party Finance in the North, 1860-1920* (Albany, N.Y., 1970); and Martin, *Enterprise Denied*, 57.

13.   I am indebted to Professor Willard Hurst of the University of Wisconsin Law School for bringing this theme to my attention.

14.   *Laws of New Jersey*, 1884, ch. 101, extended and clarified in 1888, ch. 208, and 1897, ch. 69. See Richard A. Hogarty, "Governor Leon Abbett's Battle to Tax the Railroads," *Proceedings of the New Jersey Historical Society*, 84:4 (October, 1966), 207-238.

15.   J. A. Sackett, *Jersey City: Railroad Centre of the East* (New York, 1875), 4; and Herman K. Platt, "Jersey City and the United Railroad Companies, 1868: A Case Study in Municipal Weakness," *New Jersey History*, 91:4 (Winter, 1973), 249-265. Seymour J. Mandelbaum has analyzed Jersey City's role in the transportation and communication revolutions in *Boss Tweed's New York* (New York, 1965), 9-11.

16.   The seriousness of this situation was underlined by the fact that local governments depended almost exclusively for revenue from the general property tax. In 1890 alone, 92 percent of local revenue across the nation was produced by this means.

17.   In 1903 the average tax rate per acre of nonrailroad property assessed by the local tax board was $269.39, while railroads paid at the rate of $412.57 per acre on land valued by the State Board of Assessors. (See *Fact, Arguments and Exhibits by the . . . Delaware, Lackawanna and Western Railroad Company . . . to the Commission appointed . . . to examine the whole matter of taxation in the State*, Brief of William D. Edwards [Jersey City, 1904].)

18.   Noble, *New Jersey Progressivism Before Wilson*, 12-42; and Lincoln Steffens, "A Servant of God and the People: The Story of Mark Fagan, Mayor of Jersey City," *McClure's Magazine*, 26 (January, 1906), 297-308. This essay was later included in Steffens's collection *Upbuilders* (New York, 1909), 2-46. Fagan's early political career is discussed in Eugene M. Tobin, "The Progressive as Politician: Jersey City, 1896-1907," *New Jersey History*, 91:1 (Spring, 1973), 5-23.

19.   *Jersey City Evening Journal*, October 28, 1901.

20. Mayor Fagan's commitment to social welfare is discussed in Eugene M. Tobin, "The Progressive as Humanitarian: Jersey City's Search for Social Justice, 1890–1917," *New Jersey History*, 93:3–4 (Autumn-Winter, 1975), 77–98.

21. *Jersey City Evening Journal*, August 5, 1902.

22. Corporation trust companies served primarily to advertise New Jersey's liberal incorporation laws to out-of-state companies. The former then provided their clients with the essential requirements of legal incorporation—an office and a representative (see Noble, *New Jersey Progressivism Before Wilson*, 5).

23. *Jersey City Evening Journal*, March 6, 1903.

24. Ibid., March 23, 1904.

25. For a broader view of this issue see Loren P. Beth, *The Development of the American Constitution, 1877–1917* (New York, 1971), 84.

26. James Willard Hurst, *Law and the Conditions of Freedom in Nineteenth-Century United States* (Madison, 1956), 52.

27. The railroads were represented by Joseph D. Bedle, a former state supreme court justice (1865–1875) and ex-governor (1875–1878) and by Benjamin Williamson, former chancellor of the Court of Errors and Appeals (1852–1859).

28. State, the Central Railroad Co. of N. J., Prosecutors v. State Board of Assessors, et al., 48 N. J. L. 1 (Sup. Ct. 1886).

29. The Court of Errors and Appeals was composed of the chancellor, chief justice of the supreme court, eight associate justices, and six special justices (non-lawyers), all appointed for seven-year terms by the governor.

30. State Board of Assessors et al., Plaintiffs in Error v. Central Railroad Co. of N. J. et al., Defendants in Error, 48 N. J. L. 146 (Ct. E&A 1886).

31. The lone dissent was voiced by Justice David A. Depue, a Republican member of the supreme court since 1866.

32. *Jersey Journal* (Jersey City), October 9, 1909.

33. See Lawrence M. Friedman, *A History of American Law* (New York, 1973), 316–317.

34. *Board of Trade of Jersey City Review*, 2 (February, 1903); U. S. Department of Commerce and Labor, Bureau of the Census, *Manufactures*, 1909, 780; also U. S. Department of Interior, Bureau of the Census, *Twelfth Census of the United States, 1900: Special Reports, Occupations*, 578–581.

35. Fogel, *Railroads and American Economic Growth*, 7.

36. In the Matter of Taxation of the Erie Railroad Co., 65 N. J. L. 608 (Ct. E&A 1901).

37. See New Jersey Junction Railroad Co. v. Mayor and Aldermen of Jersey City, 63 N. J. L. 120 (Sup. Ct. 1899) and the same parties in 70 N. J. L. 104 (Sup. Ct. 1903).

38. *Jersey City Evening Journal*, September 25, 1903.

39. Fagan's electoral triumph also coincided with a major victory in Central Railroad Co. of N. J. v. Jersey City, 70 N. J. L. 311 (Ct. E&A 1905). The legal issue involved the relationship between the territorial limits of a state and its sovereignty. Jersey City's right to tax lands located under the tidewater of New York Bay was upheld as being a proper delegation of state authority.

40. *Fact, Arguments and Exhibits* . . . Brief of William D. Edwards (Jersey City, 1904).

41. *Laws of New Jersey*, 1905, ch. 91. See Noble, *New Jersey Progressivism Before Wilson*, 28.

42. *Laws of New Jersey*, 1905, ch. 83. The full impact of this bill, known as the Hillery Act, is discussed in Noble, 29–30.

43. *Jersey City Evening Journal*, April 8, 1905, and *Newark News*, April 8, 1905.

44. *Laws of New Jersey*, 1906, ch. 82, 146. This problem is discussed in Ernest S. Griffith, *A History of American City Government: The Progressive Years and Their Aftermath, 1900–1920* (New York, 1974), 248.

45. *Laws of New Jersey,* 1906, ch. 120.

46. *Newark News,* November 8, 1905.

47. Friedman, *A History of American Law,* 393–394. For an analysis of similar difficulties incurred by another "New Idea" mayor, Frederick R. Low of Passaic, consult Michael H. Ebner, "Passaic, New Jersey, 1855–1912: City-Building in Post-Civil War America" (Ph.D. diss., University of Virginia, 1974), 223–239.

48. The Mayor and Aldermen of Jersey City and Mark M. Fagan v. State Board of Assessors and United N. J. Railroad and Canal Co., 73 N. J. L. 164 (Sup. Ct. 1906) and 73 N. J. L. 170 (Sup. Ct. 1906).

49. The Jersey City tax rate for 1906 was $24.90 per thousand ratables, while the railroads paid well below that figure on their first-class property.

50. Robert H. McCarter was appointed in 1903 to succeed his brother, Thomas N. McCarter, who had been elected president of the Public Service Corporation, New Jersey's utility conglomerate. The new attorney general had been counsel for the Delaware, Lackawanna and Western Railroad. During the course of the litigation the Lehigh Valley and United New Jersey railroads were represented by Gilbert Collins, ex-Republican mayor of Jersey City (1884–1886), one-time justice of the state supreme court (1897–1903), and director of the Prudential Insurance Company —the principal stockholder in the Public Service Corporation. John Franklin Fort was elected Republican governor of New Jersey in 1907 after serving seven years on the state supreme court bench.

51. Mayor and Aldermen of Jersey City and Mark M. Fagan, Prosecutors, Defendants in Error v. State Board of Assessors and Lehigh Valley Railroad Co., Plaintiffs in Error, 74 N. J. L. 720 (Ct. E&A 1907). Nine months later the Court of Errors and Appeals reversed the decision of the supreme court in the United N. J. Railroad case, 75 N.J.L. 571 (Ct. E&A 1908).

52. Roscoe Pound, "Common Law and Legislation," *Harvard Law Review,* 21 (April, 1908), 403, 406.

53. *Laws of New Jersey,* 1905, ch. 67. The purpose of the board was to determine whether railroad property was taxable by the State Board of Assessors or local taxing authorities.

54. The State, Mayor and Aldermen of Jersey City, Prosecutor v. Board of Equalization of Taxes and the New York and Jersey Railroad Co. and Manhattan and Hoboken Railroad Co., 74 N. J. L. 382 (Sup. Ct. 1907).

55. See Mayor and Aldermen of Jersey City et al., Plaintiffs in Error v. Board of Equalization of Taxes and Central Railroad Co. of New Jersey, Defendants in Error, 74 N. J. L. 753 (Ct. E&A 1907).

56. *Jersey City Evening Journal,* October 15, 1907.

57. Stanley P. Caine, "The Origins of Progressivism," in Lewis L. Gould, ed., *The Progressive Years* (Syracuse, 1974), 34.

58. Friedman, *A History of American Law,* 499.

INDEX

NOTES ON CONTRIBUTORS

Co-editor **Michael H. Ebner** received a Ph.D. from the University of Virginia, where he studied with William H. Harbaugh. His articles, essays and reviews have appeared in numerous scholarly journals, including *Labor History, The History Teacher,* and *New Jersey History*. Recent publications include "Socialism & Progressive Political Reform: The 1911 Change of Government in Passaic," in *Socialism & the Cities,* (Ed.) Bruce M. Stave (Kennikat, 1975) and "The Future of *River City:* The Contemporary Political History of Passaic," *Urbanism Past & Present* (Winter, 1976–1977). He is assistant professor of history at Lake Forest College.

Co-editor **Eugene M. Tobin** received a Ph.D. from Brandeis University, working with Morton Keller. He has contributed several articles to *New Jersey History* and *The American Journal of Economics & Sociology* on progressivism in Jersey City as well as a study of George L. Record in *The Historian*. Tobin's article "The Progressive as Humanitarian: Jersey City's Search for Social Justice, 1890–1917," *New Jersey History* (Fall-Winter, 1975) was awarded the William Adee Whitehead Prize of the New Jersey Historical Society. He was an N.E.H. Fellow-in-Residence at Vanderbilt University during 1976–1977, studying with Dewey W. Grantham. Tobin is visiting assistant professor of history at Miami University (Ohio).

John F. Bauman received his Ph.D. from Rutgers University where he studied with J. Joseph Huthmacher. He has contributed articles to *Current History* and *Pennsylvania History*. His most recent publication is 'Safe and Sanitary without the Costly Frills: The Evolution of Public Housing in Philadelphia, 1929–1941," *Pennsylvania Magazine of History & Biography* (January, 1977). He is professor of history at California State College (Pennsylvania).

Augustus Cerillo, Jr. has a Ph.D. from Northwestern University where he studied with Robert H. Wiebe. He is the author of "The Reform of Municipal Government in New York City: From Seth Low to John Purroy Mitchel," *New-York Historical Society Quarterly* (January, 1973). Cerillo is associate professor of history at California State University at Long Beach and also serves as editor of *The History Teacher.*

Edward J. Kopf has a Ph.D from Brandeis University, having studied with Morton Keller. He is the author of "Untarnishing the Dream: Mobility, Opportunity and Order in Modern America," *Journal of Social History* (Fall, 1977). Kopf is assistant professor of history at Virginia Commonwealth University.

Michael P. McCarthy took his Ph.D. from Northwestern University, working with Robert H. Wiebe. His articles and essays have appeared in the *Journal of the Illinois State Historical Society, Northwest Ohio Quarterly,* and *The History Teacher.* He is the author of "On Bosses, Reformers and Urban Growth: Some Suggestions for a Political Typology of American Cities," *Journal of Urban History* (November, 1977). He is Senior Research Associate, Center for Policy Research, New York City.

Lee F. Pendergrass has a Ph.D. from the University of Washington where he studied with Robert E. Burke and Otis A. Pease. He is the author of "The Formation of a Municipal Reform Movement: The Municipal League of Seattle," *Pacific Northwest Quarterly* (January, 1975). He teaches at Chapman Residential Education Center, Oak Harbor, Washington.

Harold L. Platt received a Ph.D. from Rice University where he studied with Harold M. Hyman. He is an assistant professor of history at Loyola University of Chicago.

Martin J. Schiesl holds a Ph.D. from SUNY Buffalo where he worked with C. K. Yearley. He is the author of "Progressive Reform in Los Angeles under Mayor Alexander, 1909-1913," *California Historical Quarterly* (Spring, 1975) and *The Politics of Efficiency: Municipal Administration and Reform in America, 1880-1920* (University of California Press, 1977). He is associate professor of history at California State University at Los Angeles.

Wayne J. Urban holds a Ph.D. from Ohio State University, where his work was directed by Bernard Mehl and Robert H. Bremner. His most recent publication is "Organized Teachers and Educational Reform during the Progressive Era: 1890-1920," *History of Education Quarterly* (Spring, 1976). He is associate professor of educational foundations at Georgia State University.